CLIMAX

CLIMAX

Why Great Leaders Need Love Affairs

AN ENLIGHTENING LEADERSHIP FABLE

by

Emily W. Liu

ISBN: 978-1937559939

Published by New Chapter Press
1175 York Ave., Suite #3S
New York, NY 10065
Randy Walker, Managing Partner
RWalker@NewChapterMedia.com
www.NewChapterMedia.com

BAND-AID® Brand Adhesive Bandages is a registered trademark of Johnson & Johnson.

Disclaimer:
The characters in this book are fictional, except the mentor and healer, the author, Emily W. Liu. All other characters' resemblance to actual persons (living or dead), organizations, places, and events are coincidental. This book is not a substitute for psychotherapy. The contents in this book and the healing steps are for informational purposes only. The author, the publisher, IFS Institute, and The Center for Self-leadership do not guarantee that anyone following the techniques, suggestions, tips, ideas or strategies will be guaranteed a result. If you need mental health support, please seek professional help. Emily W. Liu (founder of Soar to Greatness Now LLC), New Chapter Press, IFS Institute, and The Center for Self-leadership assume no liability nor responsibility to anyone concerning any loss or damage caused, or alleged to be created, directly or indirectly by the information contained in the book.
Printed in Canada.

Praise for *CLIMAX*

"This is more than just another novel. By interweaving the principles of the Internal Family Systems model of psychotherapy throughout this dramatic story of business and personal relationships, we glean insights that will serve us well in our own professional and intimate relationships. I am grateful to Emily for offering these lessons in such an engaging way."

—Richard C. Schwartz, PhD LMFT, Founder and Developer of *Internal Family Systems,* author of *Internal Family Systems Therapy: The Mosaic Mind*

◆ ◆ ◆

"This is a great book about great leaders. But it is not about a love affair; it is about finding love in yourself. Philosophers have long held that to love another you must first love yourself. With excellent case studies and a well-structured protocol for self-examination and self-help, Emily Liu asks the reader to look inside. This introspection can lead to self-awareness, self-forgiveness, and self-love. She speaks not of narcissism nor self-absorption but of a strong comfort level with one's self. She is on rock solid ground in her discussions of psychology, and her writing is smooth and easy.

Ms. Liu and I share the view that to be a great leader you must really be in touch with yourself, your character, and your values. And she rightly places love as the bedrock of that value system. Why the focus on values? A leader demonstrating a strong set of values such as respect, openness, and integrity is what causes followers to really trust the leader. 'I would follow him/her to hell and back.' In a nonromantic sense, leaders 'love' a leader of good character. Liu makes the case that the first step is to love yourself."

—Robert C. Carroll, author of
Building Your Leadership Legacy: It's All About Character

◆ ◆ ◆

"*CLIMAX* is an important read to understand how unresolved childhood traumas can negatively impact personal and business relationships. Emily Liu's ability to tell a story allows you to empathize with its characters. If you desire greatness in all areas of your life, *CLIMAX* teaches you how the Internal Family Systems Self-leadership model can help you become more authentic and self-aware, in an effort to achieve your dreams in leadership and love."

—Patrick H. Tyrance, Jr., MD MPP MBA, Harvard-trained Orthopedic Surgeon, NFL draft pick, advisor to medical and health device start-ups, and author of upcoming book, *Making the Cut: Steps to Overcoming Fear and Reclaiming Your Power*

◆　◆　◆

"*CLIMAX: Why Great Leaders Need Love Affairs* is a mirror for any leader to acknowledge one's own 'parts' in order to activate transformative awareness. Emily Liu masterfully paints a narrative that both prompts self-reflection and a deep actionable understanding of the Internal Family Systems model. Any leader, regardless of context, will surface important understandings of leadership through the tale of the two main characters."

—Dustin Liu (no relation to author), former Cornell University Student Trustee, Fulbright Scholar, student at Harvard Graduate School of Education

Table of Contents

PART III

PART IV

APPENDICES

Dedication

If you hide behind a mask or two—to help you feel good enough and help you feel like you belong—this book is for you. You are not alone; we are all perfectly imperfect. If you want a meaningful and practical alternative to living without masks to unlock your leadership potential *and* take your love life to new heights of closeness, pleasure, and spiritual depth, I dedicate this book to you.

Acknowledgments

It took a village of people and many life experiences to mature my soul enough to birth this book. My most important "thank you" is to the Universe for guiding me to fail forward and fast many times. Adversity helped me learn the lessons that birthed the necessary materials for this uniquely-angled leadership book.

I am deeply grateful for Richard Schwartz, PhD, LMFT, the founder and developer of Internal Family Systems (IFS). Without his brilliant model, this book would not have been possible. Dr. Schwartz always believed that IFS can be applied to other facets of our lives beyond psychotherapy. With this book, I strived to make his inspiring claim a reality by focusing on the connection between leadership and love.

I am deeply grateful for Doug Osber for acknowledging my potential in October 2011. After getting laid off from a twenty-seven-year pharmaceutical sales career, Doug told me I needed to become an entrepreneur.

Many thanks to my publisher, Randolph Walker of New Chapter Press, who took a chance on me during a Universe-orchestrated "random" encounter in 2014. After only a twenty-minute conversation, Randy offered me a book deal. Thank you to my editors, Rosemary Sneeringer, Ellen Winkler, and Barbara Dee.

The entrepreneurial journey requires a network of kindred spirits to support each other through life's emotional roller coaster. These are the beautiful souls I'm deeply grateful for: Theresa Velendzas, Leyla Salvadé, James Benedict, PhD, Patrick Tyrance, MD, Kenann McKenzie, PhD, Dustin Liu, Montserrat Anguera, PhD, Martin Fox, Percy Ballard, MD, Agnis Pena-Toro, and Thomas Holguin. Thank you all.

Last but not least, I give thanks to one of my fiercest champions and mentors, J.P., who calls me out when I'm out of line and challenges me to think bigger, so I can leave a legacy of cultivating greatness in the people I serve. I share your enthusiasm for the life-changing transformation you're about to discover.

Preface

You may have picked up this book because the edgy title stopped you in your tracks. *Great leaders need love affairs? Whaaat? Is the author crazy? What is this book about?* Of course, I don't mean great leaders need to have *illicit* love affairs; I am talking about a different kind of love affair, a legitimate love affair with all parts of yourself—self-love.

Becoming a great leader who everyone loves to work for is about your ability to have (platonic) "love affairs" with your colleagues and direct reports (the first chain of employees from the boss). It is not easy to shower unconditional love and validate others if you haven't done the work to love yourself, especially to love the dark and disowned parts. Without healthy self-love, it can be a struggle to climax—that is, reach the pinnacle of success and happiness—in love and leadership.

Think about the worst boss you've had. I know, your stomach may churn at this thought; perhaps you had many sleepless nights, talked ad nauseam about how infuriating this person was, and how difficult it was to interact with them. Have you ever thought about what this boss is like in their love life? Would you want to be their significant other? Your answer is probably "Heck NO!"

This leadership book aims to help you see through a compassionate lens why people are "bad" and difficult. You will also learn the root causes of incompetent leadership and *all* relationship struggles. I will show you how to improve relationships. You will understand why the spiritual journey to self-love and confident vulnerability *is* the key to manifesting (and keeping) love, money, and success.

There are many leadership books and seminars that teach you how to be a better leader. These books and workshops often say that what they teach can be applied to any relationship, including the romantic ones. I am suggesting we change the order around; I am enticing you to learn leadership skills through the doorway of love and intimacy.

The vital components for a great love life are the same as those you need to become a fantastic leader that everyone loves to follow, talk about, and work for, with the caveat that in leadership, romantic energy and physical intimacy are not appropriate.

We are in an era of witnessing many influential leaders in politics, media, business, religious organizations, education, and other institutions fall from their pinnacles of success. Instead of outright blame and criticism, we need a compassionate leadership book that explains the root causes of why these leaders failed miserably. Current movements such as #MeToo, in which victims feel liberated to publicly speak out and expose perpetrators of sexual harassment and criminal acts, have lowered society's tolerance for bad leadership. The time is ripe for a compassionate understanding of how and why some people get "toxic." They weren't born bad; their childhood's emotionally devaluing experiences and messages from authority figures and peers molded them into uninspiring, challenging, and energy-draining leaders.

The struggles faced by individuals, teams, organizations, and society boil down to a lack of Self-leadership, which is rooted in an "internal civil war" of subpersonalities in the psyche. The inner psychic cast of characters—i.e., "parts"—seek redemption and validation. These parts comprise of vulnerable child parts, beliefs, thoughts, emotions, body sensations, and behaviors. Parts can either help us or hurt us on the journey to greatness—especially in the love arena.

A dismal statistic quoted by many leadership books and studies is that two-thirds of leaders fail. *Climax* addresses the root causes of why these leaders fail and provides solutions to lasting transformation, success, and happiness. The dynamics of failed leadership and relationships are addressed through the evidence-based, psycho-spiritual Internal Family Systems (IFS) Self-leadership model developed by Richard Schwartz, PhD, LMFT. The IFS framework provides a robust and relatively simple solution to remedy individual, team, organizational, and societal leadership dysfunction. IFS is also a paradigm for living and compassionately understanding ourselves and others, especially when negative thoughts, emotions, and behaviors take over and cause damage. Please allow me to show you why and how authenticity via confident vulnerability *is* the essential ingredient to mastering epic love and leadership. If you learn how to do love right, then getting leadership right by using the same Self-leadership tools is an alluring way to become an extraordinary leader who is loved by all.

The characters in this book are fictional, except for myself, the Internal Family Systems practitioner and healer. The two main characters are a composite of struggling, success-driven leaders. Through my executive coaching practice and deep friendships, I am privy to clients' and friends' innermost thoughts regarding their deepest fears and insecurities. After hearing their secrets, the most crucial point I want to share is that every success-driven, high-achieving leader is vulnerable to fears and inferiority complexes, just like everyone else.

As you read *Climax*, acknowledge the emotions that may get activated. I will show you how to look at the triggers through the Internal Family Systems lens. As you learn about *Self* and *parts* and how your personality developed, you will be able to explain the deep-seated causes of why you are the way you are, why some people push your buttons, and why you struggle to cross the finish line of your ambitious goals. The insights you gain can create a liberating, positive energy shift and lead to formidable outcomes.

Depending on your experiences, John, one of the protagonists in the story, may seem a little bit harsh and unrelatable; unfortunately, these cold-hearted leaders exist in real life. I purposely fashioned a slightly "toxic" character to illustrate that people who appear selfish or challenging are not inherently so underneath their ego, fears, and masks. This benevolent view may seem like an oxymoron; it isn't. I invite you to suspend judgment, blame, and criticism and get curious instead of furious towards leaders, family members, current and former romantic partners, colleagues, friends, and acquaintances who get under your skin and make your life miserable.

If you see parts of yourself in the characters or get emotionally charged as you read the story, please do not berate yourself. Your emotional reaction is a sign that your dark, forgotten, or wounded parts are activated. You may not be ready to acknowledge or heal these parts yet; that's okay. You will have many self-compassion lightbulb moments when you are prepared to explore the inner psychological forces that have influenced the creation of your off-putting traits and outer reality.

The evidence-based Internal Family Systems Self-leadership model is the secret sauce for permanent emotional healing, accelerated transformation, spiritual growth, and coming "home" to center.

I have infused this book with my deepest love and appreciation for you, dear reader, so that you are empowered to achieve climactic successes in all areas of your life.

Emily W. Liu
September 2020
Boston, Massachusetts, USA

Introduction to Internal Family Systems (IFS) Self-Leadership Framework

Adapted from IFS Institute (www.IFS-Institute.com)

Human beings comprise of Self and Parts.

Definition of Self or Higher Self

"Self" is the essence of who you are. A spirit full of joy, peace, and compassion for yourself and others.

- When Self is in the driver's seat of your life, you are in harmony, feel calm, and happy because no part of you is angry or disconnected. Self is your inner wisdom and can speak *for* the parts that get activated, such as when your direct report makes you frustrated and angry. For example: She is late again with the monthly summary. A Self-led leader gets curious (instead of furious) and says (in a calm tone instead of from angry energy), "Jane, I'm curious . . . I've noticed that this is the third time the monthly productivity report is two days late. A part of me is upset because our team's productivity is affected by late reports. Don't worry; I'm not going to get angry. I would like to know what is going on, and I would like to know how I could be contributing to the lateness. Have I provided enough clarity? Please tell me how I can best support you."
- According to the developer of Internal Family Systems, Richard Schwartz, PhD, LMFT, 13 qualities makeup Self—eight "C" words and five "P"

words. The "8Cs and 5Ps of Self-leadership are: clarity, curiosity, confidence, connectedness, courage, creativity, calmness, compassion, playfulness, persistence, patience, presence, and perspective.

When the best of you, the Self, is in Self-leadership:

- You are consciously aware of what you are thinking, feeling, saying, and doing. You embody attractive high vibration energy that attracts others to you like bees to honey. You are at your best when you do not let an extreme part, such as anger, take over.
- The Self is forever there, but it can be hidden because of devaluing emotional experiences; i.e., big and little traumas, especially those that happened from birth to eight years of age.
- The Self is the healing agent for your traumatized parts that are still locked away in your inner psychic basement.
- The Self has the power to be sovereign over your *parts*. Self can direct which parts should lead in a particular situation, such as when you are near a deadline or walking down a dark alley. When a deadline looms, Self leads perfectionist, analytical, and micro-managing parts to inspire your team to get things done fast. When you walk down a dark alley in a bad neighborhood, Self tells the hypervigilant part to be front and center, with angry, dominating, and screaming parts on standby, just in case your safety is threatened.

Definition of Parts

"Parts" is an overarching term to describe the parts or subpersonalities within you. These include your beliefs, thoughts, emotions, body sensations, behaviors, and also the vulnerable child parts that were emotionally hurt. For example:

- A grown-up man has an angry part that is a dominant feature of his personality. This part developed to an extreme because he did not receive enough attention from his parents, who divorced when he was three years old. Dad hardly visited him, and Mom was exhausted from working two jobs.

- A grown-up woman's dominant traits include perfectionism and control. These parts show up in how she leads her team and how she interacts with her husband. She can be overbearing with perfectionism and control because growing up, Mom punished her for tiny homework mistakes, B's on the report card, and less than perfect tennis practices and matches. Her high standards make her work team feel like she doesn't trust them; they walk on eggshells. At home, her husband feels like nothing he does is good enough; he has emotionally fled the relationship and is having an affair.

- Some people wear layers of masks because they are not in touch with their emotions and authentic Self; they are afraid to show the full rainbow of their personality, including their vulnerabilities. Here's how these masked people are described: *emotionally unavailable, can't crack their armor, they're not real, they've got an image to protect, they don't make me feel safe,* and *they judge me.*

Your *internal* parts interact like members of a *family*, in a *system* of relationships; thus, Dr. Schwartz termed this model, *Internal Family Systems (IFS)*. The elements of you that are dominant on many days contain the material that people talk about when you're not in the room. For example:

- "Sara is hot and cold. Sometimes she's so caring and lovable, and at other times, she's judgmental and critical, especially when I ask for advice. Instead of supporting me when I have promising dates, Sara gets jealous, judgmental, and critical. She judges my dates' characters without even knowing them. She can never be happy for me."

- "My husband is such a jerk! He can't do anything around the house. He sulks when he gets home, completely controls the finances, and gives me an allowance for clothing and shoes, even though we are financially well-off. He's not present when we make love; it's all about his pleasure, not mine. In addition, I know his boss is not happy with his performance due to his controlling and selfish ways."

The Internal Family Systems (IFS) Self-leadership model guides you to reorganize and rebalance your "internal family." This reorganization means that the best parts of your colorful, unique personality come out at the right time and in appropriate doses to inspire others and follow your lead.

PART I

PART 1

Chapter 1

Soul to Soul Communication

October 2017

J ohn is on the Metro-North hour-long train commute from his White Plains apartment into New York City. He is in turmoil, feeling ashamed of recent failures. He notices tension in the shoulders and tightness in the chest. He recalls the strategy to manage the stress—*When you get overwhelmed with inner critic voices and emotions, don't stuff them down. Capture them on the phone to clear the chaos.*

As John types the caustic words of critical voices into the Notes app on his iPhone, Jill's email comes across the screen. He got close with Jill—incredibly close—as they worked together. His heart skips a beat. *What the heck does she want now? She had every right to be mad. Hmm . . . the subject line is "Oneness."*

My dearest John,

I have been meaning to send you my appreciation for our most beautiful spiritual experience.

You were so present and conscious in your divine masculine that I fully surrendered into the divine feminine goddess that I am.

I felt safe.
I felt witnessed.
I felt ravished.

I felt cherished.
I felt closeness.
I felt pleasure.
I felt bliss.
I felt high.
I felt special.
I felt sexy.
I felt safe to release the blocked river of emotions.
I felt oneness with myself, oneness with you, and oneness with the Universe.

With love for your soul—ALWAYS,
Jill

John's heart fills with love and delight, and his eyes water as he reads Jill's email three more times. *All we did was an extended meditation to powerful music. I'm speechless! Spiritual poetry. It was an extraordinary experience; I made her feel all that?! The culmination was intense.*

This loving email moves him out the inner critic state. John closes his eyes and relives the beautiful experience. He felt like a warrior protecting a beautiful, expressive woman who felt like she found God. He gets aroused. *I was so turned on with eye-gazing and breathing, our hearts beating as one.* Then his inner critic voice takes over again, reminding him of current realities and his mood sours. *Don't bother answering the email. Nothing will change. Get your financial shit together. You've been faking it for too long, and she witnessed your failure!* John gazes out the train's window as the landscape passes in a blur. *But, she saw right through my masks and loved my soul anyways. Damn! Why do I feel like cockroaches are crawling on my skin?* Then, a hopeful voice chimes in—*One day, you'll apologize and make peace with her.*

Exasperated, John covers his face with his hands, an attempt to quiet the cruel inner voices. *Okay, have faith. Your life will get better.* The train finally screeches into Grand Central Station. After a twenty-minute brisk stroll along Madison Avenue, he walks through the revolving doors to his new Senior Manager position at a midsize advertising agency. *I'm back on purpose. Love is not on my radar.*

The John and Jill fictional story is told from the third-person omniscient narrator perspective. I show you how Self-leadership and lack of Self-leadership played out in John and Jill's professional and personal struggles. When you read the call-out boxes, like this one, the first-person perspective from me, Emily Liu, the author, will also be present.

Chapter 2

Look at My Beautiful Peacock Feathers

Three Years Earlier . . . June 2014

John Robertson is excited to meet Jill Morgan, a promising new hire in his business unit who has a track record of brilliant marketing successes from her previous jobs. John's direct report, Michael Laine, the Director of Strategic Services, and HR have interviewed Jill. They inform John that she will be a tremendous asset to the company. Unless John finds something egregious, Jill will receive an offer for the Strategic Services Consultant position. Jill's responsibilities will include finding new clients and developing marketing and advertising strategies for them. This meeting with John is just a formality to bless the recommendation to hire Jill.

John is a handsome Senior Executive Vice President at Zatuck, Inc., one of the premier New York City advertising agencies. He is forty-two years old, an inch short of six feet tall, with salt-and-pepper hair, and exhibits twenty pounds of a midlife beer belly. Many have called John a George Clooney look-alike. If he didn't have the gut, he would belong on the cover of *GQ* magazine.

John dresses in business casual attire on most days, including today, with fitted slacks, designer Italian shoes, and a cashmere-blend custom-made jacket over his pressed, custom-made shirts. He loves how the women compliment and swoon over his sartorial choices. On casual Fridays, he impresses with designer jeans that hug his athletic posterior, paired with a blazer and an eye-catching pocket square. He is an influential senior executive who makes a boatload of money. John's image is the epitome of an alpha warrior—or so he thinks.

Jill is thirty-five years old, five feet six, and today she's wearing a short-sleeved, form-fitting, size-four gray dress that hugs her perfect curves. The dress lands just above her knees, showing off her well-toned legs with the help of her three-inch, leopard-print Manolo Blahnik pumps. With her wavy, shoulder-length, strawberry-blond locks bouncing, she strides into John's office like she owns the room. Her magnetism, energy, and confidence shine brightly. John can't help himself and performs a once-over, doing his best to conceal the admiration for her attractive body. John silently drools—*Holy moly! She's hot! Michael made a great decision. I've got to show her how I am head and shoulders above the average alpha guy.*

John's libido is awakened by someone who looks like she stepped out of *Maxim* magazine. The alpha part of him wants to show off. This part takes center stage upon Jill's entrance.

"Nice to meet you, Jill. I've heard many great things about you from HR and Michael," he says with confidence and a big smile.

"Likewise, Mr. Robertson. I've read so much about you through googling you. I look forward to getting to know you and learning how I can help you achieve the next level of success for your business unit," Jill says, with a fireworks combination of charm, grace, and confidence.

Jill's initial impression is—*Oh boy, I know I can make men fall like dominos when I walk into a room. I've cast my spell on this good-looking boss. Hmm . . . a beer belly.*

Jill is used to men ogling her beauty, so this boss doing the same thing is nothing new to her. She and her women friends often lament how men objectify women, but Jill usually gives them a pass, chalking it up to "primal biology." *A man as attractive and successful as John always gets a pass.*

"Let's grab lunch while we get to know each other. And please, call me John."

"Okay, John," Jill says with a big smile.

John and Jill take the elevator to the company cafeteria three flights up to have their informal "interview." John sucks in the beer belly. They eat lunch in one of the senior leaders' private dining rooms with floor-to-ceiling windows overlooking midtown Manhattan. John's peacock feathers fan wider and wider as Jill asks probing questions about his rise to the top.

John says, "I earned my marketing degree at a well-known Ivy, and then I got my MBA at the most prestigious business school in Boston. After business school, Zatuck hired me. I rose through the ranks and was responsible for the most profitable campaigns we've ever launched." Jill does her best to look attentive and interested, though she can't get a word in edgewise.

"I traveled the world," John continues, "and I was able to buy a dream home, beach and ski houses, and send my two kids to private school. My wife doesn't have to work. We have help, and she gets to pursue her hobbies. This means if you do well, you can rise to the top and live your dream life."

At this point, Jill is sickened by his ego, but she needs to play the game to secure the job. "Everything you've accomplished is so impressive. Tell me more. How did you rise to your current position?"

"Well, senior leaders noticed me, and they put me on the fast track. After only two years, I received a big promotion. And boy, did I deliver! After that success, I kept delivering results and here I am, the youngest Senior Executive Vice President ever to hold the position. I get to travel on the company jet and meet celebrities and business tycoons. *Forbes, Fortune, Success,* and numerous other publications call me an 'influencer.'" At this point, John realizes he's being braggadocios, but he doesn't care. Jill's eyes are still locked into his, and eating this up. John continues to boast about the dynamos, super-achievers, and luminaries he's met because of his position.

The Internal Family Systems (IFS) Perspective on Parts

Cars have parts, and so do computers, smartphones, and people. The people parts are the subpersonalities within, comprised of negative and positive thoughts, emotions, body sensations, behaviors, and inner child parts. For example: the part that likes to sing and dance or the part that wants to be alone to read a book. John's bragging part is front and center in this interaction with Jill. A part is comprised of its own beliefs, thoughts, emotions, and behaviors. When a part plays an extreme role, such as how John proactively shares his accomplishments from bragging energy, it comes from fear. John needs to impress Jill because he is afraid that he may not win her over to work for him. Every part has good intentions, with the ability to help us on our path. But when parts take over in extreme doses, and Self doesn't rein them in, they can eventually hurt us and set us back.

Jill is a smart cookie, and she knows from her previous career in sales and marketing that the way to win people over is to let the other person do all the talking. They will think you are their new best friend, even though you haven't said much. John's monologue took up the lunch hour, and she is pretty sure she secured the job. Jill is thankful for the time-tested influencing secrets in Dale Carnegie's classic book, *How to Win Friends and Influence People*.

As lunch comes to an end and the upbeat energy swirls, Shelly Wilson walks by the closed glass doors of the dining room and notices that John and a beautiful woman are locking eyes and grinning from ear-to-ear. *Hmm . . . What the heck is going on? Is she the new hire Michael mentioned? I hate her already.* Shelly is part of John's team and has been with Zatuck for ten years. She is an attractive forty-year-old with short auburn hair who prides herself on keeping in shape and indulging in the latest anti-aging trends. Unlike Jill, Shelly does not make men fall like dominoes when she walks into a room. She is smart, proficient, and still has a tinge of resentment from the drama she had with John years ago.

At the end of the lunch, John and Jill rise from their chairs. John reaches his hand out, "Jill, you're hired! Welcome to the team. We need your creativity. Congratulations!"

"I'm thrilled! Thank you."

"HR will give you the details on when you start and your benefits."

"Fabulous!"

As Jill leaves Zatuck headquarters, she muses—*It's gonna be interesting to work for a self-absorbed boss. I feel an incredible energy around him though; it intrigues me.*

As John takes the elevator back to his office, he thinks—*I like this hot gal! She'll be a significant contributor. I'll take her under my wings and help her rise to the top. She's a new person to fantasize about since Liz wants nothing to do with sex.* It had been three years since his wife, Liz, discovered the last affair; things are still chilly at home.

◆　◆　◆

John grew up in Scarsdale, a wealthy suburb twenty-five miles north of New York City. His father founded a successful technology business and sold it for over $100 million. John and his two younger sisters were privileged to go to private schools.

John's dad was very successful despite his narcissism. Dad was controlling, had anger issues, and was, and still is, emotionally abusive to John's mom. It was difficult for John to watch his dad mistreat mom, and others to boot. Throughout John's formative years, he walked on eggshells because he didn't know when bad moods would strike Dad. Mom stayed home and raised three children. John rarely witnessed physical affection between his parents. His mother was depressed, medicated, and addicted to wine, drinking almost a bottle every day. John often saw her sneak a drink while he did homework.

John's athletic gift is tennis. His father pushed him to enter tournaments and yelled at him when he didn't make it to the finals. Tennis was the doorway to approval. Mom was rarely present for his tennis practices or matches, usually too depressed and hungover to leave the house.

John's wounded inner child parts made him feel like he was never good enough, especially on the tennis court. When he did get into an Ivy League school, instead of congratulatory high-fives, Dad said, "Too bad; the top three Ivies rejected you. You'll have to settle for a B-rate Ivy. Good thing the tennis team wanted you, otherwise you would have never gotten into an Ivy." And his mother said, "Congratulations," without a whiff of excitement or pride. After two years of work at a digital marketing startup, John was admitted to a very prestigious business school with the aid of Dad's connections. When his parents learned of his acceptance, they finally expressed how proud they were.

John was driven and determined to secure a "corner office" position before age forty. With his ego, charm, and intelligence, he talked his way to the top. His team executed his creative, out-of-the-box ideas. Not everyone was happy with John's leadership style, but somehow, John's team managed to produce results. As his hubris and cocky attitude turned meaner and more insulting, many team members left. John couldn't accept the reality that published studies have shown that most employees left terrible bosses, not bad companies or jobs. John's attitude was—*I don't care why people leave. It's their problem, not mine!*

Yet, through all of the employee defections, John stayed in the old boys' club with his superiors. They were aware of his poor leadership style and assigned executive coaches to work with him. His bosses didn't want to fire or demote him; he was a creative genius. They didn't care how he got results as long as he achieved them. Unfortunately, none of the executive coaches seemed to get through to John to change his negative traits. He would talk over them, signaling that their methods were foolish. He would temporarily improve, then revert to his faulty patterns.

As for relationships, by the time John turned thirty years old, there was one failed relationship after another. Most of the women dumped him. The loneliness, pain, and futility of surviving several breakups finally got to him. He decided the easiest way to settle down was to win back his college sweetheart, Liz. He jumped through hoops to woo Liz with his narcissistic charisma. He got her pregnant on their fifth date, married soon after, and settled in the suburbs. They now have two boys. Liz left her PR job and devotes her time to raising the kids, yoga, and volunteering at their private school.

John and Liz's relationship has centered around living the ideal upper-middle-class suburban life in Rye, New York. A life filled with keeping-up-with-the-Joneses activities such as hosting fancy dinner parties, driving luxury cars, decorating their McMansions, bragging about exotic vacations, and showing off other symbols of accomplishments and wealth.

When John receives his low six-figures 401K retirement statements, he thinks—*I shouldn't keep withdrawing from my 401K to pay for my lifestyle.* Then his devil's advocate part speaks up—*Don't worry! You have plenty of time to accumulate for retirement. You're a seven-figure moneymaking machine. You can afford private school tuitions, three beautiful homes, and an expensive lifestyle. Just enjoy your success. You've only got one life to live, so why hold back?*

John and Liz have bought into Madison Avenue's images and messages of happiness: "Just buy this and that and you'll be happy just like the beautiful people in this ad." They join the ranks of people who enjoy temporary highs from material wealth and status, but their happiness set-point never seems to budge. As a result, they look for the next dopamine hit of elusive happiness, the way addicts do. *If I just buy this next thing and get the next promotion, I'll finally be happy!* If only John knew the real key to happiness.

◆ ◆ ◆

Unlike John, Jill came from a middle-class Ohio family without a lot of drama. Jill's parents were hands-off with their two kids. Her father owned a construction company that generated unpredictable income. Dad is the silent type, offering little emotional support or presence to his kids. Jill's dad didn't have values he felt were essential to instill in his children and was, and still is, virtually checked-out of life. Growing up, when he had something to say, he would go into the same story of how he was the captain of the baseball team in high school and college, and how he led the team to victory.

Dad's higher education was the local community college, where he barely survived academically but did manage to graduate. Since intellectual pursuits were not his thing, he was more comfortable as a tradesperson using his hands in the early days of his construction career. Most conversations with him were about his past. These conversations were meant to impress his wife and two daughters—even though he feels like a failure due to unpredictable income. When he did manage to secure a contract, he would self-sabotage financial security by spending the money on the latest electronic gadgets. He told himself he deserved to splurge after all the hard work.

Jill's mom was an elementary school teacher. She showed love by helping her kids with homework and cooking meals, yet was too preoccupied with household responsibilities to give Jill and her younger brother the quality time they deserved. Mom seemed to be barely holding it together emotionally, living life as expected of her. Working and caring for her family left no time for herself, which meant she always looked tired and worn out.

As a result of lack of emotional depth with her family, Jill felt unseen and unloved. She won the lead role in a junior high school play, and Dad was absent from the audience. Dad was out with the boys that night, indulging in beers and playing darts. Mom couldn't get in touch with him [before cell phones], and Jill was distracted, searching for him in the audience. At Jill's sweet sixteen birthday party, her father forgot to pick up the birthday cake, too busy drinking with his subcontractors.

Jill believed she didn't matter. In truth, her dad's needs were top priority. Jill was left on her own to figure out life. She attended Ohio State on a full academic scholarship and studied psychology and marketing. After college, Jill spent twelve years in sales and marketing positions at consumer products companies and ad agencies. When she realized she was good at marketing and advertising, she decided to apply to Zatuck, Inc., to earn more money and make a greater impact with her creative gifts.

In the love department, Jill unconsciously chose men who were similar to her dad—aloof and emotionally absent. Jill is single; she ended her five-year live-in relationship just before joining Zatuck. Because of Jill's "daddy traumas," it felt soothing to hear how John was smitten with her gifts and hired her on the spot. She's excited about starting a new chapter and found a studio apartment on the Lower East Side.

Chapter 3

Honeymoon Highs

December 2014

John's charismatic side knows how to make Jill feel good about herself, complimenting and validating her as he carries out his plan of feeding his ego. She feels very drawn to him. In the six months that Jill has worked on the marketing team, she feels alive with how he pays attention to her.

John approaches Jill with an idea. "I've been watching you. You know how to inject amazing ideas into client pitches. The senior leadership team desperately needs more women. Michael has shared how impressed he is with your brilliant contributions. I would love to take you under my wings so you can rise through the ranks in just a few short years. Are you interested?"

Jill smiles ear-to-ear, eyes beaming. "Of course, I'm interested! Thank you for the offer. What can I expect?"

"This means a few extra hours at the office. You and I need to spend one-on-one time together so I can show you the ropes and politics. I need to introduce you to important senior leaders. Since meetings bombard me during the day, this would mean staying late a couple of nights a week."

"I'm in!" Jill is so excited she can't contain herself. Her heart feels so warm about someone who recognizes her potential. She's been looking for a mentor like this, and she's finally found one.

Later that afternoon, John looks at his watch. "Ready?" he asks.

Ben, a fellow senior colleague he had spent the afternoon strategizing with, nods. John stands up, revealing his sneakers. John pulls his sweatshirt over his head and tells Ben, "I'm running late. Bringing my boys to the soup kitchen again. It's good to expose them to how the other half lives."

"I'm going there tonight too. See you there," Ben says. Ben doesn't have kids, so he has more time to spend at the office before going to the soup kitchen.

On his way to pick up the boys, John muses about a scholarship student he met in college. Charlie was always volunteering on several school committees, from clothing drives to pressuring campus events to donate some to their profits to charity. John was curious about Charlie's cheerful and upbeat nature and asked him if he needed any help. This is how John ended up working at a soup kitchen during his college years. When he asked Charlie about his advocacy, Charlie told him it always felt good to volunteer and give back. "When you give, you always get too," Charlie said. John never forgot him, the most popular guy on campus because of his inner light and compassion. Now, Charlie is the CEO of a large non-profit.

◆ ◆ ◆

John and Jill begin to spend more time together in his office, having dinner while discussing business. John fills Jill in on how his methods work. When Zatuck buys millions worth of advertising for clients, they accept rebates from the vendors and keep this money for themselves. The clients don't know that Zatuck receives kickbacks.

"This sounds fishy—and greedy. I thought kickbacks were illegal. Can't we get fired for this?"

"Well . . . kinda . . . technically . . . but no one has come after me. I'm a senior leader, and I can make decisions without jumping through hoops. Other agencies do it too; no one talks about it."

"Okay . . . I'm still a bit nervous. You're the boss, so I'll have to believe it. This way of business sounds like a friend of mine who worked at Silica Pharmaceuticals. Her fellow drug reps backhandedly 'bought' the doctors so they would prescribe more of Silica's drugs. As a result, the reps won sales awards and promotions. Eventually, karma came calling. Some of them were caught and fired. The kickbacks were rampant in pharma. Ultimately, the government imposed a strict code of marketing ethics and conduct for all pharmaceutical companies."

"That's pharma; this is advertising. We're not playing with patients' health. Don't worry, you're in good hands with me," John says with a wink and reassuring tone.

Jill decides not to push the conversation any further since she's still relatively new at Zatuck.

John's involvement with kickbacks alongside his generous volunteer work at the soup kitchen show opposite sides of his personality. His privileged, bloated-ego part believes he won't get caught. He thinks he's above his employees and can order them around and blame them for his mistakes. Opposite sides of a personality show how disparate parts can be; a "good" side coexisting with a "bad" side. Most people have at least one or two negative parts they're not proud of. We are complex creatures with many facets. Some negative aspects became extreme as a response to emotionally devaluing experiences that occurred in childhood and young adulthood.

Late nights at the office allow John to continue preening his peacock feathers whenever Jill gives an opening. He likes to tell old stories that shine the spotlight on how great he is. Jill can't help but be impressed and throws in a few of her stories to show John that he and Michael made the right hiring decision. John loves it when she peels off another layer of her emotional and intellectual onion. Although John still seems self-centered, the self-centeredness softens when he shows a keen interest in getting to know everything about Jill. Jill is smitten, but she knows he's a married man and off-limits, especially since he has authority over her. Nonetheless, she's flattered with all the attention.

Internal Family Systems Perspective on Self-to-Self Interactions

John and Jill are having fun. Their interaction is an example of Self-to-Self connection. John has a "soul" that is the inner essence of who he is—i.e., when he is separate from his extreme emotions, thoughts, and behaviors. When he connects to this essence, he's in Self. The Self is connected, compassionate, curious, clear, playful, and present. When John shows these qualities, Jill responds positively to the connection, and she feels safe to be more playful and reveal more parts of her personality. Self-to-Self connection facilitates deeper intimacy, vulnerability, and transparency.

Jill is an avid student of psychology. She excelled in sales and marketing jobs because she understood the psychology of persuasion. As Jill witnesses the self-centered part of John, she reminds herself that this is mother nature's way to enchant the opposite sex and ensure the survival of the species. Jill had learned and retained from her studies that evolutionarily, men are wired for competition, to be the top dog. The more successful they are, the greater the likelihood to capture the most beautiful women. Women's "primitive" brains want the most successful alpha man because this means financial resources are available to provide and protect the family. Women compete with each other to be the most beautiful. That is why beautiful women can trigger competitiveness with peers who are in the same social and educational strata. As much as the literature says women should support each other, when it comes down to it, many catfights continue due to the (frequently unconscious) primal forces of competing for alpha males' attention. No wonder it is not typical for a less attractive woman to help a colleague, friend, or acquaintance, who is more beautiful and gets more attention. The lack of "sisterhood" is the dark side of mentoring that no one likes to highlight. Our primitive brains are wired this way for survival, even though we are not living in the cavemen-cavewomen era anymore.

Jill thinks to herself—*It's interesting to observe our dynamic from above, watching John as he tries to impress me. I don't want to call him a self-centered asshole. It's out of his fears and insecurities that he does this. I'll soak it in and get a good chuckle out of it. I like being the most beautiful woman in the room, getting the attention of a powerful man like John.*

Spending so much after-hours time together gives John and Jill the latitude to reveal more of their personal lives. They head down a slippery slope, but Jill doesn't stop it from happening. She welcomes the soft touch on the arm, the firm palm on her upper back, and the prolonged eye contact during moments of silence that stirs something inside of her. She sees his soul through his eyes. Each time they stop talking, they drift into silent gaze for a few seconds. Jill wonders—*What does this mean? Oh well, stop analyzing and enjoy the moment.* Afterward, she gets chills up her spine when she reflects on the ferocity of their eyes locking. This connection feels so good after the difficulties with Jill's last boyfriend.

John can't believe how attracted he is to Jill. He's had crushes on beautiful women in the company before, but never anything like this. *Oh boy, I can't get wrapped up in another affair. I was in the doghouse when Liz caught me with Shelly. If I get reported again, I'll be out of a job*

Jill likes the way John takes the time to acknowledge her during team meetings. Jill also likes that he gives special projects that give her the opportunities to showcase her talents to senior management.

Jill taps into her psychology knowledge and the personal growth she's done over the years to figure out the unique energy she has with John. *Why is this attraction so overpowering? This is not kosher—he's my boss. We haven't even had sex. It's like we're having emotional sex. It seems like he's dying to get frisky, but that's not happening. Maybe he reminds me of someone from my past that I still have unfinished business with . . .*

◆　◆　◆

Shelly has taken notice of the time and attention John showers on Jill. Shelly thinks—*It is clear that John is smitten with her. Will he be smacked with harassment again? He's been reported several times and forced to go to "leadership rehab" classes. If he's doing to Jill what he did to me . . . yes, it was hot and heavy between us, but it was never out in the open. I ended our secret affair after a year of empty promises to leave his wife. I still have residual feelings for him. I hate that he's found a new love interest. Damn, I'm jealous! Jill is hot. Why do women like her exist? To make me feel inadequate and miserable? If he gets in trouble for harassment, it will serve him right!*

Chapter 4

It's All About Me

John is at the podium leading the quarterly meeting, droning on in his usual ways—highlighting the successes, then going into the negatives of what his business unit did not achieve.

"You guys are disappointing. We didn't meet the new business target for the last quarter. What's the matter? I thought I could count on you." John delivers the bad news in an angry and condescending tone. Everyone fidgets in their seats.

A few strong hands go up to try to defend their actions. Then a middle manager chimes in with matter-of-fact, calm energy to sum up the latest experience, "With the last two client pitches, you weren't clear on the specifics of your new ideas. We presented our ideas, and they didn't meet your standards—"

John interrupts midsentence, clearly irritated and flustered that he is publicly criticized. "Matt, I gave you all the details. Sit down, please," he says in a commanding tone. John hates it when he can't win an argument.

Someone else yells out without being called on, "John, we needed specifics!"

"Blame your managers for not giving you what you need. I gave them the vision, and it was up to them to figure things out."

Now the managers are riled up, whispering to each other during the coffee break. If a fly were on the wall, it would hear:

"What a pompous ass! He doesn't give us shit to work with."

"He's verbally constipated, can't express details clearly."

"I've known John for a long time. He never used to be so angry; the old John listened more. He must be under a lot of stress at home."

John has been able to get away with his crass ways for many years because he has middle managers who know how to manage up. They bow to him, give him accolades, and in turn, they are the ones who get significant raises and promotions. John is capable of being nice half of the time, but the other half of the time he gets overtaken by stress and fear; unpleasant parts rear their ugly heads.

Jill squirms in her seat. She has never experienced this degree of nastiness from John. *What has gotten over him? This is not the John I know. Where's his compassion?*

At the next coffee break, frustrations continue to spill out.

"Jill, I see you got an unexpected earful. Now you see what it's like to work at Zatuck. Welcome! Watch out for the big boss there. He'll stab you in the back when you least expect it."

All around the room, Jill can hear snatches of disdain.

"He doesn't listen, doesn't care, and doesn't trust us."

"He micromanages and complains but seldom compliments. But, he does show his nice side when he's in a good mood. He's not all that bad, not much worse than other impotent bosses I've worked with."

"He has an angry edge."

"Thank goodness he's not my direct boss. I would've left a long time ago. My boss protects me and takes the brunt of John's bad leadership."

As Jill listens to her colleagues throw John under the bus, she thinks—*I've seen my boss be frustrated with John. Michael figures it out and gives me his ideas of how I should go about things. It does look like Michael knows how to manage up.*

More complaints come out.

"I heard John denied unpaid leave for someone whose wife had cancer; the poor guy had to use all of his vacation time."

"He took credit for Jessie's brilliant marketing pitch."

"He's a narcissistic name-dropping Ivy League jerk."

And on and on it goes.

Mark says he's grateful Michael is a buffer from John, "Mike is such an amazing guy to work for."

"Notice how he favors certain people," Chelsea utters with a wry smirk to Mark and then looks over to Jill. "Jill, he's taken you under his wings, and we just gave you an earful of dirty laundry. What are you going to do about that? You're lucky he likes you. You'll go far if you continue to charm him," Chelsea says with a wink.

Jill looks down and says nothing.

Jared chimes in, "John is a wounded five-year-old who never got the love and validation he needed. Maybe that drove him to overachieve? Instead of hate, I feel sorry for John. Someday, things will come crashing down, and he'll have to face his demons. What goes around comes around. Law of Karma will do its job in divine time."

Maria adds, "He doesn't know any better. As a marketer, we have insights about what makes people tick and what makes them buy." Maria lowers her voice, continuing, "For years I've been studying psychology and the spiritual roots of behavior. John has deep childhood scars. He is not evolved, and he's not conscious. Living from ego, he always needs to prove to himself how great he is. I'll bet he's never been to therapy or read self-help books. Executive coaches helped him temporarily, but John always went back to his old mean ways. We shouldn't judge him for not being conscious. He doesn't know any better. I'm grateful there are a few of us here who are evolved and can see things from a spiritual compassionate perspective."

Several of those gathered thank Jared and Maria for their enlightened takes on John. They understand that he's locked in an emotional prison. As the coffee break ends, Tina thanks Jared and Maria for their insights, "I never thought of bad bosses as a deeply wounded child; it makes sense."

As Jill discovers the inside scoop on John's reputation, she feels torn. *John has been so good to me. I see his light and how wonderful he can be when his inner demons don't overtake him. My heart aches.* With this sudden, protective insight about John, Jill can't believe she has a desire to take care of the hurt little boys inside of him.

◆　◆　◆

After calling an end to the meeting, John doesn't hang around to socialize. He retreats to the office and realizes he was hijacked by negative emotions. *The financial pressures are too much. Three mortgages, two private school tuitions, credit card bills up the wazoo! No wonder I was a jackass at the podium.* He swivels the large leather chair around and focuses his gaze on a clump of trees, a small green island in the middle of the gray pavement. Another voice pipes up—*Just trust . . . things will turn around.* The next day, John decides to write an apology email.

Hi Team,

My sincerest apologies for being too direct and negative yesterday. You guys are doing a great job. Keep up the excellent work.

Respectfully,
John

Jill opens the email. Not sure if an empty apology like this can turn things around. *As a friend, I need to help him.*

Internal Family Systems (IFS) Explanation of How Parts Can Wreak Havoc

Adapted from IFS Institute (www.IFS-Institute.com)

What is a Protector?

A part becomes a protector when it goes to extremes to protect you from re-experiencing painful feelings from the past. For example, many of us have drinking parts that like to come out during Happy Hour and dinnertime. That's an appropriate time for Self to allow the drinking part to be social and enjoy how the wine complements the meal. But when the drinking part gets excessive—four to five drinks per day—and drinking part has a hard time stopping, that's when the part has turned into a protector.

Protectors can poke through and wreak havoc when you are overwhelmed with fear and shame, like they did with John during the staff meeting. John is burdened with financial and marital stresses. Feeling like a failure activated the young vulnerable part of him that felt like he could never be "enough" for his parents, as well as the part of him that felt inadequate compared to his peers. Since he was already in a bad emotional state when he walked into the meeting, his angry, controlling, and self-centered parts took over and made him look like a jerk in front of his team. Rather than conducting a productive and motivating meeting, John wreaked havoc, further damaging his reputation as a leader.

Protectors are in roles to protect you from feeling something that you don't want to deal with, such as when your spouse continually criticizes you, and you just want to drown out how hurt you feel. Drinking numbs you from feeling the emotional pain of the ten-year-old part that was criticized continuously by Mom. Your significant other's criticisms bring you back to the unresolved emotional burdens caused by mom. Angry part can come out alongside the drinking part to fight with your spouse. You may feel the "monster" parts take over when you are in conflict with your partner. Also, stress from home can be unconsciously projected onto how you show up as a leader. To dial down protectors, the Self must understand why excessive drinking and anger exist. Once the protectors feel heard by your Higher Self, that's when they permit you to heal the vulnerable exiles (the inner child/inner children) and help them unload emotional burdens. When the exile(s) are relieved and retrieved from their original terror or shame, that's when drinking and angry parts can be dialed down and not place you in precarious situations.

What Is an Exile?

Exiles are the younger parts that were exiled into the dark inner basement of your psyche during devaluing emotional experiences. They are kept hidden so that you don't re-experience the awful feelings, but they poke through during relational stresses. The exile's childhood devaluing moments can be as seemingly benign as hearing your parents say, "Why can't you get A's like your sister?" Or, when your younger brother was born, and Mom switched her attention from you to him and she said, "Play with your toys and watch this show, I have to take care of your baby brother." Or, the events can be very traumatic, such as sexual abuse, getting hit, or bullied on the playground. The emotional wounds these exiled parts suffered have programmed you with burdens such as: *I'm not smart enough, I'm ugly, I'm not lovable, I don't matter, I'm not worthy, I'm a failure,* etc.

These exiles are your vulnerable parts, or inner child/inner children that protectors protect from being triggered into feelings of past pain when a current situation unconsciously reminds you of familiar, painful energy from the past. Often, this happens when your love interest gives you breadcrumbs of affection in a similar way your dad did, or how your boss orders you around in similar energy that Dad ordered Mom around. Later in the book, you will be shown how these deep-seated emotions can be unshackled and mitigated gently with the Internal Family Systems (IFS) healing model.

What Is a Burden?

Burdens are limiting beliefs and uncomfortable emotions that imprinted during emotional experiences; therefore, these burdens are your "emotional baggage." For example, deep humiliation from getting called names by your peers or repeatedly being reminded by your parents or older sibling that you're not smart enough. Also, the cultural, world, and religious views that authority figures imposed on you can be burdens that hold you back from greatness. Examples of these views and beliefs are: "You shouldn't have sex before marriage," or "Girls are to be seen and not heard," or "Boys don't cry," or "You should never be more successful than your husband; otherwise he'll leave you."

When the child parts hear disempowering messages repeatedly, you become burdened with these limiting beliefs. As an adult, these messages and views show up everywhere when you can't accomplish your biggest goals in love, wealth, and health. If you feel stuck, you must look to the past for the root causes. The past is always in the present.

IFS is Not About Repressing Parts;
It is About Offloading Their Negative Residues from the Past

The goal of the Internal Family Systems (IFS) Self-leadership model of emotional healing, personal growth, and accelerated transformation is to reorganize the inner system so that protectors give you the permission to release the burdens and inner fury of the exiles they protect. Reprogramming your parts' beliefs via the IFS protocol also gives you a new positive "inner operating software."

This new software has the power to help you unleash the inner greatness in all areas of your life.

The Self, in its congruence and sovereignty, has the power to restore the exiles to emotional health by unburdening their disempowering beliefs and negative emotional loads. Then, the Self can help these younger parts of you adopt new views such as, "I am lovable," "I am enough," and "I am worthy!" After your exiles unburden their limiting beliefs, terror, shame, and unworthiness, the protectors will no longer need to protect them with their extreme ways of being since these vulnerable parts have been rescued from the inner basement. When the exiles' emotional intensity is fully unloaded or significantly diminished, you will feel calmer, more centered, and your magnetic Self-energy can lead the way to success. Unburdening the exiles allows protectors to dial down or change direction. The protectors usually know what new positive roles they would like to take on, such as cheering you on to take risks instead of making you afraid.

IFS tagline is: "All parts are welcome!"

Parts are most welcome in balanced doses that do not create havoc with yourself and others. Following the IFS principles do not mean you are perfect one-hundred percent of the time, or you never react. It means you are more self-aware of your emotional triggers without resorting to damaging or inappropriate outbursts. When rifts occur, you can apologize—from calm, Self-energy— *for* the parts that acted out. When you courageously and vulnerably own your shortcomings and quirks, you build deep and trusting relationships that last a lifetime.

Self-led Apology for a Part that Went Awry

If you find yourself in regret over something you said or did, use the following Self-led apology formula:

The (name the part) part had a temper tantrum when it
got triggered by (name the situation).
I'm sorry. I hope you can forgive this part of me.

Example:
"My mean part had a temper tantrum when it got triggered by not hearing from you for four days. Your silence made me unfriend you on Facebook. I'm sorry. I hope you can forgive this part of me."

Chapter 5

Get Out of My House

I t's 3:30 PM on a Friday. John is knee-deep in work when his cell phone rings. It's his wife. *What does she want now?*

"Hi, Liz, everything okay? I'm in the middle of something," he says, sounding annoyed.

"Yes, my dear, I know you're busy. I just wanted to remind you to stay at the office and not come home until eight o'clock. Remember, I told you my girlfriends are coming over at five for cocktails and catch-up. The kids will watch a movie in the media room."

"Really? I don't remember you saying that. I guess I wasn't listening. I was looking forward to coming home early to catch up on stuff on my desk before I leave for the golf vacation." *Shoot! I wish Jill weren't away at a friend's wedding. She could have kept me occupied.*

"Please, John, I can't cancel this. Everyone's looking forward to it."

"Whatever!" John says with an angry tone and hangs up.

As the afternoon wears on, John becomes more annoyed. Liz doesn't pay attention to his needs. John does have an inner critic that is often, but not always, self-aware of his negative traits. John's anger fumes. *How did I ever allow this? I hate her girlfriends. They take time away from the kids and me. I'm sure they all just sit around bashing their husbands.* He forces his attention back to the paperwork on his desk.

At six o'clock, John calls Liz. "Make sure everyone is out of the house by the time I get home. No one should be parked in the driveway; I could better pull the car into the garage. I'll be home at seven."

"No, you can't come home at seven! We're having lots of fun. You know how important my 'girls only' time is. Please don't ruin this." Liz hangs up, angry and embarrassed that John may crash the party.

At six-thirty-seven, John calls again. "Are they starting to leave? Please remind them there's no overtime chitchat. I need to get shit done before my trip!"

"Yes, SIR!" Liz yells and hangs up the phone.

Liz's girlfriends see how troubled she looks.

Several friends simultaneously chime in, "Are you okay? What's going on with John?"

"Ladies, everyone has to be out of here by eight o'clock, not one minute later. Otherwise, it's going to get ugly. You know how mean John can get when I don't honor his requests."

At twenty minutes until eight, with six friends still hanging out in the beautiful kitchen that looks like it came out of the pages of *Architectural Digest*, Liz pulls out the vacuum cleaner and attacks the crumbs on the floor. She's on a cleaning spree, clearing the wine glasses and wrapping up the remains of the food.

"Liz, don't be so neurotic, the cleaning can wait; come talk," Maggie tries to convince her to put the vacuum down.

"I can't. John goes ballistic if the house isn't spanking clean when he gets home. If his foot feels one crumb on the kitchen floor, he'll have a temper tantrum. He expects perfection."

Shocked, Maggie and a few other women think to themselves—*Thank goodness my husband is not a dictator; If I had a husband like John, I would've divorced the guy a long time ago; I'd rather live in a tiny apartment and have freedom instead of feeling like I live in a prison; I guess I have nothing to complain about with my boring marriage compared to Liz's. Whew!*

By seven-fifty, most of the ladies have left, except for three of her closest friends, Beth, Jenny, and Mary. They chitchat while Liz shows family pictures and tells funny stories. *I love these friends; they keep me sane; I can share my "John" stories. Without them, I'd have a nervous breakdown. He's getting worse with the emotional abuse. I don't know how much longer I can take this. I am attached to this lifestyle, but keeping this up is getting harder. I can't live on my own. I guess I need to suck it up for now.*

"Liz, it's eight o'clock. Is it okay for us to be talking this late? We need to get going," Jenny says.

"Don't worry. It'll be all right. John knows the three of you better than the others. It's not a party anymore, so this should be fine."

John walks in the door at precisely at that moment with a sullen look on his face.

"Hey, John," Mary says with an attempt to kiss him on the cheek. He doesn't move or smile and acts like a robot.

Beth jumps in, "I hear you're going on a golf vacation; sounds fun!" The ladies think he's just playing games with his serious expression.

John's face turns crimson with what seems like deep frustration and anger. He's blended with angry part. Jenny attempts to coax him, not thinking he's serious. "It's only us. Liz has been showing us family pictures. We won't bother you if you have work to do."

John feels like his blood is about to boil and shoots them an angry look. He starts to open his mouth. The three friends grab purses and bolt out of the house and gather on the driveway, stunned and frozen with shock, hearing the fight erupt inside. At that, they turn away, moving at once, clickity-clacking their high-heeled shoes down the driveway and dashing into their cars to escape this sad and upsetting scene.

John follows Liz up the grand circular staircase. "Liz! What the hell? I told you not to have anyone in my house when I got home. You know how hard I work to support this family. Can't I have a little goddamn peace to take care of personal business? You spend so much time with these friends. What about me?"

"It's always about you, John! I've had enough!" Liz screams and slams the bedroom door. John feels dazed, rocking on his heels. Where can he go for solace? Any thought of tying up loose ends in his home office has vanished. *Where are the kids? I need a distraction.*

He knocks on the media room door and invites Finn, nine, and Robert, eleven, to play a card game. As the door opens, he senses their trepidation, obviously on edge from hearing the blow-up between their parents. It doesn't take too much convincing to shift their mood. Staying up past their bedtime is always fun, and the boys are only too eager to blow off the movie to have some playtime with Dad. With John out of sight, Liz calms down a bit and hears their laughter. *He might be a jerk with me but he's SO good with the kids. It's time to draw a bath and drown out the whole evening.*

By ten o'clock, way past the boys' bedtime, John hugs both kids, one at each side, needing comfort and affection more than the boys do. He tells them he has a secret. "It's okay for parents to fight, guys. There's no need to get upset. Parents need to let out a little steam once in a while." Robert sighs and appears to relax. John asks the boys if they can tell him the latest jokes from school, and John exaggerates his laugh to make sure Liz hears upstairs how well he's doing with the kids. *I'm so glad I can have fun with the kids tonight. I need to do this more often.*

After saying good night, John feels unsettled by the commotion he caused with Liz and her friends. Something stirs deep inside, a feeling of spiraling financial anxiety that keeps him off balance. He just can't tell Liz the source of his frustrations. *I feel like a financial loser, not able to support our lifestyle with ease. Am I a man if I can't do that?* His breathing becomes shallow, restricted with a bit of fear, as he tip-toes into the massive master bedroom, thinking Liz is asleep on the edge of the king-sized bed; he stays on his side. *I can cut the tension between us with a knife.*

The next morning, Liz is exhausted and still angry. She ruminated on their fake and disastrous marriage and couldn't fall asleep until three in the morning. *His outbursts and petty pestering are insane. We never resolve anything because he stonewalls and never wants to talk. Gotta keep going to therapy to deal with this, even though he refuses to go. What a phony life! I didn't sign up for this!*

◆　◆　◆

A couple of days later, John starts to feel wrong about Liz's ruined party. He realizes that the monsters inside of him took over—again. But his justification muscle remains strong. He remembers that Liz spends money like crazy and does her own thing, refusing to give him the sex he needs. *It's not my fault I act the way I do. I work hard to provide a fancy lifestyle, and she still refuses to have sex. If it weren't for me, she'd be living in a one-room rental. But how long can we keep this up? I take care of the bills. She has no idea how bad things are.*

For most of their twelve years together, John didn't like it when Liz had girls' nights out or went to the gym, leaving him alone. He'd make her feel guilty when she left him with the kids. He knows he's controlling, but he can't help it. *If she wants to live the white-picket-fence fairy tale, she has to tolerate my moods.*

While these tensions and dark clouds mount at home, the bright light in John's days has been Jill. When he feels guilty about what's going on at home, at least there's a beautiful woman at work who admires him and can see the goodness of who he is. Their friendship is blossoming nicely, and she's learning a lot under his mentorship. He can't help but take credit for Jill's notable job performance.

The physical, emotional, and intellectual attraction keep increasing with Jill. Everything about her is stimulating. He imagines her in lacy lingerie, stripping her naked, and giving her mind-blowing multiple orgasms. He indulges in his fantasy more often, now, sometimes pushing aside the stacks on his desk to imagine Jill seductively dancing in front of him.

John is excited about spending time with Jill at an upcoming four-day advertising conference. John handpicked her to accompany him. The favored treatment of Jill has not gone unnoticed by members of John's business unit. They have witnessed his favoritism, and frequently gossip about John's personalized attention on Jill.

Internal Family Systems Lens on John's Lack of Self-leadership

The last two chapters illustrate John's protective parts hijacking his inner calm, where his mean, angry, and controlling traits overtake Self.

Think about a bad boss or a difficult colleague. Do you think he or she is a loving "angel" in their romantic relationship? Your answer is probably, "Heck no! I can't imagine being their partner." Or, "I feel sorry for their significant other."

Angry, controlling, and self-centered bosses or colleagues likely show these negative traits in their romantic lives, too. Conversely, if someone has a great love life, what is the likelihood that they are a peach to work for? It's probably high.

Demanding bosses and less-than-ideal romantic partners act that way because they have unresolved childhood emotional issues lurking underneath the surface. The past is always in the present. They often lack interpersonal and intrapersonal insight, which makes it challenging for them to achieve emotional regulation and take responsibility for their actions. "This is just the way I am; deal with it." Sooner or later, this attitude can cause broken relationships and careers.

People who haven't dealt with their emotional baggage—and we all have baggage—get worse over time. Think of the family member who has gotten worse as they aged. Unless they invest the time, energy, and money into therapy and personal growth, they will not improve. Finding a new job, a new partner, buying a new sports car, and undergoing plastic surgery will not save them because the same pattern will repeat over and over again. Unfortunately, their best Self is buried underneath the wounded parts. Eventually, what goes around comes around, and these people join the ranks of the two-thirds of leaders who fail. Many also fail in romantic relationships and struggle with emotional and physical health.

Triggered Exiles

Protectors protect exiles (also known as the inner child or inner children) from feeling their old shame, worthlessness, and terror. Exiles are hidden and protected in the deep recesses of your psyche. Sometimes they erupt when triggered, such as during heated exchanges or when you experience stonewalling and ghosting. When you are in emotional pain and say nasty things, storm out of the house, freeze, or cry like a baby, the Higher Self has checked out; you are now *blended* with your part(s). Another example of getting triggered is when the new guy you are dating ghosts or is inconsistent with communication. When Liz did not agree to let John come home early, he did not feel he mattered. This hurt activated the younger parts of John that felt the pain when his parents ignored him. Therefore, he felt the need to lash out at Liz to feel heard and significant.

Access to Self Can Save the Day

If John had the self-awareness and capacity to separate from his controlling and angry parts that were activated when he saw that Liz's friends were still in the house, he could have calmly expressed to Liz that he needs to relax in his own home without guests.

The Power of Unblending From Parts and Accessing Self

Dr. Schwartz, the founder of IFS, has written to his followers: "As clients learn to separate from their extreme emotions and thoughts

. . . I find that they spontaneously tap into a calm, centered state, which I call their Self—soul, essence, mindfulness. In this state of Self, clients realize that they already know how to take care of their inner exiles on their own and that those parts don't need salvation because they were never bad to begin with. I refer to this state of Self as Self-leadership."

Chapter 6

Going Around the Bases

February 2015

J ill feels happy about the opportunity to spend time with John at the advertising conference in San Francisco. John loves that he gets to walk alongside a colleague who looks like a model out of the pages of a glossy luxury magazine. People do double-takes because they look so good together. John has been diligent with an exercise and weight loss plan to whittle down his waist; ten pounds gone, ten more to go. Jill was the incentive he needed to get fit and healthy again. To Jill, John is not the narcissistic monster everyone paints him to be. *I'm so proud of myself*—she reflects. *My personality brings the best out in him. He needs me.*

On the first night of the conference, they dine at the highly acclaimed French restaurant, Gary Danko. They eat dinner leisurely as they go through an expensive bottle of wine. The wine's buzz makes them glow under the candlelight. The intensity of their mutual attraction is up a notch, and their flirting and twinkling eye contact cause big grins. It feels like a romantic movie. This entangled high vibration is the epitome of Self-to-Self energy and connection. When the bill arrives, as usual, John gives a generous 25 percent tip.

Once back at their hotel, John presses the elevator button and asks, "Would you like to see the wonderful city lights from my suite? We can raid the mini-bar and enjoy the beautiful view."

"Sure!" Jill exclaims. "I was wondering how we were going to continue this high."

Upon entering his suite, John places his iPhone into the dock, and soothing music fills the room. Then, he pours two glasses of sherry. As they look out the floor-to-ceiling window at the beautiful view of city lights, John places his left hand on the small of Jill's back. Jill's thinking—*Oh my gosh, is this really happening? My boss is making a move. I need to get out of here!* Then another voice takes over—*Enjoy the moment; he's digging you. It's been so long since you've had someone who is so in awe of your brilliance and beauty. Nothing terrible will happen. The flirting is consensual. We can keep this a secret!* The opposing inner chatter of parts compels her to remain silent. *I'll let him lead this dance.*

John and Jill carry themselves into a romantic haze. John's lips are very close to touching hers. Though his thoughts are foggy, one inner voice says—*What am I doing? I'm married, I'm her boss, and I could be fired for this.* Then, his justification voice takes over—*The last three years of my sexless marriage have been so cold. Jill is hot for me, and I'm crazy about her. I've got to break the sexual tension—otherwise, it will blow up in negative ways. Just make sure she agrees this is consensual.* John convinces himself that there's no way Jill would report this as harassment.

Jill allows herself to fall into John's arms as the Lana Del Rey song, "Summertime Sadness," plays. John turns up the volume to get the bass thumping. He places his arms around Jill's waist and looks deeply into her eyes. His hips sway to the music, and Jill follows his rhythm. Jill's thinking—*He has excellent rhythm; his hips and legs jive with mine. Syncing my body to his feels heavenly! What would it be like to climax with him? Stop thinking about sex! It's not going to happen.*

John's thinking—*Holy smokes! People tell me that when it comes to white guys with great rhythm, I'm a rare bird. This is the most fantastic rhythmic energy I've ever felt with a woman. I'll just go with the flow, with our bodies glued together, and allow the light switch in my pants to flip on.*

John reaches over to lightly kiss Jill's lips, feeling her ample, sexy breasts push against his chest. The electricity between them is palpable. *This is so hot!*

While Jill thinks—*Whoa, the hairdryer in his pants is turned up to high. The heat feels so good!*

"If you want me to stop, let me know. If you want this as much as I do, then let's not deny ourselves. We have a friendship beyond work, and we're off the clock now. I'm not your boss now, I'm your friend. I would never trespass boundaries or hurt you. Are you okay with this?" John's rationalizing part says.

Jill doesn't answer. She pulls his body closer to receive his passionate kiss. They are in bliss, and time stops.

"You're such a great kisser," John whispers between heavy breathing.

"I'm surrendering into an amazing kisser's lead. Stop talking and keep kissing," Jill giggles.

The lovers are out of the stands and onto the playing field. John makes a move to remove her blouse but leaves her bra on. Entangled, they round the kissing stage and head into a bit of shirtless petting; then John moves his hands under her skirt. Jill places her hand on John's arm and says, "Sorry, there's a padlock on my panties."

John cracks up at that moment, "That's hilarious!" Jill also laughs at her wit.

"That one came out unrehearsed," as she continues the giggle. Then she snaps out of it. "We can't do this! You're married, and you're my boss! I need to go to my room." She puts her blouse on quickly, reaches for the door handle, and exits. *Whew! That was a close call.*

A half-hour passes, and Jill receives a text. Good night Jill. Thanks for a great evening. I loved the "padlock" comment.☺ Jill replies, Good night John. I had fun.☺

At breakfast the next morning, they chuckle about their tryst.

"The alcohol took over. Seriously, it's because you're so beautiful, smart, lovely, sweet, pretty, so hot, and—"

"All right, move along." Jill blushes, talking over him.

"Stunning and charming, inside and out, you've put a spell on—"

Jill smiles and stops him with, "I get it."

John takes a sip of his coffee and says, "I couldn't help myself. Do I need to apologize for my naughtiness? We both had pent-up energy that needed to be released. We've been feeling it for a long time."

"No need for apologies. I was a willing party. I couldn't help myself, either. We desperately needed to discharge the sexual tension. You're pretty hot, John. My body was aching for you. Good thing I had enough control to get out of your room."

"Yeah, thank God!"

Jill giggles. "I love full transparency. How are we going to make it through two more nights at this conference?"

"We're adults; we can hold back. We just need to stay away from alcohol." They continue to act giddy like high school lovebirds.

Despite their intentions to behave, the second night is a repeat of the first, and Jill manages to escape after heavy groping, even though she was dying to take things to the next level.

The third night, they continue to indulge in their mutual lust, but behave again.

At breakfast, before they leave for the airport, John says, "Well, my wife can't accuse me of having an affair since we didn't go past second base. It was just heavy petting, not sex."

"Whatever . . ." Jill winks and rolls her eyes with a big smile.

"And one other thing. Because you and I have such great chemistry on so many levels, I can see us breaking away from Zatuck someday to launch a boutique agency."

Jill is a bit shocked by that statement. "Oh? That would be interesting. I've always wanted to start my own business."

◆   ◆   ◆

March 2015

In the weeks following their conference tryst, Jill's coworkers notice she is in charge of more plum assignments and given opportunities to present in front of the Executive Leadership Team. Her coworkers dislike the unfair preferential treatment.

John and Jill hold back with their physical relationship. They still enjoy the banter and fantastic chemistry.

Nine months after Jill's hiring, much to the dismay of her coworkers, Jill receives a promotion to Manager of Strategic Services, in charge of a ten-person team.

Chapter 7

Look at Yourself in the Mirror

John and his best friend from college, Antonio, meet on the patio at their favorite Mexican bar, Tequilas and Tacos. Antonio and John have a brotherly love and long history of supporting each other through thick and thin. They're comfortable enough in the friendship to call each other out on anything. After the usual niceties and three shots of tequila, the truth comes out.

"Can I confess something?" John asks.

"Sure . . . what's up? I sensed you've been dying to tell me something."

"I am seriously head-over-heels in love with someone at work. Jill is so hot and beautiful, inside and out. I almost fell out of my chair the first time she walked into my office. But it's not just that she's gorgeous; I feel a connection I've never felt with anyone before. We're like two magnets that can't stay away from each other."

"Sounds like you two are in vibrational resonance. Have you been a bad boy?" Antonio asks with a wink.

"If you promise to keep this a secret, I'll tell you."

"Of course. We can talk as deeply as women do. Your secrets are locked in a vault."

Letting out a sigh, John says, "Yes . . . I've been a bad boy. Just a little harmless fondling in my hotel room at a conference in San Francisco, but we put the brakes on. We felt like we couldn't get enough of each other. I can see myself leaving Liz for her one day. Another thing . . . it's always been a dream of mine to break away from Zatuck and launch my own business. Jill has what it takes to be my sidekick. She's wicked smart! She complements me in areas where I don't shine." John keeps smiling, "We're going to—"

Antonio butts in, "You are such a dreamer. How serious are you about Jill? You've been a bad boy more than a few times, especially with Shelly."

"Shelly was impatient for me to divorce Liz, and I can't get divorced until the kids are in college. I don't want to shuffle them back and forth, and my precarious financial position will be that much worse with divorce. Since I couldn't get divorced, Shelly reported me to HR. She said I was harassing her—without admitting we were sleeping together. I got a hand slap from HR. Then Shelly retaliated and told Liz we were having an affair. After a few years, Shelly and I did get back on friendly terms, and we're fine now. She found new love interests. Shelly's a perfectionist, and great with strategy and execution. She's someone I'll need on my team, in addition to Jill, if I ever launch my dream business."

"Do you realize what you're saying? How exactly will that work out? Jill and the 'other woman' you promised to marry would be working together? Shelly knows your patterns and can very well sniff out what's going on between you and Jill. One more slip-up and Zatuck will fire you. Look, we've been friends for a long time. Friends have each other's backs, right?"

"Right . . . what are you trying to say?"

"I see the writing on the wall. You worry me. I'm here for you, but I don't know if I can take your BS anymore. You're already on a downward spiral with your marriage and your bad behaviors at work. I've seen you blame other people when things don't go well. It's never your fault. The reality is, you're the creator of your negative outcomes."

John bats a wadded-up straw wrapper around the table and covers his ear with his other hand.

"I've mentioned this before, and I'll say it again. Do the inner work and evaluate who you're hurting—and how you're hurting yourself. Your ego is in the way," Antonio says with a loving, brotherly tone and pats John's shoulder. Despite the brutally honest pep talk, John feels Antonio's compassion.

"You know I was in a bad place a while back," Antonio concedes. "Men don't like to admit they have issues. We're supposed to be strong, right? We can power through anything. Well, not always. I needed help. When I read Lewis Howes' book, *The Mask of Masculinity*, the book explained why I was a disaster. If you keep going on like this, you could end up being another #MeToo toxic perpetrator. Hell, you could go to jail."

John scoots the straw wrapper into a planter and looks happy for the moment. He doesn't interrupt. Antonio's truth bombs have helped him navigate many challenging situations.

"I want the best for you, my friend. You know how things crashed for me five years ago?"

"Yeah . . . losing your girlfriend and job at the same time."

"After going around in circles with two therapists who didn't have the spiritual lens I needed to get unstuck, I found Martha. I'd refer you to her, but she's retired now. All I have to say is what goes around comes around. Karma will come back to bite you."

"But I finally found Jill! Are you saying if I don't get help, I . . . can ruin this?"

"Yep!"

John orders two more shots of tequila and chugs them down.

"Think of this as truth serum. Pretend I'm your clairvoyant friend, just a few steps ahead of you. It's physics and energy. You've got negative energy from childhood locked up in your emotional body. At some point, it will explode and make you self-sabotage."

John flashes on his treatment of his wife and her friends, recalling how he exploded in front of them.

Antonio squeezes John's shoulder to convey the constructive feedback comes from a place of love.

After several moments of silence, Antonio breaks the ice. "We've been best friends since freshman year. You've been there for me, and I'm here to do the same for you. Now I can sleep at night knowing I didn't hold anything back."

The two of them look around the restaurant patio, avoiding eye contact. John takes another shot of tequila.

"The way you grew up and the pressures from your dad, especially on the tennis court, are probably the root causes of your anger, frustration, self-centeredness, and the need to indulge in too much booze. Real warriors are brave enough to go to therapy. Masked phony warriors claim there's nothing wrong with them. Eventually, they self-sabotage and fail. You'll thank me later."

Silence again hangs in the air as John, and Antonio checks out the attractive waitress walking past them.

"You sound like that guy with the big teeth."

"You mean Tony Robbins?"

"Yeah."

Antonio laughs. "Thank you. I take that as a compliment. I learned a lot by watching his videos, reading his books, and going to his seminars."

"I want to say, 'Fuck you!' for being so mean to me today, but I'm not going to." John rubs his face with both hands and takes a big breath. "I need time to absorb your truth bombs."

"Tony Robbins and many other experts say, 'The quality of your relationships determines the quality of your life.' If you want things to change, it starts with you instead of blaming everyone else. Look in the mirror—you are the problem, not other people." Antonio states this in a gentle brotherly way so John can hear the message.

The two of them gaze at a couple bickering nearby. There's not much more to say. Finally, Antonio gives John one last word. "I'm done with my sermon. Since you've overdosed on tequila, I'll order an Uber to get you home safely." Antonio signals the server and picks up the check.

Feeling like crap in the back seat of his ride, John regrets drinking so much. *Antonio is right on so many fronts. I better do something about my demons. Otherwise, I'll sabotage the best thing that's ever come into my life—Jill.*

Then John mentally tucks Antonio's come-to-Jesus conversation into the back of his mind. *Can't ruminate on this now*, he reasons, *got to help with the kids' sports awards dinner this weekend.*

Men and Friendships

Not all men are fortunate enough to have the depth of emotional bond as John and Antonio have. You may raise your eyebrow with, "This is not how men talk to each other!" You are correct; this is not how *most* men talk to each other. (Some women don't have this depth of emotional connection, either.) John is quite lucky to have Antonio's friendship. A minority of male friendships are this deep. If you are afraid to share the deepest parts of you, more than likely, this means you haven't done the work to reclaim lost and forgotten parts hiding in the inner caves. You can start the self-growth journey by reading books, going to psychotherapy, attending personal growth workshops, watching personal growth videos on YouTube, or joining a men's or women's support group. If you do attend self-development workshops, the facilitators create safe environments for the mutual sharing of vulnerabilities. This environment fosters emotional closeness, and the birth of new friendships similar to the one Antonio and John have.

Many men have been conditioned through their upbringing and from cultural messages that to be a "real man," they need to chase after money, power, and sex. Eventually, this effort to satisfy the ego can lead to living a life of quiet desperation. The quest for external rewards can take over to the point where relationships suffer or are nonexistent. Our society asks men to be strong soldiers, lone wolves, invulnerable providers, and rescuers with superhero characteristics.

Chapter 8

Don't Judge Me

John is hungover in his office from his night with Antonio, whose words are still ringing. *He's so right about my shit. I've got to address it one of these days. But why does he have to burst my bubble with Jill? Okay, time to stop. Get back to work! We'll deal with this later. Jill's coming in any minute.*

John is happy to see Jill's beautiful smile and shapely body. He looks forward to spending time at a weekend off-site leadership workshop in Cape Cod, Massachusetts.

"Let's get the show on the road, my friend," John says. "I hope this leadership training isn't boring like most of the previous ones I've been to."

"Based on the description, the seminar should be interesting. I love all things related to psychology and leadership development," Jill enthusiastically says as she sits down across from him and opens her computer.

They get so lost in their project that they lose track of time. Jill notices and says, "Oh boy, we better get going before the thick of rush hour. Let's go now." John gets up and sprints with Jill to his car, parked in the adjacent parking garage.

The first few hours of the six-hour drive to the Cape were light-hearted. John "behaved" and only touched Jill's arm a couple of times. During the fourth hour, Jill, with a bit of trepidation, says, "Hey, can I bring something up?"

"Yeah, sure, what's on your mind?"

"I hear a lot of rumblings about your leadership style. Do you know what people say behind your back?"

"Kinda, but I don't care what other people think of me, I have a job to do," John says in a bit of an annoyed tone, looking at the road ahead.

"Oh." Jill feels dejected and a little surprised at how quickly he got defensive. "I want to see you succeed. I didn't like what I witnessed during the last big meeting during the coffee break—many people talked negatively behind your back. If you could only be more empathetic and listen, and be clearer and not change your mind on a whim because you feel like it."

"Please don't tell me what I need to do and how I need to change. I get enough of that at home."

"Sorry. I'm here to help. I love how we interact and how calm and friendly you are. I don't know why you have to scold me like that." Jill regrets bringing up the topic. *I just made him feel like a failure and an idiot.*

"I'm not scolding you; I'm telling you where I'm at," John says in a robotic tone. *What the fuck is she doing, talking to me like that?! I'm her boss. At least she acknowledged how nicely I treat her. I could make her life miserable, but I won't.*

To change the energy in the car, Jill calmly says, "I'm going to listen to a podcast for the rest of the ride. Thank you for inviting me to take the drive with you."

"Sure."

They finally arrive at nine o'clock at the luxurious Chatham Bars Inn resort in Chatham, Massachusetts, and settle into their respective rooms.

Giving Feedback

When you want to give constructive feedback, it is best to *refrain* from using these three words: "you," "why," or "but."

Think about a time when someone has used those words on you. Your walls probably went up, and you wanted to defend yourself. They may be coming from a place of good intentions, but they don't know how to have hard conversations via Self-leadership. In contrast, when you share your feelings using "I" statements, the other person can't attack *your* feelings. Here's how Jill could have said things differently to minimize John's defensiveness:

- "John, would it be okay if I shared my feelings about something?" (Asking permission gives the other person the power to decide if they are ready to hear feedback and prepares them to switch tracks from their current train of thought.)
- "I feel worried when I hear people talk negatively behind your back." (Jill states how she *feels* based on what she observed. Google "Feelings Wheel" for a comprehensive list of feelings adjectives.)

Instead of providing solutions or advice, ask questions to invite the other person to solve the problem.

- "What do you think about this?"
- "What do you plan on doing about this, if anything?"
- "Is there something I should know?"
- "Is there more I should know?"
- "I trust that you can figure out how to fix this. Please let me know how I can best support you."

PART II

Chapter 9

Root Causes of Leadership and Love Challenges

Emily W. Liu, the author, is now a character in the book. Emily shares her real-life backstory within the context of this fictional workshop. The omniscient narrator continues the story.

John, Jill, and thirty-eight other attendees from various industries attend Emily Liu's weekend workshop entitled: *Inspire, Influence, and Impact: The Science of Self-leadership, Success, and Self-Actualization.* Emily shows high achievers how to soar to greatness in leadership and love through Self-led confident vulnerability and authenticity via the Internal Family Systems (IFS) Self-leadership model.

John and Jill take their seats along with other participants sitting in semicircle round tables. Emily brought four fellow IFS practitioners to assist her in supporting the group's emotional needs. Emily takes the participants through icebreakers and introductory remarks, and then gets into the didactics.

"There's a widely quoted statistic that two-thirds of leaders fail. Two . . . thirds . . ." She emphasizes the impact of that staggering percentage. "This means many of you who manage teams or hope to rise to higher levels of leadership will fail. The details of these statistics are found in Robert Hogan's book, *Personality and the Fate of Organizations.* Hogan is a well-known organizational psychologist who consults with Fortune 500 companies.

"What causes incompetent, mediocre, and toxic bosses? What causes employee disengagement? What causes tension and polarization between coworkers, teams, and business units? What prevents high potential leaders from breaking through the proverbial glass ceiling? What causes the Peter Principle—that is, rising to the level of your incompetence? What causes powerful men and women to fall from their pinnacles? Well, the most important primary cause of all of these challenges is—lack of Self-leadership."

Emily asks the attendees to think about an ineffective boss they've had. If this boss is abhorrent at work, have they ever thought about what they're like in their love life? "Bet you can't even fathom being in a relationship with them, right? Do you think he or she is a good kisser?" She gets quite a few laughs from this imagery. Since Emily quickly connected with this group from the get-go, her sense-of-humor part is having a good time. She lets herself be a bit edgier when she is not training inside an organization, showing more of her sassy, colorful parts.

"Ewww . . . You couldn't pay me a million bucks to be his lover!" Susan blurts out. Laughter ensues from the crowd.

"Right? I know, everyone cracks up when I ask them to imagine this. It's highly unlikely that a bad boss is as sweet as honey with their partner, children, and extended family. Many of us, myself included, have had to learn relationship lessons the hard way. The key to repairing any relationship is to learn how to bravely and vulnerably speak for the imperfect parts that go wonky. We are *all* perfectly imperfect.

"Many of us struggle with relationships, especially romantic ones. We don't have the level of emotional and spiritual intimacy that has us flying high as a kite. So, I am enticing you to learn how to have thriving and fulfilling relationships through Self-led confident vulnerability. When you know how to be real and authentic in love through Self-leadership, you can use the same Self-leadership framework to be an inspiring leader that everyone loves to work for."

Now Emily has their attention. Every time she presents how Self-leadership can perk up their love life, participants get excited. Emily "accidentally" fell into teaching high-achievers how to be great leaders through the doorway love. When clients came to her with career and business challenges, she asked how the parts they struggled with at work showed up in other areas. Their eyes would roll, and they would invariably say, "Oh my, I struggle with that part in my love life too!" She lets them know that this is: "How you do one thing is how you do everything."

"When clients' romantic struggles were revealed, many coaching sessions switched from talking about leadership struggles to overcoming bad dating and relationship patterns. Clients loved overcoming their intimate relationship struggles through the Internal Family Systems healing and transformation model. As a result of these client experiences, I birthed my brand of teaching leadership skills through the doorway of love and intimacy."

The audience learns that lack of Self-leadership is the primary reason why relationships are hard, get stagnant, become dull, or dissolve. Unfortunately, some men—or perhaps many men—hold the belief that if the sex were better, the relationship would be better. "We have this age-old dilemma of men seeing sex as the doorway to emotional connection and women seeing the emotional connection as the doorway to sex. Maybe more sex makes a relationship better temporarily, but we know that more sex is never a long-term solution to lack of emotional safety and closeness. Just as more sex in a relationship is not going to fix a broken relationship, more surface-level leadership training is not going to fix the core of second-rate and impotent leaders." Many nods from attendees signal their agreement with this analogy.

John reflects on how Liz never gave him as much sex as he wanted. He thought sex would fix their problems, but Liz checked out during their mechanical lovemaking. *Yep, Emily's right. I haven't even had sex with Jill, and our connection is much stronger than the relationship I have with Liz.*

"Eliminating the root causes of lack of Self-leadership is the key to lasting transformation in love and leadership. 'Be the change you want to see in the world' is a quote often attributed to Gandhi. The Internal Family Systems Self-leadership framework, IFS for short, is the secret sauce to be the change, so you can make your personal and professional dreams come true. As Albert Einstein famously said, 'Problems can't be solved at the same level of thinking that created them.' If you apply this concept to leadership training, this means putting people through behavioral modification Band-Aid techniques is not going to create lasting transformation. If, after leaders learn the basics of how to be an effective manager and they don't become someone that others want to work their butt off for, this means there are childhood emotional icebergs underneath the surface that contribute to incompetent leadership. I'm taking Einstein's advice and not staying at the surface level. I'm going to show you why we need to dive deeper to eliminate the root causes of feeble leadership and romantic relationships devoid of emotional closeness."

Emily lets them know that IFS is a powerful, cutting-edge, evidence-based Self-leadership framework developed by Psychologist and Licensed Marriage and Family Therapist, Richard Schwartz, PhD, LMFT. Dr. Schwartz developed the IFS model in the 1980s. IFS has gained a lot of publicity in the last decade because studies have shown that the IFS protocol produces permanent emotional healing, accelerates self-awareness, and fosters lasting transformation.

Why Great Relationships Are Important

Emily continues. "Many studies, including the famous eight-decade longitudinal Harvard Grant Study on happiness, have shown that the emotional depth of our relationships, especially the romantic ones, is *the* most potent predictor of health, happiness, and longevity. The deeper the connection, the happier we are, and the longer we live.

"Money, possessions, power, and sex can never produce the joy and fulfillment experienced when we feel seen, seen at a level of emotional intimacy that is more naked than physical intimacy. Intimacy is 'in-to-me-you-see.' In this relational state, you can feel safe to fully reveal every layer of who you are, including your darkest secrets, deepest fears, and biggest dreams. When you dare to go first in revealing your vulnerabilities, it permits others to do the same; this is intimacy."

John and Jill both realize that they are happy after meeting each other because their friendship feels deeply connected. Jill makes a mental note that she has to refrain from sounding like a critical mother when she wants to give him constructive feedback.

"Vulnerability is the foundation of real courage, deep trust, and connection. When we're not afraid to own our shortcomings and foibles, trust and respect can skyrocket. As a result, we can become a leader and lover who inspires next-level growth and results in ourselves and others."

Emily dives deeper into what being vulnerable means. "The Merriam-Webster definition of 'vulnerable' is: 'capable of being physically or emotionally wounded.' When we open ourselves up to reveal our hidden shame, fears, and insecurities, we get scared because being vulnerable means the protective armors are no longer there. In this naked state, we are open to getting wounded with judgments and criticism; that's scary." Everyone agrees with this truth.

A homework assignment Emily gave the participants before attending the workshop was to read the NYT and WSJ bestselling book by Brené Brown, *Dare to Lead: Brave Work. Tough Conversations. Whole Hearts.* Brené is the world's most famous and leading researcher on vulnerability, shame, and courage. The purpose of assigning this book was to make them aware of Brené's hard data that proves vulnerability is *not* weakness. Vulnerability is the hallmark of warrior courage and the hallmark of daring and heart-led leaders. Emily wanted them to know the data behind the importance of vulnerability so that she didn't have to spend the time to defend how vital vulnerability is for success and thriving relationships. Emily continues, "The ability to be vulnerable requires warrior bravery, the courage to fail with vulnerability, and the resolve to scrape off the bruises to try again and again. A heart-led warrior leader learns how to be vulnerable. A leader who cannot be vulnerable is not authentic or brave, period—end of the story.

"In *Dare to Lead*, Brené cited the data that when she asked over 200 audiences for examples of courage that didn't require vulnerability, she heard only crickets. Brené pointed out that every single story of courage required vulnerability. What Brené teaches is a great compliment to how I teach you to be vulnerable via the Internal Family Systems Self-leadership framework."

IFS is Evidence-Based Emotional Healing and Transformation

The Internal Family Systems (IFS) model of Self-leadership is an evidence-based practice. In November 2015, IFS was given the thumbs up as an evidence-based practice by the National Registry of Evidence-Based Practices and Protocols (NREPP), administered by the Substance Abuse and Mental Health Services Administration (SAMHSA) of the United States government. IFS has been shown through clinical studies to significantly reduce symptoms of post-traumatic stress disorder (PTSD). Also, patients with rheumatoid arthritis experienced significant reduction in pain and depressive symptoms and improved their physical functioning and self-compassion. More studies are underway to prove the power of IFS to heal many emotional and physical ailments. You can learn about the ongoing IFS research at www.IFS-Institute.com.

Self is the Agent of Healing and Self-Love

As Dr. Schwartz developed the IFS model, he realized that IFS is not psychotherapy per se; it is spiritual healing. That is, the Self heals your emotionally damaged parts. If the Self is absent because of severe trauma, the IFS therapist or IFS practitioner (a *practitioner* is a designation for IFS-trained people who are not licensed therapists), can serve as the Self in the healing process. The Self helps us awaken to profound truths and hidden spiritual knowledge about ourselves. Self can love all people, especially yourself. (More on the Higher Self in the next chapter.)

Dr. Schwartz knew that IFS could be taken beyond psychotherapy and into leadership and personal development, to improve the dysfunctional inner lives of individuals and dysfunctional inner workings of organizational systems. IFS is a paradigm for living, which includes self-awareness, lasting transformation, and understanding others. IFS is also a compassionate framework to use for challenging relationships, group dynamics, team polarization, and organizational and societal challenges.

When you wonder why you're not feeling centered, despite having material wealth, it is more than likely because the Self is hidden and parts are in disarray. You feel overtaken by parts—that is, the subpersonalities of your protectors and exiles, who have not been befriended and loved by Self. When the Self-to-parts relationship reorganizes, you will feel like you've come "home" to center. The spiritual journey is about reclaiming the wounded and forgotten parts and letting Self be the leader of your parts.

Chapter 10

Internal Family Systems—Self and Parts

After answering questions from the opening didactic, Emily explains why the Self-leadership framework, or model, is called *Internal Family Systems*. "An organization or team is an external family of individuals in a system of relationships. The quality of these *external* relationships influences the quality of performance. Within each person, there's an *internal* system of parts or subpersonalities that resides in the psyche. Cars have parts, smartphones have parts (the apps are parts), and humans have parts. The human *parts* consist not only of our flesh and blood but also include the parts in our mind. The IFS model focuses on the parts of the multidimensional psyche. Sometimes the parts that comprise our inner world can drive us crazy with conflicting voices." She asks the audience if they can relate to this explanation; they can.

"This multiplicity of the mind does not mean we have multiple personality disorder. The internal family is comprised of vulnerable child parts, beliefs, thoughts, emotions, body sensations, and behaviors." Emily opens up her hand to illustrate this. "Your mind is like a hand. It's one thing, but at the same time, it is five things. These parts all relate to each other, like individuals in a family. This *system* of relationships is the *internal family* that makes up the traits of our personalities. Thus, the model is called Internal Family Systems."

She continues, "No matter how dreadful someone appears to be, there is a lovable and compassionate Higher Self underneath the unproductive and negative traits. The Higher Self, or just Self with a capital 'S,' is the foundation of the Internal Family Systems Self-leadership framework."

On a flip chart, Emily writes down popular synonyms for Self: *Inner Wisdom, Soul, Higher Power, Buddha Nature, Inner Light, Inner Being, Essence, Sunshine, Source, Infinite Intelligence, Heart Intelligence, Divine Intelligence, Divinity, and Spirit*. She also writes down the 8Cs and 5Ps of Self-leadership: *Clarity, Curiosity, Confidence, Connectedness, Courage, Creativity, Calmness, Compassion, Perspective, Playfulness, Persistence, Presence, and Patience.*

"The Self holds the key to rebalancing the parts in the inner world so you can be the best version of you—physically, mentally, emotionally, and spiritually. The Self has the power and courage to lead the inner team of parts to realize your biggest dreams. The Self is the witness that watches your inner child parts, beliefs, thoughts, emotions, and behaviors.

"Sometimes the Self, your sunshine, gets obscured by clouds—i.e., your *parts*. The more unhealed emotional scars you harbor, the harder it is to be Self-led. Toxic and hard-edged people—and criminals for that matter—have hardened shells, or *protectors*, which work very hard to keep them safe. Growing up, they may have been abused, neglected, and disrespected. For example, you may have tried showing your real Self by expressing the desire to be an artist instead of a doctor or engineer. Instead of feeling accepted as an artist, you were judged, shamed, or criticized. As a result, you didn't feel safe to be authentic anymore, and the real Self went into hiding. The wounded child part adopted beliefs that they don't matter and that they are not lovable unless they show up in a certain way to please caregivers, authority figures, and peers.

"When a person feels they are 'not enough' or are 'too much,' extreme traits develop, such as arrogance, defensiveness, shyness, blame, indecisiveness, manipulation, et cetera. At first, these characteristics are methods of coping and shutting out the pain of the hurt, vulnerable child parts. Over time, the coping strategies of negative traits become more robust parts of the personality. Sometimes this is helpful, sometimes not. The extreme versions of these parts can develop into *protectors*. Protectors are parts in roles developed as a result of devaluing experiences; these protectors protect the vulnerable child parts—i.e., exiles—frozen with negative beliefs, emotions, or terror.

"When burdens decrease after Self heals the exiles, Self feels safer to be front and center to lead your parts. With the presence of Self-energy, there is a higher likelihood of increased happiness and achievement of bigger goals.

"If we don't examine our lives via our parts, our lives will be difficult to change. When we embody Self most of the time, we are less fearful or closed down and genuinely more open and vulnerable. When we increase authenticity, we attract emotionally healthy people and greater opportunities. We will not attract what we want into our lives; we will attract who we are. This is the Law of Attraction; like attracts like. If we don't like what we attract, we need to make a U-turn and assess the parts of us who are responsible for attracting what we don't want." Emily repeats, "We don't attract what we want into our lives; we attract who we are," so that the attendees can let this concept soak in.

Emily goes on to share a powerful quote from Dr. Schwartz that he posted on social media: "I've found that nothing transforms a disconnected, polarized inner system into a harmonious ecology of parts, with Self in the lead, as dramatically as IFS. The Self becomes a trusted attachment figure that can resolve wounds and disappointments."

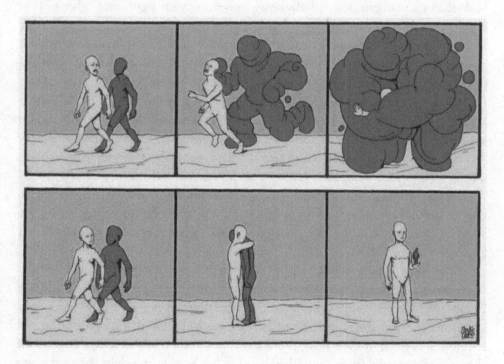

Emily continues with a cartoon she came across on Facebook. "This cartoon is by Sako Asko [reprinted with permission]—who I highly doubt was familiar with IFS. Asko has an intuitive understanding of the relationship between parts and Self. Look at the progression from left to right and top to bottom. The lighter figure represents Self, and the darker figure that grows more prominent represents one of your parts. The first box on the top left shows the protector that you dislike and perhaps don't want to acknowledge. The middle box on the top shows the protector, or part, beginning to take over Self. The box on the top right depicts when you are fully hijacked and blended with a part, and the Self is hidden. An example of this would be going on an alcohol or ice cream binge after a fight with your significant other or erupting with anger when your partner says something in an accusatory tone.

"Dominant protectors are the cause of virtually all relationship challenges, especially romantic ones. You may stonewall or get defensive or controlling when your spouse does or says something that triggers a vulnerable child part that once experienced an eerily familiar hurtful feeling. The memory of getting yelled at for a B minus in math, or getting criticized when you missed too many shots during the basketball tournament is jarred awake by something your significant other or boss said."

Emily's explanation of the cartoon lands hard on John. He thinks about how his nasty and angry parts overwhelmed him and caused Liz's friends to bolt right out of the house after he interrupted the girls' get-together. He feels guilty about how his not-so-nice parts dominate at home and work. Right now, a part is pushing up feeling embarrassed about how he has boasted his accomplishments to Jill and his colleagues. *Wow, this simple explanation makes so much sense. Why haven't I heard of IFS before? The executive coaches never explained the root causes of my negative traits. No wonder I didn't listen. They weren't solving my problems at the root cause level.*

Jill also thinks that her parts had to wear airbrushed masks to fit in with the college girls who came from upper-middle-class families. *The costumes were the protectors that helped me feel like I belonged. I was too ashamed to tell others about my blue-collar upbringing.*

"The three lower boxes depict the Internal Family Systems protocol to unblend and befriend your parts. Parts, even when they are nasty, have positive intentions. They don't know the havoc they're causing because they believe that they are protecting you since, in their mind, you are still a child stuck in old hurtful memories. Blinded by their fears, protectors may not see that you have a Higher Self that can manage the situation with calm. The last box on the right shows the Self taking the leadership reign again, diminishing the size, power, and intensity of the protective part. Back in control, the Self can choose to transform parts into new roles or let them rest or take a vacation in Tahiti. What I just described is the essence of how your internal family of parts reorganizes through Self-leadership."

Emily shows a video snippet of Disney's Pixar movie *Inside Out* [2015]. "This movie brilliantly depicts emotions as parts—anger, sadness, joy, surprise, disgust, and fear. The writers show that the cast of characters, that is, parts, all have a purpose and that no part is inherently wrong to have. Yet, there always seems to be conflict.

"To illustrate the internal civil war further, let's say you're dating. An inner critic part says, 'I can't go up to the pretty girl at the bar. I'm not good enough to deserve her!' But the alpha courage part says, 'Man up! I may not be sexy Bradley Cooper, but I've got a prestigious job, a quick wit, and empathetic nature. I'm a star at being open, honest, and trustworthy.'

"Or, in the case of many high-profile sexual harassment cases and illicit love affairs in the media today, some of them could have had a voice, a part, that said, 'Hey . . . she's cute, let's get close to her, we'll never get caught.' And another faint voice that said, 'I shouldn't do this, I'll end up divorced and taken to the cleaners.' In these cases, the louder, more immature voice took over, and the voice of reason, the Higher Self, was shoved into the corner. Eventually, karma came around for these perpetrators; they got caught. They listened to the wrong inner voices and self-sabotaged their high-profile careers and lives."

John's stomach clumps into knots as he hears these examples. He can surely relate to the inner critic. *My messy life makes sense now.*

"For those of you unfamiliar with karma, it is originally from Eastern religious teachings. It is a term about the cycle of cause and effect. According to the Law of Karma, what happens to a person happens because they caused it with their actions. It's short for describing one of the laws of physics, Newton's Law: for every action, there's an equal and opposite reaction. This means that if you do bad things, eventually, something negative will come back. If you do good things, then more good things will happen.

"Here's the reality—you can't evict the inner roommates, the parts, you don't like, no matter how much you pay a lawyer to serve eviction papers." This metaphor gets some belly laughs from the audience.

"You are stuck with the roommates—forever. But, the good news is, parts can be managed and transformed through Self-leadership, as you saw in the Asko cartoon. Every day, parts come together to form the team for that day or a particular situation. Some roommates are on deck today, while others are taking a nap, ready in a moment's notice if needed. For example, Self allows my presenter, organizing, and listening parts to be front and center to deliver this workshop. My Self-energy, filled with curiosity, compassion, connectedness, confidence, creativity, playfulness, and presence, are also here to help me serve so you can learn and transform."

At this point, many hands go up with questions. Emily answers them. The group feels relief over a shared experience—everyone can get overtaken by their parts. She let them know that when they see everyone through the Self and parts lens, it will be so much easier to minimize blame, judgment, and criticism, and get curious instead. "*Get curious, not furious* is the motto for living through Self."

Emily takes the group through a meditation to access Self, guiding them to imagine the energy they would "drop" into if they were going to interact with an adorable baby or pet—with tenderness, unconditional love, and compassion. She also has them imagine a time when they were high, stimulated, and on best behavior during the honeymoon phase of a new relationship. John and Jill both think about how energized they were when they first met each other and how high they can still get. After the participants open their eyes, she invites them to notice and feel the collective high vibrational Self-energy in the room. "We are all balls of energy. Right now, you're feeling how everyone's energy has swirled into each another. It's almost like being at your favorite concert, and everyone is happily singing and dancing together."

After that, Emily mentions that to be *aware* of the Self is one thing, but to be able to *access* the Self whenever you need it is the game-changer. "Imagine you are a boss, and several times on a particular day, employees made you angry. Someone is late for a meeting; someone turns in a sloppy report; another has given poor customer service that may result in losing business. With each disappointment, you begin to feel angry, which moves into 'This day is screwed.' Down you go, and you must vent to get rid of the anger. You take out your frustrations through blaming circumstances and other people. Everyone feels terrible, sensing a chaotic day filled with exasperation. Your agitation becomes contagious. Many employees go home feeling sad or upset, and some pass this downer energy onto their families.

"A better way is to access Self. A leader who has Self in the driver's seat changes his environment by taking a walk to the park, moving quickly through the spring morning, enjoying the blossoms on the trees framed by the blue sky. He notices he is blended with angry part. He asks Anger to separate from his body and acknowledges it. Then, he lets Anger know that Self can handle talking to the employees, with calm, curiosity, and connection. By the time he gets to the park, he feels a release. His emotional body relaxes. He sits on the bench, appreciating the flowers poking through in the garden. In that quiet moment, he turns on the meditation app on his smartphone to get grounded, relaxes his body, and settles the angry part down. This story is that of a former client. In the guided imagery through the meditation app, he imagines dropping to the floor with his grandchild, who is happily playing with blocks. He smiles and feels grateful and calm. Then he thanks Anger for showing up, lets it know that he is safe and doesn't need protection now. Self can handle the situation. He walks back to the office, feeling calm. When he arrives, he finds the team working intensely to figure out the cause of the manufacturing issue. So much productivity has happened. In the wake of 'the morning disaster,' calm and productivity were restored in his absence."

After this story, Emily answers questions and then invites the participants to self-reflect and share with their tablemates the parts that were activated from seeing the cartoon by Sako Asko. Everyone shares to the level they are comfortable.

Chapter 11

Bad Bosses (And Bad Lovers) Are Not Inherently Bad

"Many of us have heard about or have had firsthand experiences with bad bosses who are addicted to money, status, and power. Perhaps you heard gossip about their secret affairs. These bosses are not inherently bad. They show up badly because their need for control and power stems from the younger, vulnerable parts of them stuck in feelings of inadequacy, shame, and worthlessness. Adverse childhood experiences—the big hidden iceberg underneath the surface—cause leaders to become incompetent, lifeless, and sometimes downright toxic. The burdens from stressful, emotional experiences and disempowering cultural and religious beliefs can propel apathy, shyness, arrogance, and control to run the show. Sadly, these parts eventually cause the leader-*ship* to sink." Emily notices big gulps as people think about their leadership shortcomings.

Emily shows an iceberg image and lets them know that she superimposed pictures of adverse childhood emotional experiences underneath the water's surface. [Source: Shutterstock.com] "The younger parts of you depicted in this image are responsible for self-sabotage, failures, conflicts, cowardly and obnoxious behaviors, and feeling stuck."

Robert chimes in, "Wow! The image sums up the root causes of why we don't have what we want. The unresolved earlier experiences under the surface influence results."

"Yes, you are right! Here's something else I want to add about ineffective or mediocre bosses, not the toxic ones. Some shy and quiet people-pleasers can be just as feeble as the bosses who are loud and repulsive. The quiet ones don't ruffle your feathers. They can be overly nice, which is not a bad thing. However, if they can't speak up, be direct, have difficult conversations, or challenge you to perform at a higher level, they can only go so far in their leadership potential. The quiet ones have unresolved emotional struggles too, which cause them to be meek, uninspiring, and ineffective."

As John listens, he remembers how he never felt good enough on the tennis court and how he felt like a fraud getting into an Ivy League school after Dad pulled a few strings with the athletic director. John never felt as smart as his peers. He had several rounds of SAT tutoring, and his parents spent $25,000 on a highfalutin Ivy League college admission consultant who essentially wrote the college essays for him. A long-forgotten memory also surfaces about the shame he felt when he was arrested for cocaine possession during his sophomore year. Dad had to work his magic to prevent expulsion and clear John's arrest record. *I could have never gotten into Ivy League schools without Dad's influence.*

Jill wonders how the burdens of a lower-middle-class upbringing affected her relationships and leadership style. She doesn't like how John makes her feel bad about her upbringing when he boasts about his privileged life. Jill never questioned her intelligence as she scored very high on the SATs without any tutoring. She graduated fifth in her class of six hundred and gained admission into Cornell as well as Brown. But, the financial-aid packages from these Ivies weren't robust enough for her to attend either school. *There's a part of me that feels inferior compared to John and his designer diplomas. He loves to brag but never considers how that affects me, especially with the added fact that he grew up with a silver spoon in his mouth and is now supposedly wealthy beyond his wildest dreams. I'm just a working-class kid.*

Emily continues, "Leaders may have learned terrific new tools with leadership training programs. Or, they may have gone through traditional executive coaching to manage their emotions and behaviors. After these programs, many of them are temporarily motivated and energized to implement new tools. But, unfortunately, many end up reverting to their old familiar ways—with uninspiring, non-Self-led energy. This happens because the burdens of inner child parts still exist in their emotional bodies and affect the quality of their leadership.

"We are all made of energy. Think of someone's energy you love and someone else's energy that is dark and sucks the life out of you; that will convince you that we're all energy. When we detect a heavy or dark energy, it is more than likely the *energy* of low self-worth caused by exiles silently broadcasting through their aura.

"When childhood emotional burdens release, others notice: 'There's something different about you . . . your *energy* is different.' The change in energy quality happens when the emotional body relinquishes the emotional backpack. Many clients often say, 'I feel lighter. People notice something different about me. They wonder if it's my hairstyle or makeup that's different or if I've lost weight. I'm not as dark and angry.' This lighter energy is the higher vibration of Self, emanating the 8Cs and 5Ps qualities of Self, including calm, connectedness, curiosity, compassion, confidence, playfulness, and presence.

"Unfortunately, some traditional leadership development training misses the point that we are whole human beings whose emotions aren't easily compartmentalized. An unsuccessful boss receives coaching on how to change specific behaviors. Still, they may not be asked how their childhood wounds contributed to bad leadership traits. 'No . . . we don't go there with executive coaching.'"

Emily poses a rhetorical question: "If well-known leadership development methodologies are truly effective, then why do we still have two-thirds of leaders failing and the Gallup Poll showing employee engagement still at a dismal thirty percent? Sending leaders to the workshop-du-jour and sending warring couples into ineffective couples counseling without looking into the submerged iceberg of childhood burdens is like painting an old metal desk without removing the rust first. This rust also contributes to high-potential, middle-manager leaders who lack the self-esteem and confidence to reach their full potential; their negative self-talk says they're not smart enough nor good enough. High-potentials may reach a high level, only to self-sabotage because they feel like a fraud, and become a part of the two-thirds statistic of failed leaders."

Emily adds, "I'm not saying well-known leadership development methodologies have less value than the Internal Family Systems (IFS) Self-leadership framework, but the order is critical and needs to be right. That is, learn the Self-leadership foundations *first* and then follow with learning other excellent leadership tools. The foundation of Self-leadership is like the foundation of eating your vegetables for health. Let me explain. Healthy nutrition is a confusing field because there are many different camps on the best 'diet' to lose weight and maintain health. However, there is *one* strategy that *all* nutrition and health experts agree on—that is, vegetables are *the* foundation for losing weight and healthy aging. Thus, IFS is the 'vegetable' in this analogy. If your diet consists of healthy 'Self-to-parts relationships,' then everything else you learn regarding leadership and success is the yummy raspberry coulis on top of this sturdy foundation." Emily sees many non-verbal gestures to indicate that her analogy was clear.

"I love your analogy," Stephanie, sitting right in front of Emily, blurts out.

"Thank you! I thought you guys might appreciate it. In a nutshell, lack of Self-leadership is the biggest root cause of crumbling relationships—in love, business, family relations, and friendships. Lack of Self-leadership is also the cause of struggles we have with gender parity and Impostor Syndrome—that is, feeling like a fraud despite your accomplishments. We can close the confidence-competence gap with Self-leadership.

◆ ◆ ◆

As Jill soaks in the information about bad bosses, she thinks about how some of her direct reports are not as warm and responsive as she'd like them to be. *Do some of them see me as a hard-headed boss? Do I seem too polished, perfect, and unrelatable? Am*

I just as guilty as John, with controlling and arrogant parts? Maybe that's why I don't feel as much warmth from them as I'd like?

Emily guides the attendees through paired-shares and group integration. After John hears two people at his table vulnerably share their foibles, he feels safe to reveal himself. "I've been guilty of angry and self-righteous parts blowing up at home and at work." He describes the incidents where he wanted Liz's friends out of the house and where he was a jerk leading the last quarterly meeting. He receives hand-on-the-shoulder support from the person on his left and right. He admits—*It feels good to have my vulnerabilities acknowledged. I don't feel so alone.*

At lunch, John sits next to Jill as four other attendees join them. He says casually, "Hey, how's it going, my friend?"

"I love learning the psychology behind difficult relationships."

"I agree. It's enlightening information. I'm learning a lot too. I've been guilty of having many parts wreak havoc," John says from his heart.

"Yeah . . . thank you for acknowledging that. I think we realize that all of us are guilty of ugly parts taking over and making a mess." Jill reaches out with her hand and touches John's upper arm. This moment of closeness feels comforting to both.

Semantics

It has become a fad to describe people who aren't on a personal growth path as being "unconscious," which is not correct in the sense that they aren't knocked out cold. I use "nonconscious," "not conscious," and "unconscious" interchangeably. Someone who is not conscious is usually self-absorbed and usually don't have much sympathy or empathy. Some of them like to blame other people and circumstances instead of looking inward to see the role they play in challenging situations.

Self-Energy: The Secret Sauce to High Performing Teams

There's no such thing as business problems, it is *people* problems that cause business problems. The people problem *is* lack of Self-leadership. Organizations need to get the people piece of the puzzle correct to thrive. The road to higher productivity and success requires leaders to lead from Self.

- Self-led leaders command a room.
- Self-led leaders have gravitas.
- Self-led leaders influence.
- Self-led leaders inspire.
- Self-led leaders make impact.
- Self-led leaders are a joy to work for.
- Self-led leaders are confidently vulnerable.
- Self-led leaders are the obvious choice for promotions.

How Limiting Beliefs Download from Childhood

During the "programming years" that start in the womb and continue up to age eight, many parents are unaware of how their children soak up everything they hear as truth. According to the site www.UpAllHours.com, the first eight years of a child's life have the most significant impact on developing their characters. (Another resource to understand the science of beliefs and how the subconscious mind affects outer reality is Bruce Lipton's book, *Biology of Belief.*)

"The brain begins developing in the womb rapidly, forming neural networks at the rate of one million connections every second," according to the Center on the Developing Child at Harvard University.

Up All Hours explains that from the womb to age two is spent in the lowest brain state—Delta waves—as infants and small children live their lives mostly in deep sleep. Yet, even then, these young children's subconscious minds are continually being programmed.

Children between ages two and six operate mostly in Theta wave, an internal state of "daydreaming, imagination, and rapid learning." Yet, they remain in a non-rational state of thought. Whatever they are told and experience are embodied as truth.

Between ages five to eight, the brain waves speed up, ultimately changing to Alpha frequency. As their interpretive and analytical/rational brains blossom, children's imagination feels as factual as the external world because they are in the "frequency of meditation or a light trance." During the Theta and Alpha years, children remain in a continual hypnotic state. "They are being programmed by the environment, open to suggestions, and in a super learning state," as stated on *Up All Hours*.

During the birth to eight years that children dwell in the hypnotic brain-wave state, they absorb everything that happens as truth; the brain is a meaning-making machine. In the moment of hurt, a child takes on a belief to explain the event: *Mom is ignoring me because I must not be lovable.* Sadly, many parents have inadequate Self-presence to explain to their children the meaning behind emotional events. A child has no idea why this or that happened, and frequently, the child doesn't receive loving corrective explanations.

Finally, from ages eight to twelve, the Beta frequency arrives, introducing analytical and logical thinking.

When uninterpreted negative memories accumulate, they damage self-esteem. For instance, being compared to the smarter sibling is just as damaging as a child who continually hears they are wrong or stupid. All of these events contribute to building an increasing number of protective parts or masks. A parent who spanks a child, then tells them they love them, causes confusion and fear that can channel into becoming a wary, afraid, and controlling leader and romantic partner.

Even as adults, our subconscious hears and believes everything we say. Our constant inner affirmations can be positive or negative. In May of 2019, a 54-year-old Utah man, Donald Cash, completed his goal of climbing the tallest mountains on all seven continents by reaching his final dream: scaling the summit of Mount Everest. Soon after, he fainted twice and died on the mountain. Donald told his family repeatedly that he would "rather die on a mountain than in a hospital bed." His belief became reality.

In another story, a woman flew to the Midwest to attend her cousin's funeral, who just retired and died after a quick illness. The cousin loved saying, "Once I make two million dollars, I can die happy." Sure enough, as soon as he reached the financial goal, he passed away. His wife was shocked. They were about to enjoy the good life of traveling the world. Regrettably, his subconscious took his words literally and he died. The moral of the story is: be careful what you think and say!

Chapter 12

The Real Yearning

After lunch, Josh says, "I like some of my well-developed parts, especially my perfectionist and overachievement parts. They helped me get where I am today."

Emily answers, "Great point, Josh. You should honor how perfectionist and overachievement parts have worked hard to make you successful. I'm curious, have these parts ever been in overdrive, where you check things repeatedly and work until one a.m. and end up neglecting the family?"

"I do that sometimes."

"You're not alone. Many of us have been guilty of that. Access Self and get curious. What are these parts afraid to experience if they didn't work overtime?"

"I'll be criticized."

"That's a common fear many of us have. Let me explain how we can dial these parts down when they don't have a deadline. Self can negotiate with these parts to let them know when the PowerPoint is good enough so they can take a nap and give you time for self-care and time with your family. Self can help parts achieve work-life balance.

"Parts can drive you to secure the corner office by age forty, make truckloads of money with the unconscious intent to prove something to the bullies and authority figures who did you wrong. Parts drive the need for 'look at me' external validation. Many of us high achievers—myself included— have been unconsciously driven by the need to prove something to the people who have hurt us. Achievement for the wrong reasons will seldom make us happy. We get temporary highs from reaching goals, and wonder, 'Is this all there is?' Then shortly after, we're back to our baseline emotional state, looking for a brighter and shinier rainbow to chase. When you do the work to unburden the vulnerable parts that made you into a super-achiever, then it's possible to adopt a better narrative of why it's important to achieve. An example of a new story could be: 'Based on my childhood's defining moments, I developed unique gifts to be a Portfolio Manager. I did not choose this career to gain my dad's approval. I'm in it because it's my passion and moral obligation to help clients reach financial freedom.'"

As John learns the deeper layers of the IFS framework, his emotions stir. He's a bit flustered when it hits home that he's been ruthless in securing a Zatuck corner office and accumulating material symbols to prove to the bullies that made him feel inadequate. Jill has a better understanding now of why John does what he does. She has even more compassion about how his negative traits were born out of unresolved childhood emotional experiences.

◆ ◆ ◆

"I Want You to Change" Is a Cry for . . .

"There's a related topic when we talk about Self and parts. We often hear how many men enter into relationships with the wish that their women never change. On the flip side, many women go into relationships thinking they can change their men." This comment gets a roomful of knowing smiles and chuckles, and Emily laughs along with them.

"Here's the real truth about women's desire for their partner to 'change.'" The audience is wide-eyed and eager to hear an in-depth psychological explanation. "The desire to change someone is about the desire to experience more of their Higher Self, full of compassion, calmness, connectedness, curiosity, confidence, courage, playfulness, patience, and presence. When we want to change someone, we are unknowingly trying to convey that we would like to see less of their extreme parts and more of the fun and enjoyable parts in hiding. Parts to dial down may include drinking, overeating, not exercising, watching too much sports or porn, controlling behavior, self-centeredness, or fear of vulnerability. Parts to dial-up could be the courage to try new adventures, share vulnerable emotions, playfulness, presence, trying new things in the bedroom, and getting out of the head and into the heart.

"So, it's not that we want the person to change per se into a person that they are not, we want that person's Self to be the conductor of the symphony of their parts, exhibiting the 8Cs and 5Ps qualities of Self. However, you do have to honor the protective parts that want to remain in hiding until they feel safe to venture out of their comfort zone."

Several people raise their hands to say that this insight makes sense. Emily invites them to share experiences regarding the times they tried to change someone. Then, Emily guides them to rewrite the desire to change someone from the Self-leadership lens: What parts would they like to see dialed down? What parts would they like to see dialed up?

"Here's an example from my client files. Melanie complains that her boyfriend of one year, Jack, has ambiguity and fear-of-commitment parts that drive her crazy. She wants marriage. Jack deflects conversations about their future. He claims that marriage will happen eventually. Since Jack refused to join her in couples counseling, I couldn't guide him to find out what his fears were underneath the ambiguity and fear-of-commitment parts.

"The only thing Melanie could do was share with Jack how ambiguity was her kryptonite. She needs to say from her heart that when he's not clear about why he doesn't want marriage, she makes up the story that she's not good enough and that he's waiting for a better option. I guided her to say, 'Because I don't have the real reasons you don't want to commit to me, I feel inadequate and insecure. I don't feel worthy of you.' Clarity is one of the characteristics of Self. Unfortunately, Jack is not in Self. After Melanie shared this with Jack, he stonewalled; no amount of prodding got him to dial down his ambiguity and fear-of-commitment parts. Lack of clear communication became a deal-breaker for Melanie, so she broke up with him."

Ouch! Ambiguity is my middle name, John thinks to himself.

"Here are more examples. One person is neat versus her messy husband, and it doesn't bother her. His messy part is welcomed. Another person places high importance on comfort and dresses in sloppy ripped sweatshirts on the weekends. The sloppiness turns off her boyfriend, who prefers neat, tasteful chic, without holes. You get to decide what your deal breakers, turn-ons, and turn-offs are."

John likes that change is not about changing the core of who he is. It's about Self being in the lead to direct which parts should play in the sandbox for a specific situation. Jill is also enlightened with this concept and thinks about how she can ask John to be more in Self.

◆ ◆ ◆

The Core Human Need

"Validation is a very significant human need. We are starved for validation because many of us didn't get enough of it growing up. The key to self-validation is from your Higher Self. Self-validation means loving all the parts in your inner world, including the parts you would rather not look at.

"The yearning to come to wholeness is about accepting all parts of you, especially the parts you've disowned and locked away for decades. From coaching many high achievers like you, I know that some of you cannot look in the mirror and say, 'You're the greatest thing since sliced bread. You are beautiful inside and out. I love you so much!'" Every time Emily says this phrase, she sees faces cringe at the thought of looking in the mirror and saying that.

"One of the top trauma specialists in the world, Bessel van der Kolk, author of the New York Times bestseller *The Body Keeps the Score*, says, 'Lack of compassion for others is due to lack of compassion for your wounded parts that you've never looked at.' In other words, you can only love thy neighbor to the extent you heal and love yourself. Loving yourself means loving all parts of you, especially the most wounded parts. When you lovingly look at your darkness, you drop judgment and gain compassion for another's darkness.

"If it's hard to love yourself unconditionally, it will be tough to be the leader everyone loves, and be the lover who confidently engages in Self-led vulnerability, authenticity, and intimacy." Jill lets out a big sigh with these thoughts—*I don't validate my team enough. I can't remember to do it because I'm too much in my head instead of my heart.*

"Every change you want to see starts with you, which means doing the work to access more Self-energy. Your caregivers, parents, teachers, and coaches did the best they could. They didn't know how to give you validation in the way you needed it; they didn't know about Self-leadership. They didn't understand the long-term damage that judgments, criticisms, and emotional neglect could cause. They were and are broken, too. Brokenness is the universal human experience. Please forgive the people who hurt you."

By now, many participants are in deep reflection about their situations, especially about their disowned, dark, and ashamed parts. Emily guides them through a meditation that soothes the parts that could have been activated through the lecture.

Intellectually, John knows he needs to work on his parts so he can become a better leader. But, a voice says—*It's okay to push this work to the back burner for now. Things aren't that bad yet. I don't have the time now.* Sadly, John is typical of many people who do not feel enough discomfort to do the work to change for the better.

Many people need to hit rock bottom before they face themselves in the mirror. John is okay with continuing to participate in self-reflection exercises and sharing among his tablemates. He may consider the inner work necessary, but not urgent.

Jill's hope for the drive home is to have an in-depth discussion about what they learned in the seminar so they can support each other to become better leaders.

IFS Lens on Midlife Crisis

A midlife crisis is when you find yourself questioning your identity, and why you feel lost. Midlife is an existential milestone and a time of transition. This is challenging in a society that puts inordinate value on youth and material shows of success. A midlife crisis can bring on tough questions:

- Who am I?
- Why am I doing this?
- Work, eat, entertainment—is this all there is?
- How do I find my center?
- I'm old enough to have a grandchild; why does Mom still get under my skin?
- I have money, status, and real estate. Why am I still not happy?
- I haven't achieved my potential. Will I ever?
- I want to give back. What is the best way for me to do that?
- Am I doing anything to build a legacy?
- My career rocks, but why do I keep failing at love?

The Internal Family Systems model is a powerful methodology that can help you overcome a midlife crisis, come "home" to center, and become the most authentic version of you. The spiritual journey to wholeness includes integrating light and dark parts into a balanced, harmonious team, where all parts feel respected and able to express freely at appropriate times in appropriate doses. Once you give parts a safe space to express, they may whisper answers that solve your midlife crisis.

Chapter 13

Parts—Firefighters, Managers, and Exiles

"Earlier, I covered the qualities of Self. Let us dive deeper into parts. Parts is an all-encompassing word for many types of subpersonalities in the inner psyche. Parts can go rogue and become extreme. For example, many of us have a social drinking part that comes out during Happy Hour and dinnertime. This part drinks in moderation. However, some people go overboard with their drinking part and can result in addiction. When parts go into extreme, they become *protectors*. Another part many of us have is procrastination. A little bit of procrastination can help us do our best work at the last minute. However, when healthy procrastination turns into procrastination that negatively impacts career and relationships, this part becomes a protector. Protectors come in two flavors—*firefighter* protectors and *manager* protectors. Protectors protect vulnerable exiles. As I've mentioned before, exiles are the tender young parts that had devaluing emotional experiences. Protectors protect these exiles." Emily gives examples of what these parts' experiences can look like.

Exiles (Vulnerable Parts Stuck in Devaluing Early Emotional Experiences)

Exiles can have little or big scars. Common experiences of exiles include:

- Abandonment
- Humiliation
- Shame
- Rejection

- Loss of Control
- Grief
- Fear
- Terror

Manager Protectors are Proactive

Manager protectors proactively prevent you from experiencing the exile's original painful feelings. Examples:

- Control
- Judge
- Blame
- Worry
- Procrastinate

- Perfectionism
- Working too much
- Disordered eating
- Inner Critics

Firefighter Protectors are Reactive

Firefighter protectors react in response to a person or a situation that stirs up the pain of an exile. Examples:

- Compulsive Behaviors
- Addictions
- Anger and rage

- Anxiety and panic
- Emotional shutdown
- Blame and criticize

"Many manager protector parts serve positive roles—they help you get things done so you can be successful. However, some of these parts—such as judging and blaming—can wreak havoc. It's easier to judge and condemn others instead of making a U-turn to understand your contribution to a negative situation. It takes two to tango.

"On the other hand, firefighter protectors get activated when you are in situations where you feel ashamed and powerless, such as when your partner uses point-the-finger 'you' language to accuse you of doing or not doing something. The accusations make you feel inadequate, which stirs up the exiles that believed they were 'not enough' growing up.

"To illustrate protector and exile concepts, I'm going to share my story so you can see how different parts play their roles in the development of our personalities. My intention in telling my story about how I found my life's calling through my wounds is to help you see similar parallels in your story. I hope you will be inspired to make new positive meaning out of your adverse childhood experiences.

"I was 'Made in Taiwan' and exported to America at age nine, without the ability to speak a word of English, when my father's Taiwan government job transferred to the United States. The first three years in Los Angeles felt stable, quote-unquote. Our family of six lived in a two-bedroom, one-bath apartment. Despite my choppy English, I felt accepted by my peers. After my father's stint in Los Angeles was over, he was transferred to New York City. We lived in Corona, Queens, and then Bayside, Queens. We moved twice in the middle of my junior high school years. We all know how awkward junior high can be, let alone moving in the middle of the school year. During my teenage years, emotional hell broke loose.

"I tried to fit into my new environment, but it was hard. Back in the seventies, the neighborhoods we lived in contained very few Asians. I was the target of Asian slurs. The discrimination was painful. It didn't help that my family couldn't afford the clothes or the braces I needed to look and feel like I fit in. These young parts of me who felt ashamed became my exiles because I banished them into the basement of my inner psyche. These ashamed parts had burdens, the extreme emotions and beliefs of *I'm not lovable, I'm not worthy, I don't belong, I'm ugly, and Asians are not worthy of love and belonging.* Just a reminder, the exile is synonymous with the inner child." Emily checks in with the group to see if they can relate to this part of the story. She sees that they can.

"Here's a warning. As you listen to my story, some of your forgotten, tender parts can poke through as tension in your throat or somewhere else in your body. Please acknowledge these parts and let them know that when the time is right, you will do the work to hear their stories and help them recover from the past. They will appreciate the acknowledgment.

"Back to the story. The exiled parts of me felt lonely and unloved by my peers, and, on top of that injury, I also felt unloved at home. My parents weren't present; they didn't know how to support their kids emotionally. They were fighting a lot and took their demons out on each other. I was often my mother's defender when my father said mean things to her. I yelled at him for being so crass. My yelling is an angry firefighter protector part that often engulfed me in the name of protecting my mother." Emily flashes up the Sako Asko cartoon again to illustrate how angry part hijacked her on many occasions.

"Feeling so lonely and unseen at school and home, and witnessing emotional toxicity between my parents, made me decide early on that I needed to study hard to get into an excellent college so I could escape from home and never come back. My overachievement part pushed full-throttle to get ahead. This manager protector's job proactively helped me succeed in school so I could get a good job. Each of you have manager parts that have helped you succeed and prevented painful emotions of failure from resurfacing. Who has an overachieving part?" Every hand goes up.

"Where these manager parts can go haywire is when you neglect your loved ones because you work too much, and when you overachieve simply for money, status, material things, and external approval. This external validation does not bring lasting joy. Instead, happiness comes from healing the exiles and unloading their bricks in the emotional backpack. Happiness is an inner journey, rather than an endeavor to seek something outside yourself.

"Another protector who was just as active as my overachievement part was the shopping part. I suspect many of you can relate to retail therapy since Madison Avenue advertising convinces us that buying more stuff and living the good life will make us happy."

John and Jill laugh at this statement since advertising is how they make a living.

"The hard work of my overachievement part paid off. I graduated in the top one percent in a class of one thousand from one of the best public high schools in New York City, Benjamin Cardozo. I gained admission to Cornell to study nutrition, and I felt freedom on the horizon. Thank goodness the college within Cornell was a New York State school, which meant my parents only had to pay New York State college tuition rates for an Ivy League education."

At the front table, Ben blurted out, "I'm with you. I had a similar story of overachieving to get out of the house." He went on to share some details.

"Thank you for sharing, Ben. Many of us have similar overachievement stories." Others signaled with their heads that they can relate.

"Let me fast-forward. At Cornell, I managed to find my groove. I still wasn't in the cool-kids club and didn't get into the sorority I wanted. Fortunately, I found my small tribe of friends who made me feel I belonged somewhere. I thought I was over racial slurs, but they continued when I went to fraternity parties. I heard 'Look at that China girl' one too many times, especially since David Bowie's song, 'China Girl,' came out during my junior year, in 1983. I cringed every time I heard that song at a fraternity party. Invariably, a guy or two would come up and say, 'You're such a cute China girl.' Or, I would overhear guys say to each other, 'Look at that China girl over there.' Ouch! My belief that *I must be flawed because I'm Asian* hit hard.

"Because of the upsetting feelings associated with home, I rarely talked to my parents, and I dreaded going home for the holidays. During one Thanksgiving break, the minute I walked in the door, my parents were in the middle of a fight. I got hijacked by anger again, which was in firefighting mode to try to stop the emotional pain, and I ended up fighting along with them. After only twenty-four hours, with my exiles triggered by their fighting, I bolted. I took the subway back to the Port Authority Bus Terminal. Then I boarded the bus to Cornell and spent Thanksgiving weekend alone in my dorm room. This escape was the reactive 'I'm outta here!' firefighter protector that wanted to escape the little Emily's pain that was so done with witnessing emotional abuse.

"This reactive protector is like a firefighter trying to douse out a fire—the fire of growing up with parents who I was embarrassed to introduce to my friends. Let me fast forward twenty years to share the most embarrassing firefighter protector outburst of my adult life." Emily gulps to model the depth of the courageous and confident vulnerability she's about to share.

"For my fortieth birthday, when I opened my present from my parents—a pair of diamond cluster earrings—I flung the box across the room." Emily takes a deep breath and sits with a pregnant pause for the audience to picture the scene. She makes eye contact one-by-one with several people during the pause. They are mesmerized by the power of connection through how Emily let the scene soak in through silent eye contact.

"The gift seemed ludicrous. This present was so out of alignment with the minimal birthday gifts I got growing up. I immediately apologized and started crying, but the damage was done. My parents and three siblings promptly left my Connecticut home and drove back to New York City. The angry part was triggered and silently thought: *How dare you try to make up for my lousy childhood by wasting money you don't have on a pair of damn expensive earrings you can't even return because you were stupid enough to buy them during a cruise?! Get real! It would have made more sense if you asked to spend time with me to shop for a gift.*

"Of course, my parents didn't understand the source of my blow-up. The exiles that held so much anger for my embarrassing childhood were activated. My raging angry firefighter took over and threw the present back at Mom." Emily stops with another pregnant pause.

"Wow, this is so brave of you to share the vulnerable story," John said, his voice soft and full of compassion.

"Thank you. I'm modeling Self-led courageous and confident vulnerability. Notice the Self-energy through which I'm telling this embarrassing story. I'm not still stuck in the story; I'm witnessing the story. Telling your story from a higher perspective is how you own your mistakes and connect with your audience. My vulnerability helps you see that I've got flaws just like you. We're all imperfect and make stupid mistakes we regret. This story may have stirred up something embarrassing you have done where you were hijacked like I was. That part may be in your throats now. Let that part know that you are aware of it and that you're here to learn what needs to happen for you to heal. The more you understand how and why we get triggered, the more empathy you will have when colleagues, friends, lovers, and family blow up with anger and rage.

"To finish the story, I apologized profusely to Mom through letters. I never heard from her for months. Dad never had the spine to scold me, and he remained silent too. Eventually, time healed the wounds and the silence ended. Okay, let me go back into my twenties now. Eight months after graduating from college, I ended up in a dream job—pharmaceutical sales with Pfizer—where I thrived for twenty-seven years before getting laid off in October 2011.

"In this job, I was able to be my fun and charismatic self with my healthcare customers. My insatiable curiosity and empathy helped me win friends and influence people. The job was perfect for my personality. I got to know *me* and what I liked and disliked from my interactions with these customers. I developed my core gifts of curiosity and empathy as a reaction to not feeling seen and heard by my father. I became the person who was never going to be uncaring. It's no wonder my life's calling is being a motivational speaker, workshop leader, and spiritual teacher and healer. Our deepest wounds have the power to create our greatest gifts. What are your greatest gifts that have been birthed as a result of your deepest wounds?"

Jill feels at home with Emily's story. She knows that her interests in psychology and marketing grew as a result of watching her dad fail at marketing his construction business. She also wanted to understand the psychology of why Dad had a habit of stretching the truth.

Emily reminds the participants that she's not throwing her parents under the bus. After she healed her broken parts, she understood that her dad was incapable of showing up in the way she needed because of his unresolved childhood wounds. She shares that after reading his memoirs, which he wrote before Alzheimer's ravaged him, she learned that he was physically beaten by teachers and parents when he did something wrong. Emily finally figured out the root causes of why he couldn't show up as a loving parent; hurt people hurt others. She has forgiven Dad and released the childhood anger. Her father transitioned to heaven in June 2020.

"Think about someone who hurts you or gets under your skin. Perhaps it's your boss, mom, or significant other. Instead of judging, look at it through the lens of 'hurt people hurt others.' They are unknowingly projecting their hurts onto you. They feel a sense of power when they do this. Some of you may still be holding onto anger and resentments about how your caregivers and authority figures treated you. That's normal, but, those stored negative feelings will eventually erupt in some way, usually through your emotional and physical health; this is just physics. The childhood anger energy has to be released somehow. It can express via emotional instability and physical illnesses. Many integrative doctors have written about the mind-body connection in the development of diseases."

Emily continues and shares that she married at age twenty-six, had a son, and amicably divorced twenty-eight years later, in 2017. When she was forty-one years old, she went into a year-long battle with depression and anxiety as a result of a stressful work situation. "I judged and criticized a colleague's behavior towards me, and I couldn't stand up for myself. The psychiatrist gave me an antidepressant and sent me to a hypnotist to heal the little Emily's whose buttons got pushed during challenging interactions.

"The psychiatrist asked me a compelling question on the first visit. She said, 'Emily, what drama from your childhood are you reliving through this challenging work situation?' I said, 'Whaaaat are you talking about? It's all *their* fault that they treat me this way.' And then a lightbulb went off. 'Oh my God, I am reliving the emotionally abusive way my father treated my mother! The way that this colleague treated me stirred up a familiar, uncomfortable energy. I couldn't advocate for myself, and I couldn't get the right words out. I froze. I became just like my helpless, emotionally hurt mother during the difficult interactions with this person at work.'

And the shrink said, 'See, you're reliving one of your worst nightmares through this work situation. The past is always in the present.'"

The Past Is Always in the Present

Emily then invites the audience to write down the critical point they need to remember: The past is always in the present. "When someone pushes your buttons, and your reaction is automatic, think back to an earlier time when you experienced a similar feeling. Your unconscious mind, which has no sense of time, believes that the original wound is happening again.

"The brain interprets and gives meaning to the current situation, especially if it is challenging, through the filter of your childhood movies. I just gave you the example of the struggle with how my former colleague treated me and how I exaggerated the narrative that they were out to get me like how my dad was out to get my mom. The unconscious mind, out of conscious awareness, has no perspective on the challenges and pains that the conscious, rational mind does. And so, the past is always present.

"Let that information sink in. I see that some of you are gulping. Some of the difficult, get-under-your-skin interpersonal dynamics is your mind filtering the experiences through your childhood movies. Emotionally laden incidents almost always trace back to unresolved childhood stressful experiences." Emily pauses to let the points soak in.

Jill chimes in, "Thank you for sharing the root causes; it makes sense. I am analyzing why certain people push my buttons."

"I'm so glad you see this. My other colleagues who worked with this person that I didn't like were not affected the way I was. These coworkers agreed that this person wasn't the brightest lightbulb in the shed, but they weren't losing sleep over it. I was losing sleep and overreacting because of my daddy triggers.

"How do we stop the triggers? By understanding the psychology behind them and by engaging your Higher Self to take care of the exiles. When you want to judge and criticize the coworker, boss, friend, or significant other, it's essential to step back and make a U-turn and look at the frightened child parts of you who got woken up because of something they did or said.

"I share the depression part of my story to let you know that when we sweep the past under the carpet, it will show up somewhere. For me, it was depression. I swept the shame of being Asian and my painful childhood under the rug until it could no longer keep hiding; the shame exploded through this work situation. It's impossible to keep those mounds of painful childhood emotions hidden forever. It's like trying to keep a beach ball submerged underwater; it doesn't work.

"Even though my depression challenge was hell, it was the biggest gift I was bestowed. Now I know I had to go through that to tell you this story today to let you know that we are all more or less the same, with ghosts from the past that can haunt our careers, relationships, and physical and emotional health. These burdened child parts silently scream for our attention through self-sabotage—via failed leadership, failed business, disordered eating, substance abuse, mental health disorders, relationship conflicts, et cetera."

John thinks about how often he stuffed his emotions by drinking to drown out the noise from the cruel inner voices. Jill thinks about how she was addicted to exercise and restricted her calories to fit in with the size-two girls. She's not as neurotic now with her weight; she's okay being a bit curvier than she was in college.

"My depression and anxiety parts were protectors. They showed up to give me a message that my little wounded Emily's were still unhealed. For you, it could be eating too much or too little, drinking too much, working too much, shopping too much, being a controlling bulldozer, fear of success, fear of failure, fear of public speaking, persistent health issues, et cetera. Essentially, any extreme behaviors, feelings, or thoughts—parts which have turned into protectors—can hold you back from a centered, balanced, and joyful life.

"We can heal, increase self-awareness, and transform through Self-leadership. Self can negotiate with the parts that need to dial down, and mold them into new roles to help us thrive.

"Let's continue with my shopping protector story. Once I landed my well-paying pharmaceuticals sales job nine months after college, I had a shopping protector that became overactive. We all know that buying stuff can give us temporary highs—such as, after buying the Yves Saint-Laurent handbag, Jimmy Choo shoes, the big-screen TV, latest smartphone, or the luxury car. After the dopamine high dissipates, we go back to our old state." Emily notices many smiles that signal they get her gist.

"My shopping protector needed to decorate in designer clothing. Thank goodness this was a manager protector that didn't go too crazy. If I went on many shopping binges beyond my financial means to soothe the part of me that felt inadequate, this binge-shopping protector would be classified as a *firefighter*. However, because I shopped within my financial means, and shopping didn't overtake my life, this habit was a *manager* protector.

"When you look at your protectors, it's not important to get into the weeds of whether or not it's a firefighter or manager. Protectors are like soldiers guarding the doorway to the vulnerable inner parts hidden in the psychic caves. So, the shopping part was my way of showing the world that I was no longer that shamed poor girl who didn't belong because she was Asian and couldn't afford nice clothes. I can afford beautiful clothes now! Eventually, as I shared before, the reality of my buried traumas hit when I went through that bout of depression.

"To overcome my depression, the psychiatrist referred me to a hypnotist. The hypnotist had me reparent the younger part of me that felt I wasn't worthy of being born, similar to the IFS reparenting step. Under hypnosis, I uncovered the fetus part that took on the belief that I was not worthy and not enough because I was a girl and not a boy growing in my mother's belly. I still remember my grandmother's voice telling my mom that she had to keep getting pregnant until she produced sons. Asian culture is rooted in the belief that sons are more valuable. I am the oldest of four children. My sister came next and then my two brothers." Emily watches the two women of Indian descent shaking their heads, clearly dismayed with the backwardness of Asian cultural thinking. Emily then says that the feeling of worthlessness at the fetal stage was further reinforced when Mom and Dad were not emotionally there for her.

"These devaluing experiences created the core of my personality—the need to be perfect and overachieve to show that I'm worthy of belonging and that I'm lovable. The shopping part, together with the perfectionism part, were developed to make me seem perfect so that I could be accepted by my peers. There's nothing wrong with perfectionism, overachievement, and shopping parts. Where it gets problematic is when parts do their jobs solely to seek external approval. The perfectionism part could make you stay up until two a.m. to perfect a report that doesn't need that level of perfection. The shopping part could make you shop for stuff you don't need, to impress people you don't like, with money you don't have. Our social circle influences where we spend our hard-earned money." The group lets out giggles to show that they get it.

"After I healed my worthlessness traumas through hypnosis, I eventually came out of my depression. I also forgave my parents during the healing process. My visits home were no longer anger-filled trigger fests. Before my depression battle, my then-husband would say, 'Emily, I don't recognize you during these visits. You turn into someone I don't know.'"

Roberto chimes in that he turns into a monster too when he visits his parents.

"Now, shopping part no longer needs to shop to impress others. I like how my shopping part helped me develop a sense of style. I still like to shop for nice things, but now I buy them for the right reasons and not to prove I'm no longer the poor, teased Asian immigrant that no one wanted to play with. I know some of you have retail therapy parts. I invite you to examine the intentions behind the need to shop mindlessly. Treat this part with compassion."

John's throat is tight again after hearing Emily's shopping story. *Yep, I buy to impress others. Liz is guilty too. Despite my debts, I'm still above water.*

Jill feels guilty about her designer clothing spending habits. *At least I make enough money to support my consumerism. I need to have a different intention so I can dial down the shopping habit and shift more money into my 401K.*

"My point in telling you the story is to show how getting to know our parts can help us access more Self and become happy on the journey to realizing our full potential. As I mentioned before and it's worth repeating here, I hope you have noticed that I told you my life's story from the high confident vibration of Self and not from the weaker 'I'm still broken, help me!' energy. An example of a celebrity who is an ace with vulnerability is Oprah. Oprah is not ashamed to tell her sexual abuse story to millions of people. She shares this without getting into a tearful meltdown. Oprah and I courageously tell our stories from a place of strength, not from victim energy. She and I can do that because we've done the work to release the skeletons in the closet. I'm modeling for you how to confidently tell your story. When you take the risks to reveal the hardest stories from a place of courage, which is from Self, that's when deep connection, trust, and respect can significantly increase. What are the skeletons in your closet?"

Jill raises her hand and says, "It's beautiful to hear your story. I feel more connected to you because of it."

"Thank you, Jill. There is one caveat, though. It's vital to do the self-awareness work and healing before you attempt to tell the sensitive stories, especially to people you don't know well. Some of your stories will not be appropriate for the workplace; be judicious. Otherwise, if you are not fully healed, the audience can pick up on the lower vibrational, traumatized energies, and conclude you are still broken. Being so raw from an unhealed place will not inspire others, nor is it healthy. The rawness should be revealed in a healer's office first.

"Many people crave deeper connections, but they don't have the know-how. They are waiting for someone else to get vulnerable first. So, you have the opportunity to peel a layer of your onion first so that the other person can be relieved that you permitted them to say, 'Me too!' Mutual vulnerability is the birthplace of deep connection and feeling seen and heard."

Emily then finishes this segment of the workshop by talking about toxic masculinity and Impostor Syndrome.

The Internal Family Systems (IFS) Compassionate Lens on Toxic Masculinity

The #MeToo movement against sexual harassment went viral in 2017 when long-silenced victims came out in droves to name their guilty, high-profile perpetrators. It's natural to want to judge and criticize the high-profile #MeToo business, political, and entertainment offenders. There is no doubt that they did wrong, both legally and ethically, and there are victims who were hurt in many ways. Here's the IFS lens of why sexual harassment happens in the first place.

These once-powerful men in business, media, and politics were knocked down from their pedestals after self-sabotaging themselves and attacking others—mainly caused by shame and worthlessness burdens of their unhealed child parts. These exiled parts more than likely had *I'm not good enough, I'm inadequate, and I'm not worthy* core beliefs. So, outside of conscious awareness, these men developed protectors to feel significant. These protectors provided short-term benefits, yet the laws of physics and karma would bite them in the butt; what goes around comes around. Their inner (nonconscious) dialogue could have been something like: "See . . . you deserve to fall. After all, you were the little boy who didn't belong in the cool kids' club and couldn't make the varsity baseball team. You were too dumb and fat. Mom and Dad were right; you were never going to amount to anything."

Understanding the often unconscious, inner dialogue is the compassionate perspective on the #MeToo perpetrators. No one is perfect; we are all broken. Let's have some sympathy for the little boys inside of them who were shamed and made to feel worthless. Their brokenness should not detract from empathy for the victims, nor does nurturing compassion inside of us for the abuser's inner child parts mean that they get a pass for their unjust and hurtful behaviors. Learning to use the kindhearted lens helps our hearts soften and helps us accept our vulnerability.

It was the little boys who wanted to feel in control, think that they were somebody, and feel they didn't ever want to be bullied again. So, they went ahead and bullied and sexually harassed others to feel powerful. They abused to fulfill a core human need: to feel significant. They thought that the only way to feel powerful—because feeling powerless and worthless are the worst feelings anyone can have—is to have power over others. Their child parts acted out a self-fulfilling prophecy: "You're a fraud! Who do you think you are being a $200-million-dollar media mogul? You were abandoned by Dad and abused by Mom. I'll show you what you're worth. I'll make you gamble away your money, harass women, and abuse your kids and wife, so you can come down from your pedestal and own how worthless you are."

Hurt people hurt others. The consequences are massive failures, substantial legal bills, bankruptcy, and public humiliation. These bad behaviors are the reservoir of anger from childhood acting out on the open stage. Let's not forget that women can be perpetrators of abuse, too.

Many people have anger lodged in their bodies that originated in childhood. They may not be aware that this anger is what makes them feel unsettled and off-center. Anger at what your parents didn't give you. Anger at what the bully did to you. Anger at being treated like the ugly duckling. Anger at not being able to keep up with the rich kids. Anger at Dad's insistence on all A's. Anger at Mom scolding you for being a tomboy instead of a girly girl. And, anger at not being validated for just being you. Thank goodness most of us are not #MeToo perpetrators, but we may be guilty of being the demanding boss or the complicated and emotionally unavailable romantic partner.

Is it possible for these once-powerful business and entertainment moguls to regain some dignity and respect? Just as I can pick up a pallet of wood with a forklift, the big job of recovering one's Self after such extreme missteps can be accomplished by almost anyone who has the right attitude and tools. IFS is indeed one of these powerful tools.

If these fallen leaders did the deep healing work of their shamed exiles, they could gain the courage to share Self-led, heartfelt apologies. They can express how they gained compassion for their broken parts. When the audience hears that their apologies come from Self-energy, that is when things can positively shift for the perpetrators and victims.

Solving Impostor Syndrome and Gender Parity Challenges

Wikipedia's definition of Impostor Syndrome:

Impostor syndrome is a psychological pattern in which an individual doubts their accomplishments, and has a persistent, internalized fear of being exposed as a "fraud." Despite external evidence of their competence, those experiencing this phenomenon remain convinced that they are frauds and do not deserve all they have achieved. They walk around in a chronic state of guilt and fear (of being found out). Individuals with Impostor Syndrome attribute their success to luck, or as a result of deceiving others into thinking they are more intelligent than they perceive themselves to be. While early research focused on the prevalence among high-achieving women, Impostor Syndrome has been recognized to affect both men and women equally.

By now, I hope you see that the root causes of most struggles—including feeling like a fraud—come from vulnerable child parts burdened with limiting beliefs of unlovability and the feeling that they don't deserve what they have amassed and achieved. These parts were developed as a result of early, devaluing experiences. When you do the work to unload the burdens of these child parts, that's when you can stop feeling like a fraud, own your accomplishments, and go outside your comfort zone to take inspired actions to realize your dreams.

Some diversity and inclusion experts say it will take over 100 years to achieve gender parity at the rate we're going. I say that could be true—unless the powerful and effective IFS model becomes more widely taught and utilized. If IFS Self-leadership methodologies were employed, we could make significant progress, including seeing more women and people of color gain seats at the senior leadership tables.

Many diversity and inclusion leadership training programs do not address the missing foundational piece: accessing Self-leadership to release from the inner obstacles that originated in childhood. Self-leadership training would also go a long way towards eliminating men's implicit biases about women's role in society. If implicit biases regarding women in senior leadership are not revealed, openly discussed, and conquered at both the individual and organizational levels, gender parity in this lifetime is highly improbable.

Why Leadership Development Programs Fail

It is not a secret that leadership development is broken. The McKinsey white paper, "Why Leadership-Development Programs Fail" [January 2014], by Pierre Gurdjian, Thomas Halbeisen, and Keven Lane, addresses how organizations have struggled to develop their best talent. The difficulties are chalked up to leaders' lack of influence with subordinates and minimal impact with cross-functional teams that are crucial to delivering top-line business results:

". . . burgeoning leaders, no matter how talented, often struggle to transfer even their most powerful off-site [leadership training] experiences into changed behavior on the front line."

Companies continue to collectively spend $14 billion annually on leadership-development practices that don't produce lasting transformation. This article also stated that there's an elephant in the room, and the article chose *not* to name the elephant:

". . . too often, these organizations are reluctant to address the root causes of why leaders act the way they do. Doing so can be uncomfortable for participants, program trainers, mentors, and bosses—but if there isn't a significant degree of discomfort, chances are that the behavior won't change."

The root causes of why leaders act the way they do is because they are still burdened with their vulnerable childhood parts. I'm not sure what "elephant" McKinsey had in mind, but through the IFS lens, I believe the emotionally charged exiles are the uncomfortable "elephant in the room" that McKinsey chose not to state in the paper. My best guess is that McKinsey may know that childhood burdens are a significant contributor to why two-thirds of leaders fail.

The definition of insanity is doing the same thing over and over again, expecting different results. Spending $14 billion annually on leadership development that doesn't produce significant results and lasting transformation is not exactly sane. The Internal Family Systems Self-leadership model is the foundational missing piece in leadership development. The article also says:

"Identifying some of the deepest, below-the-surface thoughts, feelings, assumptions, and beliefs is usually a precondition of behavioral change—one too often shirked in development programs."

From the Self-leadership perspective, this precondition to behavioral change must be mandatory. It is typically shirked in development programs because the originators of the training programs do not know how to go underneath the iceberg's surface to uncover the parts that prevent access to Self-leadership. The IFS framework gives the powerful hows to break up the psychological icebergs that block successful leadership. If leaders fail to adopt lasting positive behavioral change after returning from leadership development training, this means that self-awareness tools via understanding Self and parts have not been taught.

How do we measure the success from Self-leadership training? One of the most straightforward measures is to look at the before and after results of 360-degree assessments. A 360-degree evaluation provides anonymous feedback about your positive and negative traits from your supervisors, peers, and subordinates.

Specific well-known executive coaches (who shall remain nameless) to Fortune 500 CEOs have mentioned in their books that they don't even bother taking on clients who like to dwell in the past since they blame their shortcomings on their parents and their difficult childhoods. These coaches often believe these leaders are lost causes. Sadly, the coaches don't realize that many psychotherapy and coaching methodologies do not recognize nor go into the icebergs underneath the surface. The outermost protector is the fear of change. Without addressing the fear of change *first*, this protector won't allow the leader to permanently transform into their best self despite participating in expensive training and coaching. Some of these leaders are not lost causes. All of them can benefit from Internal Family Systems sessions to remove the obstacles underneath the surface. Still, many well-known executive coaches do not have the proper training to help their clients remove deep-seated barriers. The IFS model is the most effective way to target and resolve these parts that limit and sabotage leaders and their leadership. Self-leadership is about leading from the heart, not from logic and fear. Self-leadership is not only a crucial ingredient for long-term success, it is a foundational leadership competency that has been missing in leadership development. If you want a beautiful house that lasts for centuries, you need a rock-solid foundation. If you want to be a compassionate, heart-led, and empathetic leader that everyone loves to works for, it's imperative to erect a rock-solid Self-leadership foundation.

Chapter 14

The Universe's Grander Plan

Emily continues her story to show the audience what is possible when you're Self-led and muster up the courage to go outside your comfort zone. "Two weeks after getting laid off in 2011, my money manager brought me into this office to give me a pep talk. Doug said, 'Emily, stop looking for another job! You need to become an entrepreneur! I never give life coaching advice, I stay behind a computer to manage money, but I felt compelled to talk to you. I've known you and have watched you for over twenty years. You've got all the skills to be a successful entrepreneur.'

"I said, 'Whaaat?' looking like Martians just landed in front of me. Never in a million years was entrepreneurship on my radar. I didn't grow up around a family business. I never went to business school. I shoved that idea into the back of my mind while I looked for another pharma sales job since my then-husband and I still had a mortgage and three years of college tuition bills for our son.

"After five months of not materializing another pharmaceutical sales job because I was too experienced, too old, and too expensive, I decided to jump into entrepreneurship, with zippo ideas on how to build a business. I opted to launch into the nutrition health coaching arena since I have a degree in nutrition. I spent a lot of money on courses and mentors to understand how to be an entrepreneur. After being a nutritionist for a year and a half and networking everywhere, I realized I hated telling people how to eat better. They knew how to eat healthily, but nutrition didn't address the internal emotional blocks, the *parts* that kept them from adopting lifelong healthy habits. Just having information is never enough. I'm sure some of you could relate to gaining all the weight back after going on diets." Emily notices several people nodding their heads with that statement.

"As I plugged along marketing myself, never did I ever question, 'Am I good enough to be in my own business?' I knew I had big ideas *and* can execute; I just needed to learn the steps. Since I recovered from my shameful past over a decade prior, I knew I had the superpowers to make it big. And of course, my money manager's encouragement and confidence in me sparked my determination. I kept going and going like the Energizer Bunny, and people responded to my vibrant, confident Self-energy. For example, after a ten-minute conversation with a woman at a networking event in New York City, she called me the next day and said, 'You are going places young lady, I just know it!' Wow! I had no idea my energy was so immediately impactful.

"I share these stories to reinforce a critical point: your *energy* sells, period! According to communication studies published long ago, it doesn't matter what you say; words only account for seven percent of communication; 93 percent is nonverbal, which means your *energy* broadcasts your truths," Emily says, emphasizing the word *energy*.

"As I kept putting myself out there, little did I know that someone I met at a New York City networking event would change the course of my life forever. I'll call him 'David.' As the friendship with David grew over six months, he revealed his deepest fears and insecurities. He had been through twenty years of therapy that rendered him stable, but his self-esteem was still low, and his new business wasn't going anywhere, despite his three Ivy League degrees. Notice how accumulating designer diplomas and fancy initials after your name won't improve your self-esteem or guarantee success and happiness."

Whoa! That comment hit home with John.

"David was seeking help. I was only trained in neurolinguistics programming, NLP, at the time, and I knew it wasn't deep enough to get him unstuck. The Universe decided to orchestrate another synchronicity collision at the yoga studio where a therapist friend said I needed to get trained in Internal Family Systems so I could solve David's issues. I had heard of IFS before from another friend, but hearing it again made an impact. I bought the IFS books and then signed up for the in-depth training. Because the Internal Family Systems Self-leadership framework is, at its core, spiritual healing, non-therapists like myself can be trained and apply IFS beyond psychotherapy in whatever areas we are passionate about.

"After I read the IFS books, I let David know that I could help him if he wanted to be my guinea pig. The IFS training wasn't starting for another two months, but David couldn't wait. If therapists were hearing this part of the story, they would be shocked at how I took such a bold step to do 'trauma' work with someone when I wasn't even officially trained. Well, I knew if I got stuck in the process of coaching David, I would stop. I clumsily followed the IFS protocol as best as I could and, because David trusted me thoroughly, he was on board. Attunement is half the battle in finding the right healer.

"I was able to guide David to access a four-year-old part of him, the exile, who was still stuck in the foyer of the house he grew up in, as his father left with two suitcases in hand when his parents divorced. That four-year-old took on the belief that he wasn't worthy of love or worthy of other things, such as success. These core burdens of worthlessness were the heavy emotional suitcases he carried his whole life.

"I guided David's forty-two-year-old Higher Self to rescue, unburden, and reparent the four-year-old. This initial session took two hours. At the end of it, David said, 'I feel like thirty pounds of baggage just released off my back. You did more for me in two hours than twenty years of therapy!' The next day, I touched base, and he said, 'This is the first morning of my life that I woke up happy!'"

Emily let the audience know that lightning struck in that moment with David in August 2013. She finally found her life's calling; it felt like a spiritual orgasm. "David continued to work with me via videoconferencing for about twelve more hours over the next four months. When I met him in person in New York City in January 2014, David said, 'Because of you and the power of IFS, I became the man I've always dreamed of becoming. I feel happy and alive for the first time ever!' I was moved and speechless.

"David got cranking with his business. The following two years, with his new high-vibration Self-energy, he manifested $20-million-dollars in assets for his business. David said that was an insane amount, practically unheard of for a newbie in his line of work. He continues to kick butt today with growing many facets of his business. Getting to know and working with his parts through IFS transformed him from ordinary and stuck, to extraordinary.

"I share David's story and my story to illustrate that when you do the work to shed old faulty programming and become the most magnificent version of you—led by your Higher Self—the world is your oyster.

"As a result of finding my center and my true calling in 2014, my clients kept saying I needed to write a self-help book that wasn't 'self-helpless,' and I needed to talk about the applications of IFS beyond psychotherapy. I wrote in my journal in April 2014 that self-publishing a Kindle was a top priority. I had no idea how I was going to write a book. English Composition was my most dreaded subject in school since English wasn't my native language. When I jotted down 'writing a book' in my journal, I didn't have any negative self-talk of 'Who do you think you are? You're not a writer! You dreaded English 101!' That journal entry was Spirit making the decision for me to write a book. My parts did not question that assignment. Therefore, I did not have any negative self-talk.

"Two weeks after that journal entry, I was at a New York City reception where I hardly knew anyone. I was invited to the event by Ben, whom I'd met two months prior. Ben was fascinated with my energy and my work, so he asked me to the party. Again, notice I said *energy* again. It's your energy, your high-vibe Self-*energy* that attracts others to you like bees to honey.

"In the middle of this reception, a man in his forties started talking to me. We didn't know each other from a hole in the wall. Randy peppered me with many questions for twenty minutes. I'm thinking to myself—*Who is this nosy bozo that wants to know every little detail about me?* It didn't feel like he was flirting, so what was up? Then, he asked if I had ever thought about writing a book.

"I said, 'Yes, I wrote in my journal that writing a book was a priority, but I don't know how to do that, and I don't have a publisher,' blah . . . blah . . . blah. Randy said, 'Stop, Emily. You don't have to worry about how to write and publish a book. You've been talking to a publisher for the last twenty minutes. I'm fascinated with you and your energy and how you are going to change the world.' Notice, it's my *energy* once again. Randy continued, 'I never do this, but I'm going to give you a book deal right now. I know you're a first-time author, and I'm going to take on all the risk. I've been asking you all these questions to understand your platform's seriousness, and your *energy* told me everything I needed to know. You'll get the contract in a week.' I was speechless. I thought I was in a dream. Whaaat? I just got a book deal?! Are you freakin' kidding me? Some authors spend a whole lifetime looking for a publisher. Miracles and synchronicities like this can be orchestrated by the Universe when your parts are in internal alignment with your highest purpose.

"Every belief, thought, and feeling has a vibration. That vibrational energy is picked up by the Universe. What you believe and think create your reality. As I've said before, 'You will not attract what you want into your life; you will attract who you are,'—that is, who your *parts* think you are. What your parts believe about you is broadcasted via your aura. Randy and Ben were sold on my energy. I walk my talk to show you the evidence of how the *energy* of your beliefs determines your success. If you have parts with doubts and fears, the Universe will *not* orchestrate the required synchronicities—for example, the events that led up to meeting my publisher—to realize your dreams. If you are left-brain and data-driven, and would like to learn the science of how beliefs, thoughts, and feelings impact every area of your life, please look up books and videos on YouTube by scientific thought leaders—Dr. Joe Dispenza, Gregg Braden, and Dr. Dean Radin.

"So, with the book deal in hand, Spirit guided me to write my first book in six months. *How to Permanently Erase Negative Self-Talk: So You Can Be Extraordinary* was published a year after that fateful meeting with Randy, the publisher. And of course, Spirit needs me to write more books so *you* can live an extraordinary life in love and leadership. My passion and legacy are about using my God-given gifts to change *your* life.

"There's a saying that you need to teach what you need to learn. It's been fascinating to learn about myself and get clear on how I want to show up for you and walk my talk authentically. Through my stories, I have illustrated how my protectors and exiles have played out in my life. Once I unburdened from the past and became more Self-led, and vulnerably and authentically showing up as my best self, the Universe took over and orchestrated my being at the right place at the right time. I had to believe in the crazy destinations I plugged into my life's GPS. I didn't have to know the hows of the exact routes I needed to take to get to my destination. All I had to do was surrender, put myself out there, and be willing to fail forward and fail fast and often. I've certainly made lots of mistakes along the way, and I'm still making mistakes so I can learn from them and let the Universe bring about the 'oh my gosh you're never going to believe what happened' synchronicities. Great things can happen to you too, when you access Self-leadership and finally unconditionally love and believe in yourself.

"Helping organizations and individuals solve leadership and love challenges at the root cause level is the beacon that gets me out of bed in the morning. Being a great leader *and* having an intensely satisfying love life is a spiritual journey. When all else fails, go spiritual.

"Marianne Williamson, a renowned spiritual teacher and author, sums up our deepest fear beautifully in this famous quote from *A Return to Love: Reflection on the Principle of 'A Course in Miracles'*:

Our deepest fear is not that we are inadequate. Our deepest fear is that we are powerful beyond measure. It is our light, not our darkness that most frighten us. We ask ourselves, who am I to be brilliant, gorgeous, talented, and fabulous? Actually, who are you not to be? You are a child of God. You playing small does not serve the world. There is nothing enlightened about shrinking so that other people won't feel insecure around you. We are all meant to shine as children do. We were born to manifest the glory of God that is within us. It is not just in some of us; it is in everyone. And as we let our light shine, we unconsciously give others permission to do the same. As we are liberated from our own fear, our presence automatically liberates others.

"Powerful, right?" Many heads nod. "It's my spiritual duty to be liberated from my fears and let my light shine so I can give *you* permission to shine, so *you* can influence others to shine their light."

Also, Emily lets them know about the dark side of allowing your light shine. She uses the example of losing weight and feeling good about yourself. "The newfound confidence can trigger some friends and family because they are watching you 'rise' above them in confidence and self-esteem. Your self-assurance can activate their insecure parts. Therefore, they may subconsciously sabotage you to stay in your place so that they can feel significant once again. 'Come on; you're getting too skinny. The apple pie is not going to hurt you,' and, 'Who do you think you are with that big business idea of yours? You barely survived college.'" The audience has smirks on their faces to signal they get the point.

"It can be uncomfortable to unleash the greatest version of you—with a healthy body and a kick in your step, land the dream job, or become the successful entrepreneur. The envy and possible isolation from your tribe can be difficult to experience. Know that your newfound confidence is something they wished they dared to express. The ostracization can leave you in no man's land while you look for a new tribe. Feeling alone after you embody and live the better version of you is *one* of the major reasons why 95 percent of dieters fail. There are many other protectors that don't like the new you. If you want to remove the invisible blocks that hold you back from success, it's important to do the work on the parts that don't feel safe when you shine your brightest light. This part is afraid that something bad will happen to you, like getting criticized for shining so brightly. I sound like a broken record now. After all, repetition is the mother of all learning, right?" The attendees agree.

"In summary, when you are proud to share the journey of how you got to where you are, through Self-led courageous and confident vulnerability, your authenticity helps you to connect deeply with just about anyone. The improved quality of your relationships translates into a happier life. The quality of your relationships determines the quality of your life."

With that conclusion, the audience erupts with applause, comments, and questions. They are very appreciative of the many lightbulb moments and parallels to their forgotten parts that were stirred by Emily's stories.

During the break, John and Jill look at each other and smile. "Emily is covering great insightful stuff," John says to Jill.

She replies, "The IFS framework is so spot on to explain life's challenges."

Chapter 15

Intimately Holding Space for Parts

At the end of the first day of training, John and Jill join the group at dinner. At nine o'clock, John whispers into Jill's ear, "Would you like to come to my room so we can have a private chat? Too many people here."

"Sure, I would love to." John texts his room number to Jill, and they leave within five minutes of each other to ward off any suspicions from the other attendees.

John's room has a couch and fireplace. He feels a wave of peace and calm wash over his body with the camaraderie and closeness he felt with the fellow participants. Jill also feels warmth and calm from the group energy. What transpired in Emily's workshop was Self-energy begetting Self-energy.

John and Jill continue to bathe in that vibrational goodness as they settle down on the couch. *I have no desire to be frisky,* John thinks to himself, as he again admires Jill's beauty. *I just want to hold her and cuddle.* Jill decides to go with the flow and crosses her fingers that John will not push the boundaries.

John slips off his Ferragamo loafers and lies across the sofa with his hands behind his head. Jill decides to sit at the edge of the couch with her leg and hip touching John's leg and hip. "Can we hold hands? I will behave." Jill feels relief with that reassurance.

"Yes, of course," Jill says as she reaches for John's hands.

"I felt seen today by the people at my table. Emily's stories hit close to home," John confesses.

"I'm glad you felt validated. Your energy is beautiful now. It feels like I'm holding hands with your soul." Jill feels electricity charging through their hands. They savor the silence and continue to look into each other's eyes.

"The little John's were stirred up a bit this afternoon. I still see my five-year-old and ten-year-old parts in my mind's eye." John closes his eyes and holds space for the exiles.

"Yes, that's beautiful. I accept you as you are, with all your parts." At that moment, Jill creates a safe space for John to express whatever wants to come out. The way she firmly holds John's hands and looks into his eyes lets him know that it's safe to reveal whatever is on his mind.

John and Jill are in a dance, where Jill holds her inner "masculine" frame for John's inner "feminine" side of emotions to pour out. This dance is similar to a parent holding space for a child to share what bothers them.

All of us have masculine *and* feminine energies. We flip from one to the other, depending on the situation. An aspect of masculine energy is holding the "container" for an experience. For example, Emily's inner masculine erected the safe boundaries for the participants to express their feminine side—that is, their emotions. Another example is when a couple dances. The best dances happen when one person leads (masculine energy), and the other follows (feminine energy).

John's and Jill's masculine-feminine energies are polarized now. When a person is in solid, masculine energy, and the other person is in feminine, flowing, emotional energy, this can create intimacy, sexual chemistry, a feeling of oneness with self, oneness with the other, and oneness with the Universe. Jill is in masculine energy, holding space, and John is in feminine energy, sharing emotions. "I don't want to get into the specific stories of the little John's, that's too heavy," John says. "I love how peaceful I feel with you honoring where I'm at."

"Of course, I will honor your wishes. I'm enjoying the energy between us too."

John responds with a wink, closes his eyes, and breathes even deeper. After five minutes of silence with his eyes closed, feeling Jill the whole time as he reflected, John opens his eyes, and says from his heart, "Thank you."

"Thank you for giving me the privilege to experience this soulful connection."

"You bet. I wish I had more of this in my life."

"Yeah, me too."

"What about you, Jill? It's your turn. What would you like to share?"

In this moment, John flips into his inner masculine energy to let Jill know that he's ready to be the "frame" or "container" for whatever vulnerabilities want to come through Jill's inner feminine.

"Thank you for opening the space. I had several parts of me activated today, too. Like you, I want to sit with those feelings as you hold me."

"I'm here for whatever needs to be witnessed," John says with smooth and reassuring energy.

"The part that got activated was college Jill, who worked so hard to impress the sorority girls and convince them that I was worthy of belonging in their tribe. Some of them accepted me and others flat out rejected me." Jill shares this as she looks into John's eyes. Her throat cracks, and a few tears trickle down.

Jill moves her body, indicating that she wants to cuddle. John turns sideways on the couch to make room for spooning. John remains silent to let her feel the "I've got you" masculine frame. He wraps his arms around her, cradling tightly like a couple who just finished making love. They breathe in unison for the next ten minutes. Jill's thinking—*The connection and energy flowing between us is like a prolonged climax. I want to freeze this moment forever!* As Jill remains in a spiritual trance, John's thinking—*I don't remember the last time I felt this connected. This energy feels better than sex! Well, sex after this would be mind-blowing, but we're not going there.*

"Let's get on the bed and give each other room to cuddle. I'm going to behave. Is this all right?" Jill loves how he took charge, respected the boundaries, and asked permission. That felt soothing and safe and helps Jill relax.

"You're good at reading my boundaries, and I feel even safer now that you've asked for permission. Thank you."

"Well, we may have been friskier in the past, but not today. I love how we're able to talk about this. I want to cuddle, hold hands, and maybe some light kissing. Is that okay?"

"Yes, I'm okay with that," Jill reassures John.

John picks up Jill from the sofa and moves her over to the bed, gently releasing her. They settle into spooning again for another ten minutes, rubbing each other's arms and torsos and avoiding the nether regions. Then, they turn to face each other with more gazing. John moves toward Jill and lightly kisses her on the mouth and face. They softly moan to let each other know how much they are enjoying the experience. *I've never felt this level of closeness before. I'm so used to 'baseball' sex, performing, and making sure my partner climaxes,* John thinks as he places another kiss on Jill's lips, without the need to engage in a deep tongue dance. "Hey . . ." John says softly to Jill, "Can I share what I'm noticing?"

"Of course."

"I'm not feeling the full surrender of your lips now. Feels like you're holding back and not relaxing into the kiss."

"Oh, I didn't know you could pick up on that energy. I had no idea I was doing it. Maybe a part of me feels guilty for being here with you?"

"No need to be afraid of anything. I've got you; you're safe with me." With that inner masculine reassurance, Jill lets out a big sigh, takes a deep belly breath, and lets her body and lips relax.

"Follow my lips as they close and open; no need to get ahead of me." *Wow, no guy has ever been so attentive to my energy, directing the dance of two lips.* John thoroughly enjoys how Jill has surrendered into his lead. He has no idea how he got into this state of leading through Spirit. He follows the energy without expectations. They feel presence, closeness, and pleasure. He slowly teases Jill into the softness of letting their lips savor the dance and the heart-to-heart connection; a deep tongue tango is unnecessary. Their sexual chakras (energy centers) light up like a Christmas tree, yet they manage to honor the boundaries.

After an hour of cuddling and heartfelt connection, Jill reluctantly says, "I have to run. I don't trust myself. I'm too turned on to stay here."

"Okay, I get it. I'm turned on, also. Good night," he says, giving her one last bear-hug embrace.

After Jill closes the door to her room, she lies on the bed and stares at the ceiling. *I feel so high, like I've transcended to another planet.* She grins ear-to-ear and hugs her pillow. *My heart is on fire with that "orgasmic" connection. That was John's Self-energy. No wonder I'm drunk on spiritual love.*

After Jill leaves, John soaks in the deliciousness of what happened. *That was a heavenly out-of-body experience. Is this what true love feels like? I'm so turned on I'm ready to explode. All we did was cuddle and kiss. Wow, just wow!*

John and Jill finally realize what being fully seen feels like, where any vulnerabilities that come up are not judged, shamed, or fixed but honored with "holding space." All parts are welcome!

After an hour of gazing at the ceiling, Jill texts: THAT was the most beautiful, intimate, and heartfelt experience I'd ever had. Thank you for holding the loving space.

John beams as he reads the text and answers: I know, right?! Thank YOU for holding space for my parts. I finally experienced spiritual intimacy. I was never able to wrap my arms around that concept. Imagine what it would be like if we went further and hit it out of the park? And maybe someday we can even open up our own business?

Jill chuckles at the baseball analogy and feels enthused about the possibility of exploring a business future together. Jill texts: I know, I can only imagine. The intimacy was intense. A business partnership sounds good to me—when the timing is right. Good night, my friend. ;)

John's still beaming with a smile: G-nite beautiful. xoxo.

Why the John and Jill Relationship May Not Make Sense to You

At this point in the story, you may have a judgment part that thinks—*This story is ludicrous! The author is crazy. The story of John and Jill is not real. No one has this kind of intimate platonic relationship at work, especially between a married boss and a single subordinate. This is an affair. Jill is so stupid for getting involved with a married boss. If this ever happened at my workplace, it would be grounds for termination!*

You're right—John and Jill's dynamic sounds far-fetched, mainly because it's a hierarchic relationship in a large company. This dynamic is more real than you might guess. Please remember that there are many varieties of platonic and non-platonic friendships and "relationships" that form behind closed doors in organizations. I ask you *not* to judge how real the story is. I developed the John and Jill characters to illustrate how the past is always present in personal *and* professional relationships. I am showing you how to become an authentic Self-led leader. This fictional story is *not* about dissecting how many HR rules John and Jill are breaking; it's about the secret to authenticity, closeness, and pleasure.

Holding Space With "I've Got You" Masculine Energy

Relationships—in business, friendship, and romance—become a challenge when there isn't a "container" to process fears, communication breakdowns, resentments, and frustrations.

As you've seen in John and Jill's connection in the hotel room, desires and boundaries were communicated. How does this apply to leadership? If a leader wants to be trusted and respected, he needs to erect the "frame" for performance expectations and honest conversations. For example, a hiccup happens, the leader accesses Self and says, "I would like to share my thoughts regarding xyz without placing blame or judgment. I'm curious about how I contributed to the misunderstanding and would like to work together to fix this." This is the leader's inner masculine part erecting the "I've got the situation under control. Here's the safe container for our discussion." When boundaries and desires are expressed through calm, connected, present, and curious Self-energy, the other person *feels* safe. Feeling safe fosters harmonious conflict resolution, increased engagement, creativity, and productivity.

Are you a leader, friend, and lover who knows how to hold the inner masculine space (without the need to fix) while the other person shares emotions, vulnerabilities, and hurts? Or, do your defensive, judgmental, and fix-it parts take over?

To learn more about inner masculine leadership, read: *The Way of the Superior Man: A Spiritual Guide to Mastering the Challenges of Women, Work, and Sexual Desire* by Davide Deida and *The Masculine in Relationship: A Blueprint for Inspiring the Trust, Lust, and Devotion of a Strong Woman* by GS Youngblood.

Also, you can learn more through my online courses: "Climax in Love: Be the Ultimate Warrior for a Goddess" and "Climax in Love: Be the Ultimate Goddess for a Warrior." To access these courses, go to www.ClimaxInLove.com.

Chapter 16

Legitimate Love Affairs

The next morning during breakfast, John and Jill exchange big smiles as they sit at different tables. It feels good to have a little secret between them. As Emily eats breakfast with this cadre of amazing leaders, she can feel the high vibration of collective Self-energy. She thinks to herself—*It's even higher than yesterday, and I can feel the "group love" in my bones. This magic happens every time a group of strangers gathers because I've created a safe container for them to share vulnerabilities. Many of these new friendships will continue for years to come.*

As the lively crowd regroups in the conference room, Emily acknowledges, "Hey everyone, I just want to share that I love witnessing the formation of new friendships. And, I also cherish the new friendships I have with you, too. No wonder I love my job so much."

"We love you too, Emily!" Matt shouts out as he refills his coffee.

John continues to daydream about last night's kissing experience. Jill sits at the table to the left of John. They can see each other out of the corners of their eyes. Jill is still reliving last night's kisses and cuddles. Jill texts: I'm blown away with the depth of your consciousness. I'm in awe of how you sensed my blocked energy and said the right things for me to relax and surrender. I felt ravished. I appreciate you.

John reads the text with the phone on his lap so the person next to him can't read it. He beams, and their eyes lock for a quick second as he texts: There's no one else in the world I would rather ravish than you. ☺ Your receptiveness to my lead felt terrific. I like being in my manly role of protecting and ravishing a beautiful woman. xo

Jill continues to feel tingly as she reads the text, with John watching her beautiful, lit-up face. She texts back: And I felt like a goddess in the arms of her warrior. We had a serious spiritual experience. ;)

John texts: **Hell yeah**! She looks up, and their eyes lock again for a few seconds. That was pure Self-to-Self connection, with presence and playfulness. Now it's time to pay attention to the training.

"I want to thank you, Matt, for noticing the love here. This energy is something you can achieve with your team when you lead and listen from Self and share expectations, desires, and boundaries. You, the leader, is responsible for creating this safe 'container' I keep talking about. When the container has boundaries and expectations, it's easier for people to be themselves because they know what they should and should not do. When you allow freedom of expression within the boundaries, this can increase engagement, creativity, and productivity. When people feel safe, they are more likely to go beyond the call of duty. Your team members will say, 'I'll go to the end of the earth for this boss! I'll follow him anywhere!' That's the power of Self-leadership."

Wonderful Childhood Does Not Always Equal No Struggles

Jeff, the CEO of a Silicon Valley technology startup, lets Emily know that some of the examples of traumatic childhoods she shared did not resonate. He had loving parents, and, for the most part, a great childhood. Jeff knows he isn't the best leader because he micromanages and often needs to have the last word, which has created many conflicts.

Emily asks Jeff if he has ever been compared to a sibling.

"Yes, I was. I wasn't a straight-A student like my older brother. I felt second best, like I was never going to be good enough in my parents' eyes. And, I never made the varsity basketball team; that failure caused my brother to tease me mercilessly. I feel like I need to prove something by making sure my startup becomes a huge success."

Emily encourages Jeff to think about other incidences on the playground, locker room, or school dances that could have made him feel inadequate. "It's not uncommon for these seemingly innocuous emotional experiences, little 'traumas,' to have significant impact in midlife. When these embarrassing moments occurred, some kids didn't feel safe to open up to Mom and Dad. Their parents didn't know how to provide the safe space for their kids to express emotions. Sadly, for many boys, they heard, "Boys don't cry. Showing your emotions is weak." As a result of this bold disempowering message, these men become emotionally unavailable romantic partners and are the stoic leaders who don't make their team members feel safe to express their frustrations.

"Your painful memories are the skeletons in the closet that show up when you try to go big, such as launching a business or going after the big promotion. Having great parents and a stable childhood with minor hiccups doesn't preclude parts from going into extreme roles.

"Jeff, your micromanagement part can irk the team. And, there's a part that doesn't feel smart enough. If these parts are not liberated of these beliefs, they can sabotage your aspirations. Let's talk later to see how I can help you."

"Your explanation makes sense. Thank you."

Emily takes the group through self-reflection and experiential exercises to meet and manage their inner team of subpersonalities. After lunch, she goes into the discussion that everyone loves, how parts affect the love life. She saves this for last because, by this time, the group has emotionally gelled, and some will feel safe to share their love life challenges.

Infidelity and Aliveness in Long-term Relationships

Jennifer, a forty-something brunette, shares that she got divorced because her ex cheated on her. "Can you interpret Esther Perel's teachings on eroticism, passion in long-term partnership, and infidelity through the IFS lens?"

Emily lets the audience know that Esther is a New York Times best-selling author of *The State of Affairs: Rethinking Infidelity*, and *Mating in Captivity: Unlocking Erotic Intelligence*. Esther is also a famous TED talk speaker and YouTube sensation.

"Many of us end up in long-term relationships where we feel that it's not safe to allow all of our parts to come out and play. When a third party comes along who makes you feel safe to express parts which have rarely seen the light of day, all of a sudden, you feel alive. If there's a physical attraction, and one person is not romantically available, this scenario can take you down the slippery slope of emotional affairs, and sex outside of a committed relationship." Emily can feel the palpable energy in the room that conveys—*Yep! I know what it feels like when someone makes me feel alive.*

Jennifer shares, "I hear you. So, I have to own my part in how I contributed to my ex's attraction to another person?"

"Yes, you do; it takes two to tango. When you feel seen and validated by a new person, it's a drug. We want more of that validation elixir because it fills up the number one human need—validation. If you want an exciting and edgy strategy to keep your relationship alive, I recommend watching a TED talk by Jessica O'Reilly, *Monogamish: New Rules of Marriage*. Jessica's recipe may not be everyone's cup of tea. Still, she shares how to bring aliveness, fun, and eroticism into monogamous relationships, to feel like you're dating many different personas within the same person. This play-acting helps partners reclaim their hidden parts. There's nothing more stimulating than tapping into parts of you that have been locked up for decades. So, the IFS lens on keeping relationships alive is that when you encourage and hold space for another's dormant parts to come out and play, continued eroticism and passion are possible in long-term partnerships."

As Emily shares this, both John and Jill realize that what made the connection the previous night intimate—more intimate than many sexual encounters—was that they felt emotionally connected; they welcomed, witnessed, and validated each other's parts.

"It's great to have our parts express, but please remember that too many extreme parts can be problematic. For example, expressing your sexy goddess part is not appropriate for the workplace."

Inner Masculine and Inner Feminine Energies

The group continues learning about energy dynamics in relationships. They ask many questions about how to communicate better and create profound intimacy. Emily encourages them to watch the "Great Love and Sex through IFS" YouTube channel she co-produces with a Harvard-trained psychiatrist, Percy Ballard, MD. Emily and Percy discuss, role-play, and teach you how to overcome relationship challenges through the IFS lens.

"Sexual attraction and chemistry are created out of masculine and feminine energy polarization. Everyone has masculine and feminine energies. These energies are *parts*." Emily shows the slides of what masculine and feminine energies look like.

Masculine Energy

- From the head
- Left brain
- Doing
- Leading and directing
- On mission and purpose

- Dominate
- Forceful
- Independent
- Confident
- Assertive

- Aggressive
- Tells
- Analytical
- Competitive
- Results-driven

- Plan
- Structure
- Hold pace
- Consciousness
- The witness

Feminine Energy

- From the heart
- Right brain
- Being
- Nurturing
- Intuitive
- Creative
- Emotional
- Vulnerable
- Compassionate
- Sensitive

- Graceful
- Collaborative
- Asks questions
- Surrender
- Submissive
- The witnessed
- Receiving
- Soft
- Flowing

"To learn more about the dance of masculine and feminine energies in sacred intimacy, please check out the work of David Deida, a modern-day pioneer in the field of spiritual yogic intimacy, and the best-selling author of numerous books on the topic. Two of his most popular books are *The Way of the Superior Man*, and *It's a Guy Thing: An Owner's Manual for Women*."

With this insight, John and Jill look at each other. John gives a wink, and they both get the aha that what transpired the night before was this Self-to-Self dance of masculine-feminine energy. John texts: No wonder we were in heaven last night! Jill replies: This explains the magic for sure. ;)

◆　◆　◆

In the last couple of hours of the workshop, Emily answers many questions through the IFS lens regarding procrastination, selfishness, fear of success, fear of failure, angry-edged people, and constructive feedback via Self-leadership. Here is the summary of what was covered.

Procrastination

"A little bit of procrastination isn't bad for most people. Some of you do your best work when you wait until the last minute. However, when procrastination is the modus operandi and is in overdrive, it can negatively affect every part of your life. Completed projects are mediocre, and your friends get mad because you're always late. The procrastination part is afraid of something and prefers avoidance. If it stopped procrastinating and lets you be on time, you may turn in successful projects that get you promoted, and you may attract better friends and romantic partners that you don't feel you deserve.

"Here's an example from my client files. Sheila's procrastination part held her back. Growing up, Sheila's successful dad went over her homework four or five times to make sure it was perfect. As a result of his care and perfection, she became the valedictorian of her high school class and gained admission to Yale. In her forties, procrastination part avoided getting back to people via texts and emails and made her wait until the last minute to finish assignments. She uncovered that if she did things at the last minute and the projects came back with a 'B' grade from the boss, at least she had procrastination to blame. If she stopped procrastinating and did the project perfectly and the boss gave her a 'B,' then it would trigger the shame of the little girl that took on the belief that 'I'm not smart enough to do homework on my own.' Procrastination protects this exile. It doesn't know she's all grown up now and can handle not getting an 'A.' She emancipated little Sheila of her false beliefs. As a result of unburdening the child part, Sheila's procrastination significantly decreased. She promptly gets back to people now and is not as worried about perfectionism. She is okay with 'done is better than perfect.'

"Here's a different story of how modest procrastination was birthed in Steve's life, a friend I met at a personal development conference. Typically, it took Steve weeks to answer texts and emails. The only person he replied to immediately was his boss since Steve's paycheck depended on it. Steve uncovered that the exile that procrastination protected was the young part that hated being told what to do. As the youngest of three children, Steve grew up in a one-bedroom apartment housing a family of five. He felt smothered and powerless. He didn't have space to be by himself. When he became an adult, he wanted to feel in control. The need to feel in control meant that Steve procrastinated by failing to get back to people. He didn't feel powerless when he controlled how much time he took to reply to texts and emails. Feeling in control reversed the insignificance he felt growing up since he was told what to do all the time. As an adult, he didn't care that not being thoughtful about clear and timely communications bothered his friends and family. He said, 'The ones who get me are not mad at me for taking so long to respond.' Steve doesn't care if he loses friends over this. However, at work, procrastination contributes to his colleagues' frustrations with his untimely responses. Down the road, procrastination could be the limiting behavior that prevents him from reaching his leadership potential."

Selfishness

"A self-centered and selfish person has little regard for others because many of their hurt child parts are still stuck in devaluing experiences. These exiles are desperate for validation and can unknowingly become self-centered to the extreme and act out to get attention. Self-centered people may seem like toddlers who are incapable of sympathy and empathy. If you want to label your boss or your mom 'selfish,' I invite you to take the high road and be more compassionate toward their negative ways. Think of them as a ten-year-old, feeling neglected, unworthy, and insignificant. They don't have self-love, so you cannot expect love, sympathy, and empathy from them."

Root Cause of Fear of Success

"The existence of fear of success part may not make sense to you. But, the bigger we go, the more this fear becomes real. Kim's story illustrates this. The root cause of Kim's fear of success came from an incident at the supermarket when she was five years old. Kim was jumping up and down on the cart, and eventually, the cart toppled over. She fell, was injured, and blood oozed from the wound. Several people swarmed around her to make sure all was okay. With Kim's five-year-old brain in a hypnotic trance, she believed that it's not safe to take risks and fail because all eyes will be on you. As a result of this belief, Kim held back from putting herself out there to grow her business. Kim's Higher Self retrieved this exile from the store, unburdened the belief, and reprogrammed her with new empowering beliefs about how it is safe to promote herself. IFS sessions with this part, and many other parts, including the fear of failure, gave Kim the confidence to take more risks in her business."

Angry Edge Is Childhood Emotional Pain

"Some people show up with a low-grade, angry edge. You can't put your finger on it, but something doesn't feel right; you don't like being around their energy. The darkness is more than likely unresolved childhood stressors. If the root causes are not mended, the body can express this low vibration through cancer, heart disease, emotional instability, or autoimmune issues. The solution to dissipate the off-putting energy is to do the work to unload emotional burdens."

Self-led Constructive Feedback and Performance Reviews

"Before you give constructive feedback, ask for permission. You don't want to blindside people with feedback when they're not ready to hear it. Example of Self-led feedback: 'Susan, I love your attention to detail and enthusiasm during team meetings. Our team couldn't function without your gifts. May I share an area of improvement that can help our team?' Stay curious; don't point fingers. 'There have been many instances where I felt interrupted. I'm curious if you are aware of this interruption part? I would like to see the interruption part diminish. You've stated that you would like to become a vice president of this company one day. When I witness less interruption, I will be more than happy to recommend you for senior leadership positions. You have a lot of potential, and I want to champion you.'

"Susan may have developed the interruption part as a result of not feeling heard growing up. She may be unaware that her interruption is excessive and career-limiting. As long as she hears the feedback, it is unnecessary to do 'therapy' around this part. However, if she wants to fully grow to the next level, it's essential to unshackle from the original, devaluing events that caused this part to interrupt too much. When leaders become aware that the past is always in the present, it's easier to zoom out and step into curious Self-energy to resolve challenges and limiting behaviors."

◆ ◆ ◆

After Emily finished answering the attendees' questions, she invites the participants to integrate the teachings from workshop. The takeaways include:

- Increased self-awareness of parts translates into less judgment, criticism, and blame toward yourself and others.

- One person has the power to change the course of an interaction. Self-leadership is the key to conflict resolution and better outcomes.

- The path to becoming an extraordinary leader (and romantic partner) starts by doing the work to have a spiritual love affair with yourself. The self-development process includes befriending and loving all parts, especially the forgotten and disowned parts.

- If you don't invest in personal growth, unhealed parts can get desperate and seek validation through "illicit" love affairs. Illicit love affairs with people, food, alcohol, drugs, shopping, sex, etc. undermine relationships, health, and career.

- The IFS motto is, "All parts are welcome!" Parts want Self to acknowledge the hard work they do. Parts want Self to lead which parts need to be front and center for the situation at hand.

Emily continues, "If you want to become a great leader, friend, and romantic partner who can inspire, influence, and impact, it starts with self-awareness of what makes you uniquely you. The more you reveal your parts from a place of authenticity and confident vulnerability, the easier it will be for others to feel safe to show more of who they are. The more parts others reveal, while you hold space for those unveilings, the deeper the connection. The deeper the relationship, the easier it will be for them to trust and respect you, follow you, and be inspired by your leadership. Self-leadership is the secret sauce to resolving just about all of your struggles.

"Great leaders need to have love affairs with their parts, first and foremost. When they are fully in love with themselves, that is—their parts—in a non-narcissistic way, they gain the abundance of love and care to shower onto others. If they don't do the work to love themselves, they can end up in illicit love affairs with people, drugs, work, shopping, video games, porn, et cetera. When you embroil in illicit love affairs, it will be difficult to climax in leadership and climax in love. Conversely, if you are a leader who does the inner work to love your parts, you are a great leader who has *legitimate* love affairs with self. Self-love and unconditional love for others give you the power to climax and reach the pinnacle of success and happiness in love and leadership."

Emily concludes the workshop by revealing the ironies of her life, with the intention that her story can help these leaders make sense of their childhood and realize the gifts of their wounds.

"At the 2005 Stanford commencement address, watched over thirty million times so far, Steve Jobs said, 'You can't connect the dots looking forward, you can only connect them looking backward. You have to trust that the dots will somehow connect in your future. You have to trust in something—your gut, destiny, life, karma, whatever. This approach has never let me down, and it has made all the difference in my life.' [Source: "Stanford" YouTube channel, March 7, 2008.]

"I've made sense of my life by connecting the dots looking backward. My life's purpose is to help you soar to greatness in love and leadership through Self-leadership. I witnessed my mom without a voice because of how my dad treated her. My dad stifled his voice, as well. He always wanted to publish his many writings, yet he never dared to go outside his comfort zone to do that, nor to seek greater professional success. My childhood's deepest wounds gave me a unique set of gifts and created the colorful parts of my personality. I found my life's calling at age fifty. My Higher Self guides me to keep going outside of my comfort zone. I walk my talk of confident vulnerability. I show you how to be vulnerable and authentic so you can feel alive and thrive.

"I do this work to honor my mother, who didn't have a voice. I'm reliving her life with a voice. I do this work in honor of my dad, who was afraid. I am reliving my father's life as if he was not afraid. I'm not afraid to push my boundaries and embarrassingly fail many times because I know that this is not about me; it's about what gets to happen to *you* when I inspire you through my stories and guide you to become your best self. I hated English and writing. Ironically, the Universe had me become an 'accidental' writer. Now I am a published author. I do this work in honor of my parents. I have connected the dots of my life looking backwards. How are you going to connect the dots of your life looking back and flip your negative stories into positive narratives? What are the unique gifts you developed as a result of your deepest wounds? How are you going to use these core gifts to make an impact and leave a legacy?

"It may take until you're fifty or sixty years old, or longer, to come full circle. That's okay. When you make a new, positive story of how you are so grateful for the lessons from your wounds, that's when spiritual lightning can strike. We are spiritual beings having a human experience. We are also humans having spiritual experiences with Self and parts. Happiness and enlightenment are not destinations. It's about the inner work journey of deeply knowing yourself and having your parts trust the leadership of Self so you can go beyond your comfort zone to leave the legacy that you are uniquely meant to leave. There is only one you; everyone else is taken. If not you, then whom? If not now, then when? Renowned poet Mary Oliver said, 'Tell me, what is it that you plan on doing with your one wild and precious life?'"

With that conclusion, the group erupts in applause and high-fives. They say good-bye to each other with big bear hugs.

Chapter 17

Parts Disrupt Secure Connection

John and Jill load their bags into the car to drive back to NYC. Jill hopes the Self-to-Self connection they experienced in his hotel room can continue. As they drive away from Chatham Bars Inn, John's energy shifts, and he seems preoccupied. "Are we still going with the plan on the Hector and Company proposal?" Jill carefully asks.

"Yeah . . . let's stick with the plan, giving the agreed percentage to Johnson Media," John replies, as his guilty part thinks—*Damn, we shouldn't be giving the kickback. But it's done all the time. Besides, I can use the extra money for next semester's tuition. I won't get fired; I'm not the only senior leader who does this.*

"Okay, whatever you say, boss," Jill says in a crestfallen fashion. *Am I being manipulated into a kickback scheme I shouldn't be involved in? If this is what makes him successful, does this mean I have to go along with it? Is my attraction clouding my judgment? Am I giving him more power and prestige than he deserves? His walls are back up now, damn it!*

John feels armored up, making Jill feel unsafe to bring out her lively, playful Self, so she sticks to surface-level topics. She places her left hand on John's forearm a couple of times, attempting to go deeper with the connection, but he seems preoccupied. *Why isn't this working?*

John keeps his hands on the steering wheel, eyes locked on the road with only an occasional glance at Jill. *I'm a hot mess with my little John's. They made me spend frivolously. If Jill ever saw my bank account, I would feel like a third-grader who peed in front of the classroom.* As much as he enjoyed their kisses-and-cuddle time, John's jaw clenches, thinking about how to fix his financial mess. He feels less of a man now with his dwindling bank account. *No bandwidth for love until my financial house is in order.* These negative thoughts broadcast a negative energy field that Jill feels. Jill feels tentative and scared and sticks to work conversations.

John is not unusual in his inability to sustain Self-energy. When a man of masculine essence, which means he identifies as someone whose primary desire is mission and purpose (as opposed to a feminine essence person whose fundamental desire is love and connection), his self-concept hinges on external accomplishments. If you're interested in diving deeper into these concepts, you can find books and videos on YouTube by David Deida, Alison Armstrong, and John Gray.

When a man (or a woman who identifies as masculine essence) reaches a certain level of success, they eventually come to a point where they want to express more of their feminine side. Being all one-sided in the long term feels too off-center and unsatisfying because hidden parts are dying to express. As mentioned previously, regardless of gender, everyone has both masculine and feminine energies.

As the long drive filled with surface-level conversations ends at the Stamford, Connecticut train station, John says good-bye with a quick hug and takes Jill's suitcase out of the trunk. Jill takes the Metro-North train to her city apartment while John continues to his house in Rye.

After Jill gets home, she calls her friend Martha to tell her about the highs of eye-gazing and the lows of the 180-degree flip in John's energy during the drive back.

"I'm sorry you feel bummed," Martha says, "I know you have high hopes about his guy and his offer to move you up the corporate ladder. All I can say is he sounds like a manipulator, engaging you with his charm and deceptive schemes. You rationalize his behavior because you're smitten. Disaster might be in the making. A zebra doesn't change his stripes." After a pause, Martha continues, "Maybe he got quiet during the car ride because he felt so guilty about all the wrong things he has done in his life. He didn't want you to see his guilt and shame."

"Thanks for the criticism and the negative outlook; I thought we were friends," Jill says. "I was asking for support. He wouldn't have gotten this far in his career if he was a shyster. I must go. I'm tired; I need to catch up on my sleep."

Jill was hoping for a bright light on the situation, but it didn't happen. *Maybe Martha is right. Perhaps I am seeing him through rose-colored glasses. Maybe all the negative water cooler talk about John is right. Why can't I see this? Is this because I can look into his soul and see the vulnerabilities and goodness underneath his armor? We had an orgasmic spiritual experience in his hotel room, without sex. Okay, voices, please shut up. I need to sleep. Damn! I better take a sleeping pill to silence the chatter!*

Jill feels distressed and conflicted. She's fascinated with a married boss and embroiled in a web of illegal bribes to secure business. *I need to share the turmoil I feel. I don't think he will bark at me if I speak from the heart.* She approaches him on their second day back at work.

"What's going on, my friend?" John says in a friendly business tone.

"I felt disconnected from you during the ride home from the Cape. It felt like you were holding things back."

"It's not you. I have a lot on my mind. We're falling short on new business this quarter, and my ass will be kicked if we don't deliver. And, I've got stress on the home front."

"Okay, I hear you. There's something else I'm concerned about."

"What's that?"

"All the wheeling and dealing we're doing with clients and vendors. I thought it was illegal to be involved in rebate schemes. I know you've said everyone does it, but something doesn't sit well with me. My intuition tells me we're going to get in trouble."

"Don't worry. We've been doing this for ages. Your job is not on the line." John stares into her gorgeous eyes and holds his gaze five seconds longer. He is calm and connected toward her. Jill feels chills up her spine.

"Okay, I guess I feel better now. And another thing, I'm going to use what I learned from Emily to stay curious instead of judging and criticizing."

"Okay, what else?" John's a bit worried about what else Jill wants to throw at him.

"Since you've admitted you have parts you're not crazy about, I'm curious . . . do you plan on doing any work with Emily? You need to rein in your self-righteousness. People don't trust you because you're not a man of your words. You say one thing and rarely follow through with—"

John raises his hands to cut Jill off, clearly aggravated with her "you" tone. "I don't have time for this right now, and it's none of your business if and when I plan to work on myself or change how I lead. So much for your plan to not be judgmental and critical. You have no business talking to me this way."

Damn! I think I just screwed up with the boss. I used too many accusatory "you" words. "Sorry about that, I'm just trying to be a friend and look out for you," Jill says in an apologetic tone.

"I appreciate it. I need to get on a phone call."

"Bye . . ." Jill leaves in a sad state. *All I wanted to do was let him know I support him, but he didn't hear it that way. He felt judged. His armor shut me out. Damn! I blew another interaction.*

IFS Lens on Why John Shuts Down

John's parts are not feeling worthy of Jill since he's not being honest about his most significant stresses—finances and living beyond his means. Once again, lack of vulnerability, lack of clarity, and his on-again, off-again protectors make Jill feel unsafe. Jill doesn't have the right to know the details of his personal life. However, given the level of intimacy they've experienced, John could be more forthcoming about his stressors without divulging the details. But, he's afraid and doesn't know how to do that without feeling ashamed. Instead, it's easier to be hot and cold and shut down. When someone erects protectors and stonewalls, the receiver frequently fills in the blanks with negative worst-case narratives, usually blaming themselves and their character flaws.

Chapter 18

Chipping Away at the Emotional Iceberg

J ill is quite intrigued with the Internal Family Systems model of permanent emotional healing and accelerated personal growth. She decides to work with Emily in private sessions. Even though she had many years of therapy working on her "daddy issues," she still feels these aren't fully resolved. She wants to understand why she has the incredible chills-up-the-spine insane attraction to John—a vibration and magnetism she had never experienced with previous boyfriends.

After spending the first IFS session sharing her family of origin story with Emily, Jill is ready to go deeper. She wants to know why she judges John so much.

Emily takes Jill through a visualization to get in touch with her parts. The meditation is adapted from Dr. Richard Schwartz's *Introduction to the Internal Family Systems Model*, 2001. [Reprinted with permission.]

Path Visualization: Getting in Touch with Parts

Get into a relaxed position and close your eyes. Take a few deep breaths. Notice your breath as you inhale and exhale, and inhale and exhale.

Imagine you are at the base of a path. It can be any path you are familiar with or one you have never been on before. You will meet your future self. This version of you doesn't have fears and insecurities and lives your dream life.

The goal of walking on this path to your future is to identify the beliefs, thoughts, and emotions—the parts—that currently hold you back.

You are at the base of this path now with your parts—that is, beliefs, thoughts, and emotions. Ask these parts to remain at the base and allow you to head out without them. If these parts have fears and concerns about letting you go on the path, reassure them that you won't take long. Let them know that they will benefit when they allow you to head out on the path without them. If your parts object, see if you can arrange for the scared parts to be cared for by those who are not afraid. If not, and parts remain scared to let you go, then don't go. Instead, spend some time discussing their fears and concerns. Ask the parts what they are afraid of if they allow you to go off on the path without them.

If you do sense permission to go, head out to meet your future self. Notice as you go whether you are watching yourself on the trail or on it such that you don't see yourself; you only see and sense your surroundings. If you are watching yourself, that's a signal that a part with fears is present. Find the part that's afraid and ask it to relax and return to the base. If it doesn't want to return to the base, spend time exploring its fears.

As you continue on the path, notice whether you are thinking about anything. If you are, ask those thoughts to return to the base so that you increasingly become pure awareness. As you continue on the path, check periodically to see if you are thinking; if so, gently send the thoughts back. As each thought and emotion leaves you, notice what happens to your body and mind. Notice the space you sense around you and the kind of energy that flows through your body.

Keep going on the path until you meet your extraordinary future self. When you reach that self, invite him/her to tell you what he/she wants you to know about shining your light and greatness. [Pause here to have a conversation with your future self.]

When it feels as if you have spent enough time with your future self and are ready to go back to reunite with the parts waiting at the base, begin to return to the base. See if it is possible to hold the spaciousness and energy you felt with your future self as you get close to your parts again. When you arrive at the base, meet with your parts, see how they fared without you, and ask what they need. When that process is complete, thank your parts for letting you go, if they did. If they didn't, thank them for letting you know they were afraid to let you go. Take some deep breaths and come back into the present.

◆ ◆ ◆

Jill: "I want to work on the part of me that judges. I judge my parents and John, a lot.

Emily: "Okay, let's see if judging part is willing to unblend from you."

What is Unblending?

Imagine the last time you were angry at someone—perhaps your partner, mother, or boss. You probably felt angry part as sensations in your body—clenched jaw, feeling hot, heart rate increasing, wanting to curse and scream. Anger took over your body. You *blended* with anger; you were anger through and through. To heal the excess anger or the angry-edge, you need to ask the part to leave the body so it can be in front of you. Perhaps it looks like a devil or blazing fire. You can google an image of the devil or fire on the smartphone and look at it to represent the angry part. When you feel the angry part leave your body and see it separated from you, you have successfully unblended. The Path Visualization is one way to externalize—i.e., separate or give space—between Self and parts. The next step is to access Self's curiosity so that Self and Anger can get to know each other. This conversation with the part will feel like you're talking to an inanimate object, and you are. It's Self getting to know one of your parts that gets triggered in certain situations. Befriending the part establishes the Self-to-part connection so that the part can trust Self's lead to manage stressful situations.

[Go to www.ClimaxLeadershipBook.com to watch real-time IFS sessions.]

Emily: "What does Judgment look like?"

Jill: "Judgment looks like an old lady with white hair and glasses."

Emily uses her phone to search for an image of an old lady with glasses and white hair.

E: "Look at this part on my phone. How do you feel toward her?"

J: "I'm annoyed."

E: "Can annoyed part take a seat next to you to give you space to befriend the old lady?"

J: [Closes the eyes to imagine.] "Okay . . . Annoyed just chilled out. Now I'm curious about the old lady."

E: "Ask her what she wants you to know about her judgment role."

J: [Looks at the part.] "She says it's her job to judge and criticize, especially when people don't show up for me. This part wants John to be a better leader and likes to tell him I'm not happy with his leadership style."

E: "What is the judgment part afraid would happen if she didn't do her job of judging and criticizing John?"

J: "That he will fail miserably, and I would blame myself for not being smart and caring enough to help him."

E: "Does the way John shows up remind you of someone from the past?"

J: [Looks up at the ceiling.] "Ahhh . . . my dad."

E: "Often, we are energetically attracted to someone who reminds us of our caregivers' good and bad qualities. Many bestselling relationship books have shed light on this. We have unfinished business from our formative years. It sounds like this is a case of trying to redeem your childhood through John, by trying to get him to show up in the way you wished your dad had shown up for you. Many of us have some version of this story. Does this make sense?"

J: "Oh yeah, it does." [Buries her face into her hands, then grabs a tissue from a side table and wipes her eyes.]

E: "The crumbs of validation you get from John make you feel like you're getting paternal love. When John is present and loving, it probably feels like home because it feels like sitting on your daddy's lap and receiving attention and love."

J: "Wow, that's what I felt when John and I were kissing and cuddling in Cape Cod. I felt taken care of." [Grabs more tissues and feels calmer with this profound insight.]

Emily lets Jill know that it's vital for her Higher Self to be the primary healer of her exiles, the child parts that didn't feel loved enough by Dad. Then, when Jill is ready for a conscious, evolved partnership, both parties can share their triggers so that the secondary healing can happen within the context of the relationship. Since we were all wounded in relationships during childhood, the most transformative healing happens within a loving relationship. The triggers never go away, but the good news is that they can be diminished and managed with awareness and conscious communication.

E: "When you think of Dad, how do you judge him?"

J: "Dad's a loser who never reached his full potential, and he was seldom there for me. He was checked out in his man-cave most of the time. Mom was emotionally checked out too. One Christmas break from college, I invited my boyfriend to meet my family. After he left, Mom said I could do better than him. Afterward, she and I got into a huge fight and I avoided her for six months."

Emily goes into teacher mode and lets Jill know that Mom's judgment of her boyfriend has nothing to do with Jill. Non-Self-led parents can say hurtful things, despite the best of intentions.

E: "I'm so sorry to hear that. In some cases, I have found that moms who can't be happy for their kids project their unhappiness onto their children. They have good intentions, but their kids' successes can be hard because if they haven't achieved as much as they'd hoped, some parents project their inadequacies onto the kids. So, they criticize and point out what you haven't achieved: 'When are you ever going to become VP? Haven't you been at that job long enough? Your brother achieved VP status in three years!' or, 'Your sister's an MD, and you're only a PhD, which means you're not a real doctor.' And, for moms who are jealous of their youthful, beautiful daughters, they can be overly critical in an attempt to feel better about themselves."

J: "That makes sense. Mom is forty pounds overweight and dresses in sweats and baggy clothes. No wonder she likes to put me down."

Emily reminds Jill of "the past is always in the present" concept. When someone doesn't treat you right, step back, take the bird's-eye view, and get curious instead of furious about the interaction. What part did you play, if any, to make them defensive and critical? What fears and inadequacies could they be unconsciously projecting onto you?

E: "When you judge John, are you unconsciously judging Dad?"

J: "I guess I am. John's energy reminds me of him because Dad was quite a braggadocio—and delusional, like John. Dad would say how great an athlete he was and how he led the team to victory at the high school baseball championship. He would say how someday he's going to be rich from winning construction contracts from wealthy clients. He's been dreaming big for years, and the success never happened. Whatever money he earned went out as fast as it came in. John does brag like Dad, and he's hot and cold with our connection.

E: "Now do you see why John's a magnet for you?"

J: "Yes, I do! He is putting my unhealed issues with my dad right in my face, and the part of me that wants to fix him feels compelled to engage."

Emily loves it when clients have lightbulb moments. After Jill explained what she knows about John's mom, Emily lets her know that aside from John's attraction to Jill's beauty, there is something about Jill that could be reminding him of unfinished business with his mom or dad.

E: "Your fierce attraction to John illustrates the concept of the exile-to-exile energetic magnet. Unconsciously, you both want to get validation from each other to finish out childhood issues. The exile-to-exile dynamic can be a source of eroticism, sexual tension, and long-term passion. This dynamic explains why someone who was abused or witnessed abuse is magnetically drawn to abusers. They go into the relationship unconsciously, hoping that they can 'fix' this person, representing the perpetrator who hurt them. The familiar negative energy feels like 'home.' This explains why some people are attracted to 'bad' and emotionally unavailable partners and not attracted to kind people who check off all the 'good catch' boxes. Many of these magnetic relationships have a hard time surviving the drama-laden, up-and-down turmoil. These couples need Internal Family Systems counseling. IFS methodology gets to the root causes of the struggles instead of offering another surface-level communication tool that seldom produces lasting transformation."

Chapter 19

Exiles Want to Heal and Play

Emily shows Jill an image of yearning from the 2015 Burning Man art festival, created by Alexandr Milov. [Reprinted with permission.]

J: "Wow! This picture captures so much. The little Jill wants to come out to play with the little John, but we have protective armors on."

E: "Yes, this is the state of many relationships in quiet desperation. Couples don't know how to overcome their childhood fears and insecurities, so the real, fun, child-like parts don't feel safe to play in the romance sandbox."

Emily continues with the IFS protocol.

E: "Please ask the judgment protector what she is afraid would happen if she did not do her job to judge John."

J: "He would fail. I want him to succeed. He's a genius, but his toxic masculinity is in the way. It's interesting how I can see through to his soul and not have the malignant reactions that some of my colleagues have."

E: "You realize that the Self in you can see the Self in him?"

J: "Yes! And I am seeing the parallel with my dad. My compassion for the brokenness of my father is the same for John's brokenness."

E: "Your need to 'fix' John and have him realize his leadership potential is a projection of your desire to fix your father."

J: "Yes, I see that." [Tears stream down the face.] This IFS work reaches deep."

E: "If John miserably fails as a leader, then what is your judgment part afraid will happen?"

J: "I would fail with him. We do want to partner up and launch a business. We'd make a pretty sweet dynamic duo."

E: "And if you guys fail in this venture, what painful childhood memory would that stir up?"

J: "The shame I felt watching Dad not reach his potential while my peers had more successful fathers than mine. I get it. I want to redo my childhood through John to make sure he and I succeed."

E: "That makes sense. Does this part realize that the very thing it wants to prevent—failure—is the very thing it can cause?"

J: "What do you mean?"

E: "The more you judge and criticize John, the more likely he will shut down and avoid doing the work to become Self-led. His leadership derailers—parts in negative roles—can make him fail personally and professionally."

J: "Okay, the part gets it now. It needs to stop judging."

E: "You can't fix him, nor can you fix Dad. Your judgments and criticism can sound like you've turned into his mother. He will shut down, freeze, or lash out."

J: "He shuts down. [Pauses to see what the part wants to tell her.] The judgment part is sorry that she's been so critical. She was only trying to help."

E: "Please remind her that Self can take care of the situation and get curious instead of furious with John. I'm curious, could you also be judging a part of you that you see in John that you don't like?"

J: "Huh??? Wait . . . I used to be a braggart in college, trying to fit in with the rich prep school kids. I boasted about how I finished at the top of my class, that I had the smarts to be in their circle."

E: "Now you're judging this braggart part of you?"

J: "Yeah, I judge all braggarts I come across. Aha! I get it now. No wonder I don't like it when John gets self-centered. It reminds me of Dad, and it reminds me of how I bragged so I can fit in with my peers. Darn it! It comes down to judging myself and how much I loathe this braggart part of me; it's not the real me. I'm embarrassed I had to do this to fit in! I never did fit in because the girls saw right through my phoniness."

E: "Bingo! When we judge someone's part, we are judging that part within ourselves."

157

Jill takes a breather and wipes away tears as she processes all of this.

J: "Yuck! What do I do with John now?"

E: "Be courageously vulnerable and tell him why you did what you did. Apologize for this part of you acting out at his expense."

J: "I'm going to have to think about that. And I need to apologize to my team too since I've been judgmental with them also."

E: "As you've heard me say in the workshop, Self-led vulnerability is the number one source of power, influence, and impact. And in love, the courage to reveal what's happening for you is a powerful key to resolving conflicts and building deep emotional intimacy, with leads to great sex. Self, with calm and playful energy, can say, 'The judging part of me now wants to say you're such an asshole.' I just named the judging part and spoke *for* it with playful energy."

J: "Yeah, I get it. I can playfully speak for my parts and still get my point across."

E: "Exactly."

J: "I want to experience full-out cosmic sex one of these days, as an end product of radical honesty. [Gives Emily a wink and smile.] By the way, I should be getting my 360-assessment results any day now."

E: "Please show me the results so I can help you with Self-led apologies. What do you want to say to the judgment protector now?"

J: "I'm holding the judgmental old lady's hand. 'I get how you needed to show up to protect me, but I'm no longer a child. I'm thirty-six years old with a track record of success. We're hurting John and others when we judge and criticize. We need to zoom out and have compassion when people don't meet our standards. Emily says the best way out of the negative dynamic is to get curious and connected, so John feels safe to drop his armor. It's not my job to fix him.'"

E: "Excellent! You shift out of the need to fix and give John space to work through his inner gremlins—which may not happen until things get terrible. Your job is to do *you* right and get into your spiritual center, and tell yourself that every conflict is happening for your soul's growth. Here's something else you need to also keep in mind. Just because you worked on this part today, it doesn't mean you'll never make another judgment mistake. You will judge again, but you can nip things in the bud and promptly apologize for judgment part. Everyone will keep repeating the same patterns, but with IFS work and insights, these parts can chill out more often and let you lead from Self.

Often, when I'm analyzing a difficult situation with a friend, instead of coming from a place of judgment, I will say, 'The judgment part of me wants to say xyz about his behavior.' Speaking *for* the part from Self diminishes the critical judgmental charge while honoring the part, as in 'all parts are welcome.'"

J: "I get it. Thanks for clarifying."

E: "Okay, in the meantime, we need to find and liberate the exile that this judgment part protects. Is the old lady ready to show us the part she protects?"

J: "She protects the younger Jill that felt neglected by Dad. And I think this is the same part that tried so hard to fit in with the college girls through bragging. Bragging part is holding hands with judgment part."

E: "Braggart and Judgment have played together for a long time."

J: "Yes. I see seven-year-old Jill in the kitchen, wearing a white and yellow dress. She's pouting because she's upset. Mom is cooking and not paying attention to her. [She brings her adult Self into the kitchen to be with the seven-year-old part.] I'm there with Jilly."

E: "Here's a bit of neuroscience insight. Notice how you see the scene so clearly, right down to what the seven-year-old was wearing. That illustrates the concept 'neurons that fire together, wire together.' Significant emotional events get seared into our minds. For example, on September eleventh, when the World Trade Center tragedy occurred, we remember exactly where we were, who we were with, what we wore, and what the weather was like because it was so emotional."

J: "Fascinating! That makes sense. I remember all the details of September eleventh."

E: "As you can see, my role is to safely guide you back into the original devaluing scene to befriend, reparent, and unburden your exiles. This connection with your younger self is the key to releasing the negative beliefs imprinted into your hypnotic brain. At seven-years-old, she tried to make meaning out of what happened. When new neural firings of love from Self happen today, the past painful emotional charge releases. The release can range from tears to lessening of body sensations. The memory in the kitchen will always be there. However, the original charge won't be as strong or will be completely gone.

The next time this exile is triggered—and she will be—it will be easier to *unblend* from her, speak *for* her triggers from Self, and Self can give her what she needs to feel better. If the trigger comes from your significant other, he can be that secondary healer to let her know that he loves her. This loving interaction fosters epic intimacy. The book written by Dr. Richard Schwartz [the founder and developer of IFS], *You're the One You've Been Waiting For: Bringing Courageous Love to Intimate Relationships,* goes deeper into these primary and secondary healing concepts." [The book is only available on the IFS-Institute website: www.IFS-Institute.com.]

J: "Thank you for the book recommendation and scientific insights."

E: "Let's come back from the science detour and get back to healing the seven-year-old. It's great you have so much Self-energy now and can safely move into the scene without much prompting. So, how are you feeling towards seven-year-old Jill?"

J: "I want to hug her. She's been so alone."

E: "Go ahead and do that. Let her know who you are. And when she's ready, ask her to share her story."

J: [Tears flow as she reconnects heart-to-heart with a wounded part of her.] "She tells me Daddy didn't pay attention. When she showed him a drawing from school, he only said, 'That's nice,' without any enthusiasm or curiosity. He didn't know how to show love. He would have her sit on his lap as he droned on about himself. He wasn't curious about her; it was all about him."

E: "What beliefs did she adopt as a result of those experiences?"

J: "She says, *I'm not lovable*, and *I'm not important*."

E: "Anything else?"

J: "No, that seems to be about it. And now, I see the older version of her. As she grew older, she re-experienced how unimportant she felt amongst the sorority girls."

E: "Can you go into that scene to let college Jill know who you are? See if that girl is interested in reuniting with seven-year-old Jill."

J: [Takes a couple of minutes to access the scene.] "Yes . . . they want to reunite."

E: "Are both of these exiles interested in leaving those scenes and entering into the present with you?"

J: "Yes, they want to come to my apartment. I'll bring them there and show them around. [Closes eyes and imagines showing them where she lives.] They're happy to be reunited. They hold hands as I update them about what I've accomplished. I'm showering them with love. 'I've got you, girls. I will always be here for you. We need to forgive Dad. He didn't know any better because he's emotionally scarred too, and he lacked Self-leadership.'"

E: "That's beautiful. Continue to have whatever discussion you need to have with them. You can bring in judgment and braggart parts too."

J: "Okay, my protectors are with them. [Continues with her eyes closed, silently talking to them.] Now I get how the wounds of these younger parts contributed to growing my judgment and braggart parts."

Emily reminds Jill, "the past is always in the present," and "what is hysterical is historical." Jill updates and reassures her exiles and protectors. She helps them understand that if they don't dial down the judging and bragging, they will sabotage success in love and leadership.

E: "How are they feeling with your update and letting them know that you've got their backs?"

J: "Now I see the relationship of how these two younger parts were protected by my judgment and braggart protectors. These parts kept seeking external validation through judging and bragging. Sadly, they created the opposite effect and turned people off instead. Now I understand how John can't give me the validation I want if I criticize and judge. These exiles made me seek external validation because I wasn't giving the exiles the internal validation from my Higher Self."

E: "Correct. When the exiles feel validated by you, judgment and braggart parts can take long naps or take on new roles on your inner team. Are these exiles ready to release the *I'm not lovable* and *I'm not important* burdens?"

J: "Yes!"

E: "How would they like to unburden their wounds? Let water wash it away? Let wind blow it away? Let fire burn it off? Or, whatever other way feels right to you and your parts."

J: "I see the burdens as an emotional backpack loaded with school papers and drawings that Daddy didn't acknowledge. They want to throw the backpack over the Brooklyn Bridge, and they want me to take a picture of them throwing the backpack into the river."

E: "Go ahead and help them unload that over the bridge."

J: [Eyes close as she imagines helping her parts throw the emotional backpack into the river.] "I'm going to find a picture of the Brooklyn Bridge and a backpack, and pin them to my bulletin board to remind me of the significance of what we did today. I feel so much lighter now. A weight has been released from my back, literally and figuratively."

E: "That's beautiful. It would be great if you could find a picture of seven-year-old Jill and college Jill and add them to the bridge picture."

J: "Great idea!"

E: "Now that you've unloaded the *I'm not lovable* and *I'm not important* beliefs, what new beliefs would you like to invite in?"

J: "We'd like to bring in: *You are lovable, you are important, what you say matters, you don't need to judge or brag.* Oh, that feels so good."

E: "Terrific! Now, let's see what judgment and braggart parts want to say. How are these parts feeling about what we did with the seven-year-old and college parts?"

J: "Judgment and Braggart are happy that the exiles are no longer stuck in the past and have unburdened."

E: "Are these protectors ready to adopt different roles?"

J: "Judgment old lady says she's ready to retire the role and take on a new job to remind me to zoom out and get curious instead of judging."

E: "That is a fine new role. Because all parts are welcome in the IFS model, sometimes judgment will rear its head again, especially with John. Self-leadership can step in to manage the situation, and compassionately speak *for* the part when it wants to judge something or someone."

J: "And braggart part says it has been so tired of bragging that it would rather take on the role of humility."

E: "What a positive change!"

J: "Okay . . . I'm emotionally exhausted from what we did today. We went so much deeper than traditional therapy. I talked in circles for many years without resolution. I finally see how the depth of IFS can help me be the best version of me."

E: "Great! We got into your emotional body and healed at the root cause level. The Self is the key to healing, transformation, and manifestation."

J: "I loved how safe it felt to go back into the original memories. Now I see how the childhood icebergs underneath the surface can finally chip away, so my leadership can reach new heights."

E: "Now, you sound like me! [They laugh.] That's the brilliance of the IFS model. Your protectors permitted us to go back into the original, emotionally-charged memory, and that permission is why it felt safe and easy."

J: "I need to chill out and take a nice bubble bath, then meditate and journal."

E: "Good plan. What's your biggest aha from today's session?"

J: "Instead of judging others, I need to do a U-turn and look at myself— to uncover the dark parts of me that I judge, and to heal the exiles that Judgment protects."

E: "Fabulous! Good work, Jill."

At home, as Jill sits in the bathtub soaking up the insights from the IFS session, she feels at peace and is grateful that it's the Self who can shower love and take care of her parts. *Getting to know myself through the IFS lens is indeed a spiritual journey to wholeness and enlightenment.*

[To watch real-time IFS sessions, please visit www.ClimaxLeadershipBook.com.]

Chapter 20

Perfectionism and Shame

At Jill's next IFS session, she shares that she feels sucker-punched after reading the 360-degree leadership assessment feedback. She plucks it out of her tote bag to show Emily that several of her direct reports said she was self-centered, critical, judgmental, impatient, and too much of a perfectionist. Emily lets Jill knows that all is not lost; she can redeem herself and shift how people feel about her by vulnerably admitting her foibles and committing to positive change. The feedback reflects Jill's lack of Self-leadership.

Emily takes this opportunity to talk more about Brené Brown's research. "The importance of reading Brené's research and data on why vulnerability is power, not weakness, quiets the most skeptical leaders about the importance of confident vulnerability. Brené shared during many interviews and speaking engagements that she sees perfectionism as unhealed shame from early childhood experiences. Many high achievers are guilty of perfectionism. There's nothing wrong with striving for excellence; it's how you go about it that can be problematic. Looking and acting like you've got it all together can make the other person feel inadequate; they feel they can never measure up. One of Brené's most famous quotes is: 'As a shame researcher, I've learned that wherever perfectionism is driving us, shame is riding shotgun.'" [Source: *Dare to Lead: Brave Work. Tough Conversations. Whole Hearts.* 2018, p. 78.]

Jill: "Ouch! I had to wear the perfectionism mask to show that I'm not a trailer park blue-collar gal."

Emily: "Protectors create the very thing they fear—failure and rejection. Hurt people hurt others. Your capacity to love others and your team can only grow to the extent that you do the work to fall into a healthy love affair with yourself. It's hard for teams to be high performing when they don't *viscerally* feel like you really care about them. They can disengage, gossip, and lose sleep because they sense your self-centeredness and lack of empathy. You may say the right things, but in their hearts, they don't *feel* your love and authenticity. In other words, they don't feel your Self-*energy*."

Emily guides Jill to imagine her derailing leadership parts—Self-centeredness, Judgment, Impatience, and Perfectionism—sitting around a conference table. Jill lets these parts know that despite their positive intentions, their extreme behaviors caused loss of trust and respect. These parts feel the love from Jill's Higher Self, and are willing to transform and take on more productive roles instead.

E: "Now that these parts feel heard by Self, are they ready to show you the vulnerable parts they protect?"

J: "Yeah . . . oh boy, it's the same exiles we worked on before—where she didn't feel important or loved enough by Dad, and the college part where she felt inadequate compared to her peers."

E: "These two exiles are the most emotionally vulnerable parts of you. Do you see how these parts show up everywhere? Not only with John but with your team when you start to feel unimportant and unloved?"

J: "Yes, I see that."

E: "The more you're aware of these triggers, the easier it will be to manage them when they resurface. Please look at these parts, update them, and ask what they want you to know."

J: [Closes her eyes and goes inward with her parts.] "Hey . . . I forgive you for contributing to my negative leadership traits. We don't need to wear masks; we need to be real and vulnerable. We're going to share with the team where our bad behaviors came from so we can be more relatable. Vulnerability is the key to gaining trust and respect back."

Jill lets Emily know that her protectors and exiles are on board with cooperating with Self to improve the situation. Jill accompanies these parts in her mind as they go back to the Brooklyn Bridge to unload the rest of the *I'm not important* baggage. It seems like the first time the parts unburdened the negative beliefs, the beliefs weren't fully unloaded. They can let go of the need to be in off-putting roles of self-centeredness, judgment, impatience, and perfectionism. Jill's Self, not her derailing parts, can lead her team to greatness. Emily adds, "Often, direct reports may be afraid to speak their truths because they fear that the boss, who can be unconsciously seen as the parental authority figure, may judge, criticize, and not listen. The leader must create a psychologically safe space for team members to express their concerns. Team members need to viscerally *feel* from the leader that 'all my parts are welcome!' This is like a Self-led parent holding space for their kids' emotions without judgment or criticism. When a leader can hold space like this, they are in platonic 'love affairs' with their direct reports. When team members feel seen and validated, they will likely go above and beyond the call of duty. When a leader catches himself in parts instead of Self, they can graciously own it and say, 'Sorry about that. My interruption and judging parts got out of line. Please forgive me.'"

Fixing Sub-Optimal Leadership Starts at the Top

We bring our whole selves to work, which means we unknowingly bring some of our broken parts from childhood into the boardroom. The worst of the bad bosses are controlling, defensive, argumentative, self-centered, and more. Through the IFS lens, traits labeled as "leadership-derailers" do not mean you're a lost cause. Your extreme parts are not *all* of you. In the IFS arena, you are not labeled as your part. We name the negative behaviors (parts) that acted out. For example, you're not a controlling or self-centered (narcissistic) boss. Instead, you have controlling and self-centered *parts* in extreme roles. You need to find the root causes from childhood that caused these behaviors so that these parts can calm down and be less controlling and self-centered. These parts are welcomed to come out in small doses at appropriate times, through speaking *for* the part *from* Self-energy: "The self-centered part of me wants to say . . ." If you are blended with a part—such as anger—this can make others feel uncomfortable and unsafe. Self-leadership, unblending, humility, and apologizing for rogue parts can save your reputation.

We need to be compassionate towards people who are not in Self and lack the resolve to admit they are broken and imperfect. Sadly, many think they are perfect, but they are the most broken. They have many protective layers—armors and masks—shielding them from admitting their foibles and imperfections. Here are other common characteristics that can derail leaders:

- Emotional liability (rapid or dramatic mood swings)
- Avoiding truths (white lies of omission)
- Disconnection and stoicism
- Perfectionism
- People-pleasing
- Arrogance
- Judgment and criticism
- Self-centeredness
- Argumentativeness and defensiveness
- Poor listening and inattention

These traits cause employee disengagement, low-functioning teams, emotional misery, and loss of productivity. David Dotlich's well-known book, *Why CEOs Fail: The 11 Behaviors That Can Derail Your Climb to the Top and How to Manage Them*, delineates how many of the aforementioned behaviors contributed to well-known business tycoons' embarrassing public failures. This *Climax* book goes deeper than Dotlich's book to identify and overcome the root causes of the negative behaviors so that you don't become another casualty in the two-thirds of leaders who fail.

For an organization to positively change their leadership culture into one that is comprised of Self-leadership and high emotional intelligence, the commitment to change needs to start at the top. The CEO has to be on board, and they have to engage in the Self and parts inner work. If senior leadership is not on board with

Self-leadership training, then achieving the organization's highest human capital and performance goals can be challenging.

When leaders have the guts to own their negative traits and apologize through Self-leadership, they become real and gain trust, respect, and influence. It is difficult to fake your way through an apology if you haven't accessed Self-energy; your team can smell the phoniness a mile away. It's not the words you say; it's the intention and *energy* behind the words and how you make them *feel* that make you believable or not believable. Self-energy always saves the day.

The more authentic and confidently vulnerable you are, the more powerful you become. It may be counterintuitive, but the fact is that by revealing and owning your weaknesses, you show real warrior courage and leadership.

To learn more about how to become an extraordinary Self-led leader and lover, sign up for either "Climax in Love: Be the Ultimate Warrior for a Goddess" or "Climax in Love: Be the Ultimate Goddess for a Warrior." You can access these courses at www.ClimaxInLove.com.

Chapter 21

From Bad to Great Boss via Courageous Vulnerability

"I'd like to open this meeting by addressing the elephant in the room." Jill pauses and notices that all eyes are locked onto hers, including her boss, Michael.

"I've been a crummy boss, blind to how I've been making your life miserable." Jill makes eye contact with each of them. The thick energy in the room can be cut with a knife.

"It was eye-opening to read the feedback from my 360-assessment. I had no idea how weak my leadership has been. I take full responsibility for your misery and less-than-optimal team performance. Your radical honesty helps me take steps to become a better leader. By working with a Self-leadership executive coach and spiritual healer, Emily Liu, I made a U-turn and realized my shortcomings. I caused your defensiveness and fear. If I were in your shoes, I would be afraid of me, too." The self-deprecation evokes a couple of half-smiles.

"The collective feedback said I'm cold, not relatable, too perfect, judgmental, and critical. With Emily's guidance, I uncovered the root causes of my negative traits." As Jill deepens into vulnerability, she hears and feels sighs of relief. Jill takes a deep breath and asks, "I see frozen faces. Are you good with what I'm doing here?"

Jason says, "I'm grateful you're opening up. Anyone else grateful?" Jason looks around, and Jill sees that they all concur. "Keep going, Jill."

"Thank you. I'm relieved. I'm responsible for creating the emotional and psychological safety on this team so you can be engaged, do your best work, and have fun. I haven't shown you how I do really care—and that I see you, hear you, and

173

have your back. I apologize for my bad leadership parts. I'm sorry." Jill's team visibly relaxes their shoulders and faces as they feel her heart-led apology.

"Thank you for owning your part. We admire your courage and vulnerability," Jason chimes in again.

Emily's right, Self-led vulnerability works, and fast! "Thank you for being present and holding space for my vulnerable reveals. It means the world to me," Jill places both of her hands on her heart to show her appreciation.

"I've learned from Emily that we all wonder, 'Does she hear me, does she see me, and does she care about me?' Oprah's speech from the last episode of her iconic show made the point that after interviewing thousands of people, she realized that our number one core human need is *validation*. I didn't know. I promise to do better."

Jill notices that no one is distracted by their phones. She senses a deepening connection.

"Embodying Self-leadership means I'm calm, connected, curious, compassionate, clear, present, and patient. My energy determines whether or not we are a high-performing team. Unfortunately, my selfishness has turned you off."

Jill shares some of the insights from her IFS sessions. "We all unknowingly bring unresolved emotional issues to work and project them onto each other, especially under stress. Being a Self-led leader means I will calmly speak *for* my feelings, thoughts, and frustrations and *not from* them. Instead of judging and criticizing, I will be curious, compassionate, and present to hear your ideas, deepest thoughts, and feelings. I want you to feel safe to tell me what's going on, so we can come up with solutions together. When I offend you, I may not be aware of it. I permit you to call me out on the part that is pushing your buttons and tell me how it makes you feel so we can nip things in the bud before things get messy."

James joins in and says, "That sounds great! How exactly do we do that?"

"Emily Liu will conduct workshops to teach us how to use the Self-leadership tools to have courageous conversations and resolve conflicts and misunderstandings."

Henry says, "This was very courageous of you to take responsibility for your lack of Self-leadership. I feel closer to you because you've been so open. Keep up the good work."

Everyone nods and claps softly to show solidarity.

"Thank you so much, Henry. I appreciate your feedback. Emily will show you that we are more alike than different; all of us have parts that act out and cause havoc at work and home."

As Jill concludes the meeting, she feels a shift in the group energy—an energy of optimism. *When I admitted my faults and imperfections, I felt the trust and respect increase.*

Jill's team is all abuzz during lunch, talking about the positive change they felt during the morning meeting. Marissa says, "I think I'm finally going to enjoy coming to the office. I feel it in my bones that she will follow through with her promises." With that comment, the team members give each other high-fives.

◆ ◆ ◆

During the multi-day Self-leadership training at Zatuck, Emily shares one of the simplest and most important communication tools to check in with each other and nip potential conflicts in the bud. "The check-in metaphor that can work for *all* relationships is, 'How's the weather between us?' The 'weather between us' response options are—

- Sunny: no friction;
- Partly Cloudy: have one or two minor issues bothering me;
- Cloudy: have brewing problems that need to be cleared soon;
- Thunderstorms: I'm about to lose it if we don't talk now!"

Chapter 22

You Represent My Dad

Since the Cape Cod workshop, John has kept his distance from Jill, keeping their relationship professional, with only occasional flirty banter. As much as Jill wants to recreate the emotional intimacy in John's hotel room at the leadership retreat, another Self-to-Self spiritual experience has not presented itself. Jill feels compelled to reach out via text: Can we have a heart-to-heart about something important? John replies: Sure thing, stop by my office at the end of the day.

At 5:00 p.m., Jill nervously strolls into John's office. After a few pleasantries, Jill shares, "I'm still seeing Emily Liu. She's been so insightful, helping me recognize blind spots so I can overcome them and be Self-led. The reason I did the work to understand the root causes of my leadership deficiencies was to have a heart-led vulnerable discussion with my team. Since that discussion, the team dynamic has improved significantly. We're more cohesive and productive now."

"That's great! Michael said he was impressed with how vulnerable you were. He received a lot of positive feedback from your team members. I'm glad our CEO contracted with Emily to conduct workshops. Everyone needs to understand the power of Self-leadership."

"I agree." Jill takes a big breath as she finishes this update. "So . . . can we talk about something I'm concerned about?"

"Yes . . ." John says tentatively. *Is she going to beat me over the head again?*

"I'm sorry for criticizing your leadership."

"Apology accepted. I know your intentions come from a good place."

Wow. He is present, and not in asshole, checked-out parts.

"Yeah, I'm well aware of my blind spots," he continues. "I've worked with several executive coaches to address my blind spots, but their methodologies didn't work for the long haul. Now I know from Emily's workshop that I need to engage in deeper work. I'll work with her when I'm ready. Now is not a good time."

I wish he could see that working with Emily sooner rather than later would be helpful. Damn! Jill feels her heart sink to her stomach. *He admits it is necessary; he just doesn't get that it is also urgent if he cares about leadership effectiveness. Okay, I need to honor this part of him that's not ready to work on himself yet.*

"Okay, whatever floats your boat. I have more to share."

"Go ahead."

"It's about the part of me that gets frustrated when you don't show up as the best Self-led leader I know you can be. Well . . . through my IFS sessions, I found out it's related to my frustrations with my dad. I was disappointed with how Dad floundered. When you are not at your best, it reminds me of how frustrated I felt towards my father. Because I care so much about you and your success, I projected my anger and disappointment with Dad onto you. I tried to redo my childhood through you because you energetically remind me of my deepest wounds with Dad."

Even though John is technically one of her bosses, the relationship they have transcends the boss-subordinate dynamic. They have flipped into peer-to-peer dynamic. John is fully present, with his eyes locked on Jill. As she shares her truths, she places her hand on his forearm to connect deeper.

"I don't want to see you fail. I know your brilliance is destined for greatness. I feel sad when I witness your curt interactions with others. I feel sad when I see others affected by your parts. Please understand that I'm giving this constructive feedback out of love and concern for your success," Jill reassures him from heart-led energy.

"Thank you for being so honest with me. I cringe when you beat me over the head. I value our friendship. I shut down because your frankness is a lot for me to absorb, even though I know you're coming from your heart. It's easier to hide in my man-cave than to address my issues. I can't believe I'm saying all of this to you." Jill takes a deep breath and keeps her eyes locked as John holds her hand.

John continues, "As I reflect on 'the past is always in the present' message, I have to admit that how you judge and criticize me is familiar energy. It's how my depressed mom criticized my narcissistic dad and vice versa; they were oil and water."

Jill thinks—*Wow! No wonder we have this magnetic bond of two little kids wanting to redeem their childhoods through each other. The energy between us feels familiar.*

"Thank you for sharing that insight. I'm grateful you don't attack when I get bold like this. I'm sorry if I've offended you."

"I get how you're coming from love. I forgive you. Can I hug you?" John asks.

"Of course."

Their prolonged hug feels spectacular for both of them. John's thinking—*Oh, I wish this would never end, and we could get back on a bed to cuddle and kiss.*

Jill thinks—*This feels incredibly good, but I've got to do the work to release these romantic feelings. He's not available, and this is never going to work. But I can't believe the way he holds space for me.*

Jill breaks the embrace and steps back with excitement. "I have to share something about my 360-assessment. I get it now that my team saw me as a bad boss because I couldn't hold space for them to reveal more of their personalities. You're holding space for me, I feel heard and seen, and I feel I matter. I need to sharpen my active listening skills instead of thinking ahead about what I want to say. You are in Self and present with me right now, thank you."

"See, I can be a great leader after all. But I do agree, I'm not as Self-led as you—yet. When I'm ready to do the work with Emily, I'll call her."

"Okay . . . I hope it will be soon," Jill says with an edge of disappointment.

With that, they give each other one final hug and separate. Jill's mind spins as she slips into the crowded elevator. She's disappointed. *It could take ten years before he embarks on inner work! I guess he hasn't hit rock bottom yet. Okay, judgment part, stop screaming in my ear about John!* But then she flashes back to what Emily said—*Just let the Universe orchestrate the journey of what is or isn't supposed to happen between you and John. Surrender!*

PART III

Chapter 23

A New Door Opens

June 2016

In two years of working for Zatuck, Jill finds the work rewarding and challenging, especially with all the politicking, and managing John's labile moods. Jill's Self-led communication continues to improve as she progresses with Internal Family Systems (IFS) inner work. Knowing that everyone is comprised of Self and parts makes it easier for her to see the birds-eye view perspective to interpret challenging situations.

John, on the other hand, is still in denial to some degree. He understands the IFS model but is not interested in fully embracing Self-leadership. It feels more comfortable to wear masks. His home life retains the same pattern as before—a façade of keeping up with the Joneses and robbing Peter to pay Paul.

Jill is still disappointed that she hasn't been able to experience another intoxicating high like the Cape Cod weekend. John fantasizes about Jill all the time. He hopes that one day, he can be with the love of his life. Jill has the same fantasy but is not optimistic it will happen any time soon. Still, when they look into each other's eyes, they feel spiritually connected.

After finalizing a pitch for a difficult client, John and Jill and a few others who worked on the project celebrate this completion over Happy Hour. John, tipsy with flirty energy and confidence-in-a-glass, whispers into Jill's ear, "I can't stand how insane and intense my attraction is for you. Each time I look into your eyes, I see your soul."

"I'm flattered," Jill responds with wide-eyed twinkle and a big smile.

"And, if I could, I would carry you into bed right now." John smiles and winks.

Jill is turned on by the verbal foreplay. *Finally, some lustful, playful, and heavenly Self-to-Self connection.* "I was wondering how you felt about me these days since you seem aloof. I hate to admit it, but I'm still enamored with you too. But, we have to behave right now; colleagues are watching us."

"I know I'm behaving. One day—I have no idea when—the yin will merge with the yang, and we'll fuse our energies again," John confesses with slurred speech.

"And the lid will come together with the pot," Jill adds to the spiritual poetry.

"And then the dish will run away with the spoon . . . I'm getting carried away, thanks to four beers."

"Ha-ha, I guess that makes me the dish. I think you've had enough to drink, my friend."

"You're so gorgeous. You make me melt, and you get me excited whenever you're near me. That's why I have to be aloof; I attempt to escape our magnetic attraction."

They giggle like two kids on the playground. "Okay, it's time to get home to your kids. I'll walk you to the train station to make sure you get on the right train." *The emotional foreplay is so arousing! I feel loved and connected once again.*

◆ ◆ ◆

Two days after their flirtatious outing, John and Jill get called to Human Resources. "We have bad news," Liam, the HR director, announces. "We have legal grounds for terminating both of you. As you know, our company policy states that kickbacks are grounds for dismissal. Our internal investigation shows that both of you have been involved in quite a few schemes. Please gather your personal belongings. Security will walk you out of the building in one hour."

John and Jill look at each other in shock, with their mouths open. They don't have a rebuttal; they're caught.

"Tomorrow, we will let you know about your exit packages. You will be kept on the health insurance plan for six months."

◆ ◆ ◆

Jill slams John's office door behind her. "What the hell, John?! I had no idea we were breaking the rules when you asked me to sweeten the pot. I read the policy during the new-hire orientation but didn't pay attention to the details. I thought you knew what you were doing since you're the frickin' SVP! I didn't question your integrity or your actions. I can't believe you dragged me into your scheme with no concern for *my* risk."

"I'm sorry. I didn't mean for this to happen. Someone must have reported us to HR. There are people hold grudges against me. Too complicated to explain. It's water under the bridge; there's nothing I can do now."

"Nothing you can do?! What am I supposed to do for a job?"

"Calm down. You know, this is not the end of the world. Wait, it's divine intervention. Geez, I can't believe I sound spiritual now. You know . . . we've kidded around about going into business together. We have complementary skill sets. We could be co-founders of a kickass ad agency. I've always had out-of-box ideas that couldn't be executed at Zatuck. Some clients need a different kind of boutique ad agency. What do you say? Let's go for it."

"I need to process what happened before I think about any idiotic proposal." Jill's teeth clench, and she is seething, trying to hold in the anger.

"Jilly, you are sooo cute when you're mad."

"Arrggg!" She stomps out the door.

◆　◆　◆

At home, Jill tries to come to terms with what happened. *We got fired! The nerve of him to do that to me.* Another voice says—*You know, he's right, this is divine intervention. Here's your opportunity to become an entrepreneur. John will have more substantial capital from his severance to get the business started. But, you'll have to establish firm working agreements.* And yet another voice speaks—*But, you still can't take the romance anywhere—he's married. Are you sure you want to do this? Does this have disaster written all over it? The sexual tension will get in the way of success, especially with no HR policies and boundaries to limit you.* Then the rational part says—*Oh come on! You can control yourself. You'll be okay.* These warring parts!

After a couple of weeks coming to terms with getting fired and more IFS sessions with Emily, Jill decides that she can do business with John, as long as they establish firm boundaries.

◆　◆　◆

Jill meets with John at a Starbucks in SoHo. "I have good news, my friend," she begins. "I'm all in, with the condition that we create boundaries and agreements."

"Yippee!" John picks her up and twirls her around. She fixes her skirt and clears her throat, looking to see who may have viewed this spectacle. She continues, "We are co-founders; you're not my boss. We'll have high standards of ethics in all of our business dealings. And we need to address the pink elephant in the room, head-on."

"And what elephant is that?"

"Both of us know how deep, extraordinary, and magnetic our connection is. We cannot continue to be frisky because you're still a married man."

"I respect your wishes," he says with a mischievous grin. "I wish my marital situation was different. I can't get a divorce now. It would be too complicated and too disruptive for the kids. I'll keep my parts in my pants, I promise," John says with a wink.

Jill shakes her head and laughs. *God, I so desperately want to go to bed with him right now. Why can't this energy between us dissolve? This chaos will make sense five years from now.*

"One more thing . . ." John says, "to get the business cranking fast, we need Shelly as COO. She's so good with operations. She's a great executor and stickler for details. Let me see if I can lure her away."

Jill's heart plunges to her stomach. She never liked Shelly. Shelly gives off a negative vibe. *I'll bite my tongue and tolerate Shelly. Besides, I have the upper hand. I'm the co-founder; she's working for me! John is right, she does have great skills that can help us be successful.*

"Okay, if you think Shelly is the best person for the job, I'm all for it."

"Great, happy you agree."

◆ ◆ ◆

After a few more days of reflection, Jill realizes that getting fired was a gift. Time to text her thoughts to John: Can't wait to experience the magic of what our collective smarts and energies can produce. It will be so much fun to play in this sandbox.

John smiles as he receives the text and replies: I'm so lucky to have a co-creator who's beyond amazing! ;)

Jill feels happy and flows into the connected energy: YOU are amazing too! And it's a bonus that you're hot and sexy. ;) I'm in awe of you.

John beams with that compliment: The Universe brought us together for a reason, and we're going to make a name for ourselves. LOVE being on this epic journey with you. And with our million$, we can contribute to those who are less fortunate.

Jill's loving his softer side: LOVE, LOVE, LOVE it, my friend! xo

John thinks—*She makes me feel so good about myself!*

Chapter 24

Sailing in Choppy Waters

Shelly is thrilled that John asked her to join the business. They get along very well, and she released the major grudges over their affair eight years ago. She moved on with new relationships.

The business launches with John taking the helm. They are in the conference room in a co-working space in SoHo. "Okay, my distinguished coworkers, let's figure out how we're going to build an amazing brand and have fun at the same time. Since conflicts and creative differences will be inevitable, we need to establish communication protocols to become a high-performing team."

After an hour of brainstorming and discussion, they come up with Roles and Expectations. Here's the summary:

- John is the lead visionary who steers the ship; Jill is the co-visionary and strategist who asks the tough questions to determine which ideas are realistic to execute.
- Shelly, the COO, operationalizes, and executes the details of the plans.
- They are all responsible for business development.
- They check-in daily to prevent misunderstandings and conflicts.
- They agree to use the IFS framework to speak *from* Self *for* parts.

For the first three months, the excitement of the new business has everyone on their best behavior. They use their network to bring in an initial slew of clients. But as the days go by, Shelly becomes increasingly irritated with the flirty energy between John and Jill. John and Jill go for long lunches and come back with happy smiles.

I don't like that she gets all the attention. Knowing John, I can't help but wonder if they spend their long lunches in a hotel room, like he and I used to.

John developed a new idea for a client, advertising on Total Request Live for an off-beat TV ad for products and accessories, three for the price of one; this is for artists and musicians. He presented the idea to Jill and she executed without Shelly's input. Shelly muses—*This is not cool. Did they discuss the idea at lunch and purposely left me out?*

Feeling slighted, Shelly dominates the next team meeting, interrupts Jill often, and questions her ideas. John takes notice but doesn't think the power struggle is affecting Jill.

As Shelly drones on, John continues to validate her. "Shelly, I never saw it from that angle—what a great idea!"

Jill is irritated—but bites her tongue. *Shelly's blended in a part . . . Shelly's in a part . . . stop getting annoyed.*

As the weeks and months go on, Jill notices that Shelly and John get friendlier than usual. Shelly initiates long lunches with John, and Jill hears them giggling as they walk back to the office.

Jill thinks—*Do I matter to John anymore? He's not checking in with me like he used to. Am I crazy to think that he can be attracted to her again?*

Jill does her best to rein in her jealous part's feelings. John has mentioned that he and Shelly are good friends, but Jill can't find alone time with John anymore. *He holds back on eye-gazing and touching my arm. He literally took my orders to not be frisky. I feel abandoned. Oh goodness, my parts are insecure now.*

At the next weekly meeting, Shelly interrupts Jill again for the umpteenth time. Jill can't take it anymore, and her feisty part takes over and says, "Shelly, who the hell do you think you are, cutting me off every time I try to say something?"

Jill is hijacked by feisty part because her exile feels abandoned. After all, John isn't paying attention to her to the degree she would like.

John says, "Jill, calm down. Do you need a breather?"

"No, I'm fine!"

"Let's end the meeting now," John says.

Jill hurries to the bathroom to hide her meltdown. She doesn't know why she's so triggered. She visits Emily.

◆ ◆ ◆

Jill gives Emily the blow-by-blow details of what's happening in the business. Emily responds with, "Even though you know how to access Self and Self-energy, there still will be times when your parts get triggered, especially with someone you care about. Because you have a special connection with John, everything he does and says is filtered through fear of loss, fear of abandonment, and fear of rejection. Remember how we determined that John represents your unfinished business with dad?"

"Yes."

"Even though you feel he's ignoring you and being less affectionate, who knows what's going on in his mind. Maybe he's ignoring you as a way of compartmentalizing his crazy love for you. He can't have you now, and he's not interested in a full-blown affair. Maybe the only way he can handle it is to run away from the attraction. Again, we don't know what he's thinking, and we should refrain from making assumptions and creating icky and triggering false narratives. We're all guilty of filling in the blanks with negative stories when another person doesn't give us radical honesty and clarity. There's a saying that 'the more we care, the more we conceal.' The more someone conceals, the more the other person fills in the blanks with worst-case scenario stories. Those negative stories build up like a volcano, ready to erupt with nastiness the next time your buttons get pushed."

"Yeah, I get it. No wonder my angry part blew up at Shelly. It makes sense that he can't be honest with me. I've concealed things with old boyfriends to uphold a certain image. I was afraid I'd lose them if I revealed the truth."

"That's human nature. As much as you want him to reassure you that he's still crazy about you, he's unable to do that. His supposed rejection of you has you interpret this as your dad rejecting you. You don't feel seen, so the attention-seeking and angry parts of you took over and had a temper tantrum to put Shelly in her place. Her flirtatiousness activated your insecure parts. Your exile felt the fire of abandonment, and your firefighter protector erupted their volcano onto Shelly."

"I get it. My insecurities got the best of me. I guess I should apologize to John and Shelly."

"Yes, that would be good. Now let's do the IFS work to take care of the little Jill that was triggered in this incident."

◆　◆　◆

After the IFS healing session, Jill sends an email to John.

John,

I'm sorry for my blowout with Shelly. I got overtaken by my parts.

On another note, in the spirit of transparency, my frustrated part needs to express what I learned why Jim Highland hesitated to sign on with us. Jim said, "How you do one thing is how you do everything. John is not dependable. It takes days before I get a response. I feel like his babysitter, having to reach out to see if my emails went through."

I feel the same way as Jim. I don't receive timely responses from you either. This makes me wonder if you know what you're doing. Have you been bluffing your way to the top? Okay, I know my judgment part just spoke up. Judgment showed up to get a point across. ☺ I feel like what I say often falls on deaf ears. I hope you can see that lack of Self-leadership is negatively affecting our business. I think the gifts I bring to the business are not fully appreciated. Even though we claim to be superior to other boutique agencies, clients do not experience excellent results and take their business elsewhere.

I want to be on a journey with a leader who is impeccable with his words and acts on what he says in a timely fashion. Can you deliver on your promises? I'm afraid of failing, and that's why I may sound harsh in this email. I'm sorry.

Yours truly,
Jill

If Emily read this email, she would say that this is not all Self-led. At least I admitted my judgmental part was activated. I want him to see how frustrated I am.

John gets triggered by this email. *WTF! She criticizes my competency and accuses me of bluffing my way to the top.* He restrains himself and decides to shut down instead of retaliating with a nasty comeback. In this case, his "flight" part wins out over his "fight" part. John's response:

Jill,

Thank you for your insights. I'll consider your feedback.

John

Jill feels dismissed again and is acutely disappointed with his curt reply. John hasn't cracked the door open to be approachable. Their parts are in a battle, via email. Jill needs to escape his energy and holes herself up at the Starbucks downstairs. At the next two weekly staff meetings, John is conveniently absent, "Have the meeting without me. I have to go to parent-teacher conferences."

Jill continues to engage in bi-weekly IFS sessions to get to know more of her parts to overcome the triggers. John is not ready to face his inner demons. His chaotic inner life shows up in lackluster business results. Emily tells Jill that she may have to make difficult decisions regarding the business partnership. Jill wants to get things off her chest and fires off another email.

John,

I appreciate your friendship. I admire you when you are present and listening. I hope we can get back to the fantastic connection we had in the early days at Zatuck.

I continue to be frustrated with our working relationship. I take initiatives on your vision. I know you're not into hearing the details of how I'm doing it, so I don't bother you with them. What irks me is that after I work my butt off, you change your vision midstream without asking for my input. Then, Shelly is off and running with your new ideas. We are supposed to be a team, but your actions show that my role as the co-founder is irrelevant.

When I ask for clarity, I can't follow your thoughts; you're all over the place. I feel like we're dancing the tango with two left feet, and I keep tripping over you. I need you to be more explicit, so my brain can fire on all cylinders. When I'm left in the dark, I can't do my best. I'm confused. I don't know what is expected of me anymore, and my frustrations make me blow up. Underneath my anger is sadness, fear of rejection, and fear of loss.

I don't want this business to fail, and I don't want to lose our friendship. I must be doing something wrong to create this problematic dynamic, and I want to fix it. I know new businesses are ridden with ambiguity and chaos, but I'm going berserk with too much doubt, confusion, and lack of clarity. All I ask is to for you to share the colorful details of your vision so I can think and act accordingly.

I'm looking for a felt sense that it's safe to talk to you about my innermost thoughts. For the last few months, I've felt like there's a fortress around you. I'm a little afraid of you, and I feel like you're rejecting me. Peace out.

Your co-creator in crime,
Jill

John reads the email and thinks—*She does have a point. I'm too vague and have a hard time articulating the details. My brain isn't wired that way. I can't engage with her. I've fucked up so much already. I'm drowning in shame.*

Jill,

Thank you for letting me know how you feel. I'll keep your comments in mind.

Warm wishes,
John

Jill receives the terse response, and her heart sinks. *I guess his forehead has a sign that says, "Don't bother me!"*

◆ ◆ ◆

Back in therapy, Jill shows Emily the recent emails to John—after the fact. Emily lets Jill know that "Parts of the emails are not Self-led. She commends Jill for the parts of the email that were written from Self. Many men hide when they are flooded with emotions, criticism, and shame. Their nervous systems can't deal with the emotional triggering, so it's easier to shut down. Please do not send emails when you're is in a *part*. If you can wait until you're calmer and in Self—which may take twenty-four to forty-eight hours—the email has a better chance of being written from Self."

Jill knows it's best not to ask for a conversation when she feels frustrated. But, since John doesn't have an interest in talking things out, she has to resort to emails.

Emily continues, "Moving forward, it's best to record and send your thoughts using the iPhone voice memo feature. Written words alone cannot convey the totality of the message. It's easy to negatively misinterpret texts and emails, especially when they contain negative feedback."

"Okay. I will send voice memos."

◆ ◆ ◆

As more months go by, Jill's frustration and impatience grow even bigger. John continues to hang out with Shelly. John thinks—*Shelly is so easy to be around. She gets me and doesn't have any hidden agendas.* Then one day, out of the blue, John is chirpy and in a happier mood. Jill takes this opportunity to ask for a heart-led conversation.

"Hey, my friend, there's a part of me that's afraid to have this conversation," Jill says with a quiver in her voice. John drops into his heart. He takes her hands into his to make her feel safe. "There's nothing to be afraid of. I want to hear what you have to say."

Wow, his loving soul is present right now. Why does he get bipolar with me—most days he's in armored parts and then suddenly he's in Self? "I feel ghosted, and I feel you favor Shelly."

"I'm sorry you feel that way. It was never my intention to push your buttons. Shelly and I go way back. What else is bothering you?"

"When I watch you guys banter and spend long lunches together, I wonder if our special connection is gone."

"No, it's not," John reassures Jill.

"Your aloofness has me wondering."

"I see how you could feel that way."

"It bothers me that she continues to interrupt me and won't fully hear what I have to say."

"I see that you get upset with her constant interruptions. She thinks out loud; it's just who she is."

"Okay . . . but I still don't like it. I feel disrespected. I admit that Shelly is pretty good at what she does."

"Yes, she is. And most importantly, you don't have to worry about the connection you and I have; it's still extraordinary. I think the world of you. But I can't act on our attraction; I'm still married. A strictly business relationship is in order. Otherwise, I don't trust myself, and I may not behave," John says tenderly.

"Thank you for sharing and being vulnerable. But, there's still a part of me that's afraid of your energy. When you're not in Self and blended with a part, I get contorted and scared."

"It hurts me when I hear that I make you afraid." He squeezes her hands for a few seconds to reassure her how special she is. "I'm not sharing all the toxicity that's going on at home with Liz. She's been on my case about everything. We've been fighting a lot, and that's why I'm checked out. She tears me down and calls me nasty names. I'm just not in a space to give you the time and energy for deep connection. In other words, my aloofness has nothing to do with you. And my friendship with Shelly is purely platonic, and that's why it's easier for me to interact with her."

"Okay . . . that makes me feel a little better."

"I respect you too much, and I know you wouldn't want to have an affair while I'm still married. Plus, I'll get taken to the cleaners if Liz ever found out about us. I have no idea what our future is. All I know is that we've got to make this business work. I have big financial responsibilities."

"Remember what Emily said during the Cape Cod workshop?"

"Remind me, please, since she had a lot of great nuggets of wisdom."

"The past is always in the present. I feel like Shelly is the Queen Bee, and I'm the target of her meanness. If I didn't care, I wouldn't be so emotional about the time you spend with her. If I feel solid in our friendship and know how much you adore me, the little Jill's will feel important, and my angry part can stay asleep. I'm happy when I feel heard, and I know that it's my job to take care of my young exiles."

"Good. Acknowledging you is all it's going to take?"

"Yeah . . . it's not complicated. This honest and transparent conversation right now makes my parts feel seen and heard. Thank you."

"It's the least I can do for you. I'll remind myself to do this more often. Is that okay?"

"Yes, please!" Jill says emphatically.

Jill feels relieved to share her deepest thoughts. John heard them and held space for her.

"Can I share what else I need from you so my blowups don't happen?"

"Of course."

"I would like daily, or at the very least every other day, check-ins to see what the weather is like between us. If I start to feel disconnected, I will tell you that it's not sunny; the clouds have rolled in, and we need to have a conversation."

"Okay, that's fair."

"Can you start validating me more publicly like you do when Shelly speaks up? I feel like the ugly stepchild when Shelly gets public acknowledgment, and I don't."

"I want to acknowledge you, but there's a part of me that doesn't want to publicly focus my attention on you in front of Shelly and the interns."

"I love how you're using parts language! Why is it hard to pay attention to me?"

"Because I care so much, I don't want to give anyone the idea that I feel special toward you. The last thing we need is gossip."

Emily's right, the more they care, the more they conceal! "That makes sense. I'm feeling so much better with this conversation, reassured that you haven't emotionally ditched our friendship," Jill says with a smile.

John grins. "I'll see what I can do to rein in Shelly when she interrupts. Can you apologize to her for the blowups?"

"I guess it's the least I can do. Thank you for your presence to hear me out."

John looks deeply into Jill's eyes like an eager lover and gives her a heartfelt extended hug. Their breathing syncs up for a full minute. Jill thinks—*Holy cow! I don't want to break away; this feels so good. I'm so ready to have make-up sex right now!*

John's thinking—*OMG! This is heaven. The eye-gazing and hugging feel like I'm on cloud nine. I'm dying to rip her clothes off and make love.* And then another thought pops in—*Stop it! Wait until you're a free man.*

Jill leaves the conference room feeling joyful. *He doesn't reject me when I have temper tantrums. We have make-up conversations that make me feel closer.*

◆　◆　◆

As beautiful as the repair conversation was in the conference room, John flipped back into his armored parts within a few days. Business-only surface conversations ensue, which makes Jill feel ballistic again. She's tired of getting dry crumbs, even if their relationship status is friendship and business only.

At her next IFS session, Emily reminds Jill that people who haven't invested in doing serious inner work have a hard time sustaining Self-energy. John can be connected, compassionate, curious, present, patient, and playful when he feels like it, but sooner or later, his protective parts dominate again.

Emily shares concepts from a book by Louann Brizendine, *The Male Brain: A Breakthrough Understanding of How Men and Boys Think.* "Men are wired differently than women. They can't focus on more than one thing at a time as women can; they compartmentalize. The 'Jill' compartment is probably tucked away in a remote corner of John's brain. His priority right now is to make money, pay bills, and keep the household sane.

◆ ◆ ◆

Jill reaches out to Shelly and apologizes for blowing a gasket. Shelly accepts her apology. Everything ought to be okay since John reassured her that he does not favor Shelly. But Jill's intuition tells her that Shelly's energy is still mired in possessiveness regarding John.

Men and Women Have Different Priorities

"Am I succeeding or failing?" is many men's primary question to themselves. "Am I loved?" is many women's central question. Evolutionary biology says that men are wired to be hunter/gatherers, and women are wired to seek love and be nurturers.

In a hetero-normative relationship where the man is someone who prefers to lead, protect, and provide, when he hears his partner say the four words, "We need to talk . . ." this can be kryptonite to his ears. Many men interpret the "we need to talk" request as: "I'm failing; that's why she wants to talk!" (Regardless of gender, the majority of people cringe at hearing these four words. Defenses automatically go up.)

As many females' primary quest is to be loved, when her partner pulls away, seems distant, and doesn't want to talk, she interprets this as, "I'm not lovable anymore, and that's why he's distant."

Many men need to hide in their man-caves to think and process their emotions before they talk, that is, if they even know what their feelings are. The confusion makes them stay silent and busy *doing* instead of feeling emotions. Author John Gray has written many books regarding gender differences, including his bestseller *Men Are from Mars and Women Are from Venus.* John Gray also has many videos on YouTube you can learn from. Alison Armstrong is another well-known author who helps women understand men's developmental stages.

A way to overcome disconnection is through vulnerability. The woman can say, "I'm a little afraid to say this. I'm *feeling* disconnected. I miss our connection. I want to know how I can improve my communication so I can feel closer to you. What do you think we should do about this?"

The last line, "What do you think we should do about this?" allows the man to be in his natural masculine mode of fixing problems. "What do you think" can make it easier for the man to respond instead of reacting defensively.

To learn more about how to become an extraordinary Self-led leader and lover, sign up for either "Climax in Love: Be the Ultimate Warrior for a Goddess" or "Climax in Love: Be the Ultimate Goddess for a Warrior." You can access these courses at www.ClimaxInLove.com.

Chapter 25

Green-Eyed Jealousy Monster

Shelly spends a lot of time with John implementing his out-of-the-box ideas and minimizes her engagements with Jill. Shelly seems to have co-opted Jill's co-founder role, and Jill doesn't like it.

Jill's self-concept is sinking now, and her business prowess has weakened compared to what she used to bring to the table. When she tries to cooperate with Shelly, Shelly utters underhanded snarky remarks about how she and John are like two-peas-in-a-pod and can read each other's minds. "After all, Jill, John and I worked together on several of the most successful campaigns at Zatuck." Shelly's mean girl part thinks—*Stick it up your ass, Jill! I'm gonna push you out. I'll show John he made a big mistake asking you to be his co-founder.*

John ignores the deteriorating relationship between Jill and Shelly, telling Jill to work it out like a big girl. The emotional distance between John and Jill continues to increase. To deal with stress, John drinks more, doesn't sleep well, and is weathering into an older man with bags under his eyes and burgeoning love handles.

Jill stops by his office and remarks, "You seem so distant. Do you want to talk about it? I know things are hard at home. I'm here to listen and support you."

"I appreciate your concerns, but can you give me space? I need to deal with this on my own." John's thinking—*Oh, God! I can't let her know what's going on. We're close to bankruptcy. Liz has been charging up a storm to keep up with her friends and to spite me. I can't reveal this. Jill will see me as the ultimate failure. Once I get divorced, why would she want to be with a financial loser? It's best to keep my distance and fake it 'til I make it.*

In the meantime, Jill can't shut her inner thoughts off. *I hate feeling so disconnected. It feels like daddy is ignoring me all over again. Now I'm almost sure John's not as well-*

off as he made himself out to be. How can he keep up with his lifestyle? The money isn't coming into the business as fast as we'd like. He's checked out, and Shelly is stabbing me in the back. Why the hell am I still here?

◆ ◆ ◆

Jill and Shelly enter the conference room for a team meeting, and, as is often the case, John is not coming. Shelly asks Jill, "May I say a few things before we discuss business?"

"Sure. What's up, Shelly?" Jill says casually, not detecting any animosity.

"I've been noticing that you still ask John a lot of questions as if you're tentative and don't know what you're doing," Shelly says with a slightly critical tone.

"I ask a lot of questions because I'm confused and need clarity. I can't seem to get any straight answers. He's either vague or doesn't answer my texts and emails. It seems like he's not interested in this work anymore."

"He's very interested. Remember what I said to you before? He and I are two-peas-in-the-same-pod. I can read his mind and finish his sentences."

Jill feels punched in the gut. Shelly's been extra flirtatious with John in the last few months, and John seems to participate in the dance. Jill has overheard him saying more than once, "Shelly, you have such a gift for connecting the dots and seeing the blind spots that neither Jill nor I can see. I very much appreciate your unique genius. Couldn't do this without you." Jill would cringe while Shelly ate up the compliments.

"You aren't suited to be a co-founder. You don't have as much experience as I do. You bring the meetings down with your immature and insecure questions." Shelly's steely hazel eyes stare coldly at Jill. "I have nothing more to say. You need to work on yourself and address your self-esteem. I should be the co-founder since I have a Stanford MBA, and all you have is a state school degree!" Shelly strides out of the room.

Jill is stunned. She stands there with her jaw open, trying to comprehend the venom that was just spewed on her. *What the fuck just happened?! She's triggered by me and had to vomit meanness.* Jill whispers under her breath, "This is ridiculous." She reaches for the phone to call John, who is on his way to the new wing's dedication at the children's hospital, where he helped raise $300,000 in funding. Jill tells John what just occurred.

"Take a deep breath and step back. It sounds like Shelly is triggered. She didn't mean what she said. That's just Shelly for you, in one of her moods."

"She's jealous of the friendship you and I have and is projecting all of that bitterness onto me. I know she's jealous, but I have a part that feels very hurt."

"I would never have asked you to be my business partner if I didn't think you were capable of doing it. Sorry, I have to cut this conversation short. I've reached the hospital. You'll get over what she said."

"Are you going to say something to her?"

"No, it's not my place; it's between you and Shelly."

Jill hangs up, disappointed. His tone did not reflect any grave concerns about the blowout. *I need to rethink whether I want to continue with this agency. I'm not convinced we can turn the sinking ship around.*

◆　◆　◆

Jill pays a visit to Emily to work through the anger over the Shelly drama. Emily says, "Women are sometimes cruel to each other because beautiful, charismatic, smart women can threaten insecure women. When Shelly feels threatened—in this case, threatened about not receiving attention from someone important, i.e., John— she can go into her mean girl part and project her low self-esteem so she can feel significant once again. Your Self-energy and inner light can bring Shelly's insecurities to the surface. It's like reliving junior high school woes. The past is always in the present, remember?"

"That makes sense. I'm not perfect; I made a lot of mistakes with my former Zatuck team. How do I stop Shelly's tirades?"

"I'm so happy you were able to improve as a leader. When Shelly acts out, refrain from participating in the dance. I know this can be hard to do at the moment when you want to defend yourself. You can calmly say, 'Shelly, when you are back in Self, I would be happy to resume this conversation. I'll give you space to work through your emotions.'"

Emily takes this opportunity to read out loud an email from one of her forty-something male friends after he read a blog post she wrote about inner and outer beauty. His email said:

"When you talk about beauty coming from the inside, it's true. Ask any man if he knows a woman he does not find beautiful (he might find her ugly), but for some reason he finds her irresistibly sexy. He will tell you he can think of several women like that. Guys often talk to each other this way: 'I know she's not that attractive, but there's something about her . . .' This is coming from some inner quality that is being reflected outward. There's also the opposite—women who are objectively beautiful but don't have sex appeal. They're just there, like a beautiful painting or sculpture, but they don't inspire action. These women lack inner beauty. Some women have both inner *and* outer beauty. These are the women who make men CRY!"

"Wow, that is so powerful! Maybe I'm making John cry?"

"Maybe you do. Sophia Loren summarized it the best in her famous quote, 'Nothing makes a woman more beautiful than the *belief* that she is beautiful.' This means being more objectively beautiful than Shelly can be threatening if she hasn't done the work to believe in her unique beauty."

"I will remember that powerful quote for sure. Thank you, you're a lifesaver!"

"When you are not afraid to show your rainbow—which includes the beautiful and ugly parts—and you dare to apologize *for* parts when they eject distasteful hurtful words, that's being real."

"Yes, it was so powerful when you guided me to own my bad leadership parts with my team. I gained a lot of new friends that day, and I'm still in touch with many of them."

"There's power in what you're doing with John, being the initiator of vulnerability. He's not ready to reciprocate because he may be frightened of what full-on vulnerability will do to the exaggerated warrior image he has built up. I'm sure there's a part of him that feels like a fraud. Many men's bravado is a coverup for feeling inadequate. I've mentioned Brené Brown's book, *The Gifts of Imperfection: Let Go of Who You Think You're Supposed to Be and Embrace Who You Are* [2010], in a previous session. Brené says, 'When you own your imperfections, it invites love and belonging; it allows the other person to say, 'Me too! I want to own mine too.'"

Once again, Jill feels reassured with Emily's higher-level perspectives. Jill has no idea what John's deepest insecurities are. All she knows is that he wears a façade for self-preservation.

At Jill's next IFS session, she discusses how she is getting better with Self-led communication. But, because she is so attached to an outcome with John—and being attached means she's afraid of losing him—it is hard to be Self-led all the time. John's avoidance of heart-to-heart conversations stalls the progress in their rupture-repair cycle. Emily tells Jill, "When you send texts and voice memos to John, please focus on your *feelings* instead of analyzing everything. Men want to help you not feel bad; it's their nature as protectors."

"Ohhh . . . damn! My analysis part keeps getting in the way of sharing my feelings."

"Stick to your feelings. When you own how you feel, John can't challenge your feelings—they are yours. If you truly want to succeed as business partners, you two need business partners' couples counseling. Having a business together is harder than being married to each other. In marriage, you can sweep your issues under the rug to be dealt with later, if at all. In business, if you sweep your issues under the rug, the pain will show up in lackluster business results or failure. Remember, there's no such thing as a business problem—all business problems are *people* problems."

"That makes so much sense. Unfortunately, John coming to therapy with me is not going to happen."

"I know. In the meantime, when your protectors overtake you in the middle of the night, you can type the thoughts out from that part with one big caveat—do not send the text or email! When you are in a better place in two days, rewrite it from Self. You'll see that it was a part that wrote it and not Self. Trust me, waiting a few days until you've calmed down and then rewriting it with Self speaking *for* your feelings instead will be much more productive."

"I'm grateful for the reminders. I have you to vent to and get me back on track!"

"You've got this, Jill."

Chapter 26

Confession of Intensity

Finally, after a few weeks of John's Self missing in action, he decides to have a conversation with Jill and tells her the truth. Even though he hated receiving her emails, he did appreciate some of her psychological analyses, which were spot on. But, he will never openly admit she is correct. He needs space to release feelings of inadequacy. *Admitting to Jill what is underneath my armor will give her too much power. She's already busted my balls enough. I can't even step up as a leader when the going gets tough, but yet, these hiccups make me want her even more.*

Jill is nervous about the meeting. John sits across from her, with thirty pounds of belly fat hanging over his pants. He stopped dressing like a GQ model and now looks unstylish and sloppy. *He's no longer sexy, but I must have compassion for his home situation. He's numbing out on food and alcohol. Okay, stop judging already!* She straightens up and waits for him to begin.

John is aware of what softens the edges and makes Jill melt. *I need to take her hands into mine.* John cups Jill's hands and looks into her eyes.

"Jill, my friend, thank you for the emails. I hear your messages, and I'm going to try to improve."

Jill thinks—*Try to improve? Really? "Try" means he's not serious about it. Okay, stop it, just listen.*

"As I've shared before, I've been ignoring you because of the struggles at home. I know it's not a good excuse since you see me spend time with Shelly and others in the co-working space. I've been trying hard to run away from the intensity of my attraction to you. Our mutual attraction is not doing any good for our business; it's in the way. The more I try to run away, the more you keep after me with your long-ass emails and voice memos. I'm triggered when I read them because the messages hit home—I know I'm not a Self-led leader. At times, I *am* a moron. Honestly, I only skim your emails because it's too painful to read what an asshole of a leader and friend I've been. Your honesty and vulnerability—unfortunately—or maybe fortunately—increases the attraction. Running away from the attraction isn't working."

Jill's heart melts with his openness. She tears up.

"Please, go on."

"When we're in a good place, you make me feel alive because you touch vulnerable places inside of me. I want to make love to you so badly, not in the traditional going-around-the-bases way, but in a spiritual way. You're not a sex object; you're so much more. I know I want to do things differently, but I can't act on my feelings right now. I didn't know what spirituality or spiritual connection was until I met you. You wouldn't know it, but I can't stop thinking about you twenty-four/seven, no matter how hard I try. That's all I have to say for now. I apologize for my asshole behaviors and will try to improve."

There he goes again with the word "try." Can I believe anything he says? Okay, critical part, please step aside and let Self handle this. Jill looks into John's eyes for five seconds to get centered and connected to his soul.

"Thank you for your honesty. I appreciate that you mustered the courage to explain everything." Jill decides to flip into business mode. "Please be conscientious about communication, especially regarding clients. Otherwise, our venture will flop," she says stoically. "See you at the team meeting."

As she walks out the door, Jill thinks—*Well, two steps forward for now. Let's see how long it takes before we go backwards again. I like that he validated how deeply he's in love, but I don't trust him, and I've lost respect.*

John thinks—*Wait a minute. I saw that she received my vulnerabilities through the watery eyes, but then—she changed her tune in the end? She ended up in business-only mode, and her energy shifted to apathy. Did she fall out of love with me because of my incompetent behaviors? Did I fuck up the best thing that's ever come into my life?*

◆　◆　◆

Feeling rejected by Jill after expressing so vulnerably, he experiences vulnerability hangover. John emotionally checks out, retreats to his man-cave, and mindlessly flips through TV channels.

Despite the mutual admiration and lust, neither John nor Jill feels emotionally safe. Surrounded at work by a tight-lipped, two-faced business partner and his disapproving toady Shelly, Jill reaches out to her close friends, Amy. Amy knows how to soothe Jill's disappointments and confusion.

Jill met Amy at her job before Zatuck. Even though Amy and Jill don't speak often, whenever they do touch base, they pick up where they left off, understanding every nuance of the other's experiences. The last time they communicated was when Jill was fired and decided to go into business with John. Soon after that, Amy's mother needed help moving into an assisted living facility. Jill gave her the space to tend to her mom's needs, not wanting to bother Amy with more "John challenges." Amy is good at cutting to the chase without sugarcoating. As hard as the truth can be, Amy's truth bombs come from love.

After a few minutes of niceties, Jill updates Amy on what has happened since their last conversation. Amy tells her, "Remember our last talk. I warned you that you shouldn't do business with John until you do love right. You need to consummate the attraction to get the business going in the right direction. The rest of the details, like getting divorced and the next steps will reveal themselves. It's hard for the business to crank upward when the energy is blocked with mutual attraction and marital challenges."

"I couldn't hear you the first time because I wanted to do things my way. Why does our love connection need to be explored first?"

"Because . . . I'm speaking from personal experience. I never told you this but my husband of ten years . . . well . . . we had a seven-year affair before we got married. Ssshhhhh . . . only one other soul knows this secret. People thought we started dating after Frank got divorced."

"What? How did that work?"

"While in business school, I was hired as an intern at Frank's fast-growing import-export business. Sparks flew from the beginning, but I denied them. He was married and 15 years older. After I finished school, I went back and became his top sales rep. He said he wanted me to become his COO one day but needed to wait until I learned the ropes. So, he said, 'We need to figure out this energy between us. Otherwise, the business will suffer if we don't address the sexual tension.'

"Eventually, we had sex and carried on with an affair. The sexual chemistry was out of this world. Even though Frank was married, he lived in a separate apartment. They had not had sex for years. He waited until his sons were in college to divorce. For years, Frank stayed at his studio in the city while his stay-at-home wife, a busy mom and school volunteer, lived in the suburbs. There was no way she could find out about the affair since they lived apart. The city apartment was initially Frank's place to land after late-night meetings, but eventually, he lived in it ninety percent of the time. His wife didn't challenge him; she was happy not to have him home. I didn't feel guilty about the affair, and after a couple of years, I became the COO. Frank and I waited until his divorce finalized before we went public with our relationship. So, take it from someone with experience; it will be hard to do business when there's charged mutual attraction that cannot be released. That energy will pop somewhere, and it sounds like it's getting reflected in poor business results. Exploring romance should be a top priority."

"Thanks for the input. I'm not sure we can overcome the challenges; we're too deep in the pothole. I don't know if consummation is something John will go for," Jill says in an exasperated tone.

◆　◆　◆

Jill mulls Amy's advice over the next few days. *She's right! I feel guilty for being stone cold after John bared his soul. It's time to bare my soul. Maybe he'll consider my new proposal. The whole idea of starting this business came out of our chemistry, and suppressing the chemistry is also suppressing our company's potential for success.*

Jill decides to write her deepest heartfelt thoughts about John. She records the thoughts in a voice memo. To make sure the message is from Self-energy, Jill gets Emily's blessing before sending the voice memo to John via Dropbox.

Hey John,

I want to flesh some things out, so you're clear about where I'm at. I promise this is all good stuff.

I think it's been hard for us to work together because of the sexual tension. I feel that we need to take care of what our bodies desperately want and then use the synergy of a harmonious union to benefit the friendship and the business.

Emily helped me understand why we feel so deeply for each other. I believe our chemistry is rooted in a karmic contract, which is way beyond the physical. It feels like we are the lock and key for each other's next level of transformation and consciousness. If this indeed is what it is, the journey will not be a cakewalk because we need to work through our triggers with professional help.

Spiritual gurus say love is the doorway to self-actualization. Love can expose our deepest fears, insecurities, and shadows so that we can remove these inner blocks and achieve wild success. Our challenges have given me the courage to be vulnerable and speak my truths. I have never felt safe to express all that I am in any of my previous relationships.

I've also been digging deeper into the quantum physics of spiritual relationships. The Universe brought us together because we are a vibrational match—two halves of a single unit—the yin and yang, the feminine and masculine, the light and dark, the contrasting childhood upbringings. We can help each other transform into awakened conscious souls so we can play our most potent, earth-shaking symphonies.

When you share your loving Self-energy, like you did when we were in your room during the Cape Cod workshop, I am high-as-a-kite. I feel beautiful, alive, seen, and heard. I feel I have permission to be all of me—the good, the bad, the sexy, the badass, and the ugly. No wonder I'm hooked on you.

John, I want you to know that despite our difficulties, I respect and admire you. I am deeply grateful for the karmic lessons I'm learning through you. I want you to know that you are the only one who holds a very special place in my heart, stirring my soul as no one else has ever done. Are you ready to experience joy-gasms with me on our magic carpet ride? The Universe is calling us to achieve climax in every area of life by embracing our attraction, not avoiding it. It's so worth exploring; I hope you agree.

John is in a depressed slump as he works from home. His email dings with a message from Dropbox. He clicks on it and finds a voice memo from Jill. *Why can't she leave me alone? I can't deal with this now.*

John waits until the family is in bed and gets curious about what Jill has to say. As he listens to the voice memo, he's thinking—*OMG! I can't believe what she is saying. Hmmm . . . she does make sense.* But another voice jumps in and says—*She's out of her mind. I'm not ready to have an affair. I need to focus on the business and bring in the money. I can't afford this lifestyle anymore. I'm about to pull the kids out of private school.*

John freezes and doesn't know what to say in response to Jill's beautiful and vulnerable message. He feels a slight shift in his depressed energy and gins up the motivation to take his kids on a trip for their Spring Break.

When John sees Jill after returning from vacation with the kids, he says, "You're such a great communicator. You need to record books for Audible. I have to run to a doctor's appointment. Catch you later." And, he's off.

That's the acknowledgment I get for spending so much time putting my thoughts together and pouring my heart out? Jill cries herself to sleep that night and stays in a funk for weeks to come, with minimal interactions with John. *He's more cold than hot. I can't take his unpredictable hang-ups anymore. What an unconscious phony! I deserve more than this!*

Chapter 27

Ecstatic Surrender

Two weeks after sending the voice memos, John and Jill speak with a prospective client at The James New York hotel in SoHo. The meeting didn't go as well as they'd hoped, as the energy between John and Jill wasn't right. "I don't get the sense that they are going to hire us," John says in a sad tone.

"Nope, they're not. They didn't seem impressed with our proposal." They walk down the corridor to the coffee shop to decompress.

Reflecting on the conversation with Amy, Jill musters up the courage to say what needs to be said, since John never gave her a real response to the voice memo. "As you know, I've been so patient and frustrated. I think the main reason we can't harmoniously work together is that we've got too much sexual tension. It's time to release this. I can't bear it anymore. I don't care that you're married."

She leans across the small table towards him. "I want to get naked, now!" Jill says with a sultry tone and piercing gaze.

John's eyes grow big, and his jaw drops. *Am I hearing what I think I'm hearing? Holy shit! I know she said that in the voice memo. She means business, right now!* "I'm game, end of discussion! Let's get a room here, pronto!" he says. With Jill's boldness, John's energy flips into love and connection.

They ride the elevator in silence and anticipation. John slips the key into the door. They place their work bags on the desk and hastily turn toward each other. John's hands cup Jill's face, and proceeds with passionate, slow kissing.

After a half-hour of tender groping and kissing, John takes a small step back and says, "I can't have sex with you; I'm guilt-ridden."

"Okay . . . but I'm disappointed. What can we do that will not make you feel guilty?"

"How about we breathe and meditate as we did at the Cape?"

"I'm game. Let's use the meditation app on my phone."

They sit in the lotus position on the bed with their backs to each other, breathing in synchrony for the next forty-five minutes as the music moves them. *God, I want her so much right now, but I can't!* And Jill thinks—*I want him so badly.*

Twenty minutes into the meditation, Jill tears up. The music penetrates her soul and brings up feelings from their journey—from anger to sadness, frustration, and joy. She needs to be held. John hears her sobs, uncrosses his legs, lies on top of the crisp, white down comforter, and spoons with her as the weeping gets louder and louder. He holds her tightly as the music continues—no words needed.

Jill feels comforted with John's tight embrace. John feels like a protective concrete wall containing her feminine raging emotional ocean. They are in a polarized masculine-feminine dance, where the masculine is consciousness and the witness, and the feminine is emotionally surrendered and is being witnessed.

When the meditation ends, Jill says, "Can we process what came through me?"

"Sure," says John lovingly.

They sit across from each other, holding hands, as Jill wipes away the last of her tears. John eagerly awaits her reveal.

"The parts of me that held so much anger and frustration toward you were released with today's tears. Even though I had many nights of crying myself to sleep, it wasn't enough. I needed your presence to release the pent-up frustrations. Through the tears, I realized I had been such a badass with my controlling and needy parts. These parts showed up in my accusatory emails. I'm sorry." John continues his loving gaze, which makes Jill feel safe to share more.

"I accept your apologies," he says. "I have a part to play in our struggles. I'm having a hard time being Self-led. I have so many parts that need work. Unfortunately, the challenges with my wife overwhelm my emotional and mental capacities."

"I get it. I appreciate your presence today."

"Thank you. You deserve so much more."

They continue the connection through placing their respective right hands on each other's hearts and left hands clasp each other's right hands. After a minute, they lie down and realize that the sexual energy desperately needs to be released. Jill thinks—*This feels so good, I want to have sex right now!*

"Can I pleasure you?" John whispers to Jill.

"I thought you didn't want to—"

"Shhh . . . no need to talk."

Jill gets the message and lets things flow. Jill respects John's stated boundaries of no penetrative sex. They hand-pleasure each other. Jill reaches a transcendent altered-state climax, with most of her clothes still on. "That was the best orgasm I've ever had!"

Oh my, I am *a warrior right now!* "I felt your powerful tremors. They were beautiful," John says as he plants a soft kiss on Jill's lips.

After Jill's climax, she uses her hands to help John finish, but after fifteen minutes, John shifts out of Self and into a performance part. His thoughts are all over the place, and he can't have an orgasm. John lets her know that everything is okay, he's satisfied. They go back into spooning and stroking each other's bodies, as Jill sheds tears of joy from feeling so nurtured. *It would have been nice if he could have come. It's okay; this is still beautiful.*

◆　◆　◆

On the train ride back home to Rye, John is dazed, processing the beauty of what transpired. *She made me feel so masculine. She trusted me and allowed herself to surrender into the rawest of emotions. That wasn't just about an orgasm; it was a spiritual experience that needed to happen through sex. I felt one with her and one with myself. That was intense! It took all that I had to hold space for her emotions. I don't deserve someone as evolved and beautiful as Jill. I've got to get a grip. Time to disconnect, forge on, and get back on my financial footing.*

Later that night, Jill calls Amy and shares what happened in the hotel room. Jill stays on a spiritual high for a few days replaying the tryst, yet wonders if their future dynamic will change. *I have no idea if this experience will improve how he shows up.*

◆　◆　◆

The next day at the office after their rendezvous, John is back in business mode, doing the hard work to figure out where future business will come from. The financial outlook is bleak.

John and Jill return to minimal interactions. It's as if the intimacy never happened. After talking about business development, John says, "I want to be completely transparent. We had a beautiful experience. It was something we needed to get out of our systems. However, I need to clarify that I'm not interested in doing it again and taking our relationship further. This is a recipe for a disastrous divorce."

"Sure, I understand," Jill says in a calm tone.

Jill can't stop thinking of her transcendent orgasm and how that made her feel. She's in awe of the most beautiful spiritual experience she's ever had. Jill felt so seen and validated because she felt safe to completely let go. Reflecting on the experience, she realizes she felt oneness with herself, oneness with John, and oneness with the Universe. *Is this what enlightenment feels like? I'll have to capture what I felt and send it to John someday.*

Chapter 28

Leaving for Greener Pastures

September 2017

John and Jill have been in business for fourteen months. Jill can't take his "bipolar" ways anymore. Sometimes he's in good spirits, but most of the time, he is in parts and ego. Jill has no hope for the future anymore. John has risen to the level of his incompetence, another Peter Principle victim. He is crashing hard and unwilling to work on himself to unburden the childhood demons causing the downward spiral. *I'm tired of making excuses for him. I'm tired of trying so hard, only to be met with stonewalling and rejection. The occasional presence of his loving, fun, and flirty Self is not enough to sustain this friendship and business partnership.*

Jill shares with Emily, "I've been too patient, waiting for him to step up, and he can't. Clients leave due to his lack of follow-through and lack of clarity. He dropped the ball so many times. One client threatened to sue us for not delivering what we promised."

"That is certainly lack of Self-leadership."

"Yes, when I called him out recently, he got mad and unfriended me on all social media channels. He finally lost it and said, 'Leave me the fuck alone! Everyone wants a piece of me. My wife is threatening to leave me bankrupt, and now you're on my case?!' After this blowup, I said, 'Shelly, you deal with this jerk! I'm done!' Shelly's expression looked like: What's up with her? Do I get John to myself now? Yippee!"

"Jill, you're not in Self now. Please ask the angry part to step aside and bring Self back."

"Okay, let me breathe." Jill takes a few minutes to calm down.

"What is the decision you need to make about this situation?"

"I need to write an adios letter and divorce from the business partnership." Jill slumps over and covers her eyes with her hands.

After a few minutes of crying, she takes a shaky breath and looks up at Emily. "Wow! It felt so freeing to say that; it's time."

"Just make sure this 'Dear John' letter is from Self."

◆ ◆ ◆

Dear John,

I guess this is a real 'Dear John' letter. I've been contemplating our journey and decided to eject from this turbulent plane that is obviously in a downward spiral. There seems to be nothing I can do to pull it out. I need to find a place where my gifts are celebrated and not just tolerated—or worse. I don't belong here.

I know I'm capable of amazing things, but I feel small and unsafe to be me when I feel unheard and unseen. I've been working my ass off, only to have clients take their business elsewhere because they complain that you don't deliver on your promises.

I hate that I sometimes have to shrink into a turtle's shell and be tentative, asking questions like a five-year-old because I don't know what mood is underneath your stoicism. I feel like I'm walking on eggshells, reliving my worst childhood nightmares.

How could I (we?) have been so delusional to think that this friendship and business partnership was a match made in heaven? How could I have ignored all the red flags?

What kept me going longer than I should have is seeing flashes of your most *lovable* warrior and *brilliant* true *self*. That is the John I *adore, appreciate, trust,* and *respect*. You will continue to be my *hero* . . . *When* you show up in *self*. You are *more than enough*. You don't need to activate hyper-alpha mode to prove something. How we relate to each other doesn't work for me. I've been patient, hoping that I could experience more of your Higher Self.

Thank you for giving me the gift of the lessons I needed to learn the hard way. It's time to eject. With this good-bye, I need to accept that I may never see or talk to you again. I am willing to leave all aspects of you behind so that I can feel centered again. I am reminded of Carl Jung's famous quote: "There is no coming to consciousness without pain. People will do anything, no matter how absurd, to avoid facing their souls. One does not become enlightened by imagining figures of light, but by making the darkness conscious."

It is with great sadness and LOTS of tears that I disengage from our friendship and business. I'm leaving this turbulence to find clear skies where I can soar. I deserve to be treated so much better than how I'm being treated now.

I look forward to the day when our amazing souls can meet again and have a do-over. It will be so beautiful. I wish you the best life.

Sayonara,
Jill
xoxo
P.S. Please remember I will forever LOVE your soul. Maybe in our next lifetime, we can work this out.

Jill looks it over and thinks—*Well, this email seems to be written from Self. I'm leaving in some parts-led communication so he can see how hurt I am.*
John opens the email, skims it, and thinks—*Oh well, I don't need her anyway!* He sends a reply:

Jill,

I agree we should part ways. The writing was on the wall for a long time. I'll FedEx you the partnership dissolution to sign. Good luck.

John

Jill receives his response within a half-hour of sending the email. She reads the terse response and mutters under her breath, "This *is* truly the end."

◆ ◆ ◆

Jill consults with Emily on why bad stuff keeps happening. Emily repeatedly reinforces the same message. "When people don't address their childhood stressors—that is, the exiles that drive their bad behaviors—they keep attracting situations that make them self-sabotage over and over again. Self-sabotage is the protectors' way of reinforcing core childhood limiting beliefs, such as, *I'm not enough*, and *I'm not worthy*. The past is always in the present! What is hysterical is historical. Some people need to hit rock bottom and lose everything before they decide to work on themselves. Having you come into his life exposed the emotional cockroaches in his underwear. You've caught John with his pants down. He's too ashamed to own up and clean up his incompetence."

Jill laughs at the "cockroach" metaphor.

"I know, everyone cracks up when they visualize cockroaches in the underwear. Because John hasn't dealt with those cockroaches yet, the last thing he wants is for you to see them. He needs to join a men's group and go to IFS therapy to heal shame and inadequacy. After those cockroaches are exterminated, and John feels like his underwear and body are squeaky clean—after tumbling and unburdening in the IFS washing machine—that's when he will access more Self, with balanced, instead of extreme, parts. As a result, he'll gain the courage to own up to his shortcomings and apologize for his parts. When he finally does the work, no sooner, this is when your friendship can get back on track."

Jill continues to giggle at Emily's sense of humor. "I can't stop laughing at your metaphors; they make sense."

"Thank you for allowing my funny part to shine. In the meantime, you made a smart decision to disentangle. Move on. If it's meant for you guys to be together in the future, the Universe will orchestrate the synchronicities. When you are not attached to an outcome, because you're not in fear, that's when good things happen.

And, a business breakup is similar to romantic relationship breakups. When the triggers come up, they must be promptly handled. The conflicts and inability to resolve differences will show up in lack of business earnings, tension-filled work environments, and employee disengagement. If you want a small business to succeed, you must hire the right transformational spiritual mentors from the outset to navigate the inevitable emotional rocky road to success. For newbie solo entrepreneurs, they can invest in all the fancy marketing programs they want: 'Just follow my step-by-step program, and you'll become a millionaire just like me.' Unfortunately, many waste oodles of money buying 'hope' and hiding behind, 'I just need this one new program, and I can finally get moving and make it big!' And guess what? Most of these businesses become a statistic mentioned in *Entrepreneur* magazine: 75 percent of startup businesses fail. Remember, you will not attract what you want into your life; you will attract who you are. Business problems are *people* problems."

Jill feels deflated, cradling her face with her hands. "The message is loud and clear, Emily. I attracted him so I could deal with my daddy issues and so much more."

♦ ♦ ♦

Within a month of Jill's good-bye letter, the boutique ad agency that John and Jill co-founded goes belly-up. John manages to pull himself together and finds a senior manager position at a midsize ad agency. His salary is a third what he made at Zatuck, but it's enough to pay the bills. The boys are no longer in private schools, and John has sold their vacation homes.

Why Some Visionaries Can't Articulate the Details

Sadly, John and Jill's partnership did not survive. If you want to learn the secrets of a successful business partnership, it's essential to read *Rocket Fuel: One Essential Combination That Will Get You More of What You Want from Your Business* by Gino Wickman and Mark C. Winters. The book explains why a visionary can go bankrupt if they don't have a brilliant COO or co-founder with complementary skill sets. Many visionaries have a hard time articulating the details and are not wired to carry through with strategy and execution.

According to *Rocket Fuel,* many visionaries' minds are full of color and detail with their big ideas. But, when it comes to articulating the details, they are verbally constipated and have a hard time painting the colorful picture in their minds with words. They can only share the low-resolution, cloudy, black-and-white versions of their creations, which frustrates the right-hand person who tries to execute the vision. John is a visionary who can't articulate the details of his ideas. This is why John had many communication challenges at Zatuck and with Jill. As the visionaries describe the cloudy, vague vision, they think everyone should be able to read the details swimming in their minds; they can't. As a result, confusion and chaos can follow, and failure is possible.

PART IV

Chapter 29

Thank Goodness for Male Best Friends

Jill goes into a funk after her breakup with John. She understands the IFS psycho-spiritual explanation of why John's inner demons prevented harmony and bliss, but she needs a man's perspective. She calls one of her closest male friends, Pierre, who lives in Paris.

Jill met Pierre at a personal development retreat in Bali a year before she joined Zatuck. Pierre is a former investment banker turned yogi who is on a path to become a better version of himself. They developed an instant friendship and kept in touch about their careers and relationships every few months. Using Zoom videoconferencing on her laptop, Jill looks into Pierre's beautiful blue eyes and says, "I need a male perspective on why John is such a jerk and pushed me away. I wanted things to be great between us, and it was an uphill battle." Jill is emotional and near tears.

"Mon chère Amie . . . let me tell you why some men do what they do when they meet the woman of their dreams, the woman that knocks their socks off. You've told me how John loves to peacock his accomplishment feathers. You've told me he poured his heart out, and you felt a tingly soul-based connection. You two might be soulmates or he might be your spiritual twin, the masculine missing half of you. I know it's woo-woo labeling, but sometimes we need a label to make sense of things."

Jill says, "Yes . . . another one of my friends called it a Twin Soul relationship. She said John and I have complementary emotional luggage, and that's why we have a love-hate dynamic. He does feel like the missing half of me."

"Maybe he is; Spiritual Twins, Twin Souls, Twin Flames, maybe even a False Twin Flame, whatever you want to call it. As I've shared in the past, I met my twin soul years ago. Let me share the deeper layers of the story. The intensity was too much, and I had to break it off. She pushed my buttons and activated embarrassing insecurities. Brigette was the most beautiful woman who ever came into my life on every level—physical, intellectual, emotional, and spiritual. For ten months, we were hot, hot, hot!" Pierre's sexy French accent emphasizes how hot things were. "The connection and the cosmic sex were exhilarating! Even though the sex was great, a part of me felt like my manhood was never big enough or hard enough for her—I mean this in the literal and metaphorical sense."

"Really? Are men that insecure about their manhood?"

"Don't know if it's all men. Blame it on porn. I know, it's sick. I never felt my cock was inadequate with other women until I met Brigette. I must reveal that I triggered the hell out of her, activating her biggest insecurities and fears. She may have been beautiful on the outside, but her inner beauty could not rise to match the outer beauty. You realize that macho-alpha, seemingly uber-confident men, are perhaps the most insecure men you'll ever meet. I hear that beautiful models are some of the most insecure women you'll ever meet. Many of my former banking colleagues were so insecure; it was sickening. John peacocks like these men, right?"

"Yes, often."

"I was guilty of egomaniacal peacocking too. My ego got me fired from a lucrative career. It was a rude awakening, but at least it was an awakening. I wasn't a show-off spendthrift like my peers; I socked away millions. I decided to quit corporate work and began the yogic spiritual path to find enlightenment. After Brigette, I'm not sure I'll ever have the capacity for another deep relationship because she was fine, five-star French cuisine. I can't do fast-food shallow, nonspiritual relationships anymore. I've settled for three-star cuisine now because it's easy and safe, with negligible drama. Maybe someday I'll find the courage to reach out to Brigette again and have my dream five-star relationship."

"Wow, that's a great metaphor. I've watched many videos on YouTube that say the same thing—our greatest insecurities and fears get triggered when we meet the person we're most attracted to."

"Yeah . . . Brigette sends me emails and text messages now and then, and I don't respond. I don't want to get her hopes up, at least not anytime soon since my soul can't handle the intensity. The insecure part of me will always be wondering, 'Will she continue to love me even when I don't feel man enough and successful enough?' Therefore, it's safer to push the woman away first."

"This is eye-opening to hear how men question if they will continue to be loved during the hiccups and failures."

"Yeah. I'm convinced that that is the number one reason why men push extraordinary women away. This is why I did awful things to push Brigette away because I believed I didn't deserve her. She was too good to be true. She wanted marriage; I didn't. I was afraid that once she saw all of who I was, I will be exposed as a fraud. If she took the initiative to leave me, I'd be crushed into a deep depression.

"In the end, I told her marriage was not something I wanted because I saw my parents go through a nasty divorce. I couldn't commit. My parents' divorce had me adopt a belief that love doesn't last. I pushed her away first, so she never had a chance to reject me later. If I'd bared my soul and she decided she didn't like my naked insecurities after all, then her rejection would ruin me. Yes, I own up to Emily's metaphor you told me about through text—I've got emotional cockroaches in my underwear." He laughs, "No wonder I had to push her away first so I could put my armored underwear back on."

"Ha-ha! At least we're laughing about this!"

"I let Brigette know I needed to pursue my newfound spiritual calling and told her I'm not wired for long-term monogamy. Did I want to walk away? Hell NO! She was the best thing that ever came into my life. It was painful to watch her meltdown after we broke up. She kept texting, emailing, and calling, but I ignored her. I armored up. I couldn't let myself be that vulnerable again.

"One time, I was open and shared how I was suspended at university for getting caught with marijuana. Brigette didn't say much, but her judgmental expression and silence told me everything I needed to know. She couldn't hold space for my imperfections and vulnerabilities. I desperately wanted her to accept all parts of me, and she showed me it wasn't safe to do so. She had a lot of emotional growing up to do, just like me. Some Twin Souls don't make it if the fears and shadows haven't been examined and removed. Brigette and I didn't seek counseling because I was too proud to admit there was anything wrong with me. It was easier to run than to do the serious inner work. We were too immature to understand that our unhealed traumas were the root causes of all the havoc. It was best to part ways.

"Because Brigette didn't react well to my first attempt at real vulnerability, I didn't tell her the truth—that I was fired for insubordination and cursing my boss out during a heated argument. I tried to get a new job, but I couldn't. I conveniently left out these details; white lies of omission, I suppose. I was afraid she would leave me if I told the truth. Instead, I told her that I chose to quit and got on a spiritual path."

"I'm learning so much from your innermost thoughts. I appreciate your radical honesty."

"Thank you. I felt that if Brigette were to reject me, it would bring up my painful abandonment issues. My mother abandoned my brother and me after my parents divorced when I was three. Now, it's easier to imagine Brigette with someone else because I'm the one who rejected her first. I told her she needed to move on and find her life partner. I was able to see her inner beauty and the potential she had not realized. She was still an emotional bébé chat [French for 'baby cat'] who needed a few more life experiences to become emotionally mature. After all, she was ten years younger than me."

"That makes sense."

"During our relationship, she pushed my buttons every time I saw her flirting or engaging with another guy at a party, or with men in our social circle who were richer, smarter, and better-looking. I knew I was attractive enough, but still. The little boys inside of me made me sweat, my heart pounded, and I froze because I didn't know how to overcome the jealousy. I would get passive-aggressive, and we would end up in another fight. I couldn't muster the courage to admit I was jealous. Unfortunately, this was one of the many challenges that erected walls between us."

"Fascinating . . . tell me more."

"I'm not proud of many things I've done. At twenty-eight, I got a girl pregnant from a one-night stand. She didn't want to abort, so I gave her a lump sum of cash to take care of the child. One of these days, I'll look for the kid I never met. During that time in my life, I got high and drunk a lot, and I slept with more beautiful women than I can count. I wasn't intimidated by their beauty because I didn't allow myself to get emotionally hooked. Brigette would be mortified if she ever found out what a playboy I was."

"Yeah . . . I get a felt sense that John has many secrets he would never share with me."

"Everyone has secrets. My spiritual journey has taught me that women who don't have their judging and criticizing parts front and center are women who have been through therapy—good therapy—not just the 'going around in circles talking to yourself' psychotherapy. And these women are also immersed in spiritually-oriented personal growth programs. When they've done the work, they can hold space for me to show every ugly wart I have and vice versa. When a man has done the inner work, he won't freak out when the woman expresses her deepest truths. They can handle the emotional storms without checking out."

"That's a truth bomb!"

"Yes. If I can find a beautiful woman like you who I'm intensely attracted to physically and emotionally, who makes me feel safe to reveal what I'm telling you right now, I would be more inclined to drop my masks. I'd rather die than suffer intense loss from a once-in-a-lifetime Twin Soul love."

"I get why you had to break it off with Brigette."

"Brigette will always be with me in spirit for the rest of my life. I know she loves me like no other person she's ever loved. I can't speak for all men, but my friends and I have discussed how safe it feels to date women one or two notches below our dream girl. The 'safe' ones don't stir up as many insecurities, and it doesn't hurt as much when the breakups happen. The vulnerabilities that Brigette stirred up were the same parts of me that self-sabotaged my career. Now you understand why many men become scared, insecure little boys when they meet their intelligent, ambitious, and beautiful soulmate."

"This makes so much sense," Jill says with a sigh of relief. "I feel like I'm in the power position because I'm a little spiritually ahead of John, and he's the runner, running away from his Higher Self and our deep connection. I keep chasing after him, to no avail."

"He sounds just like the old me!"

"Does this mean there's nothing I can do to influence John's decision about me?"

"There's nothing you can do. John must be ready to rise to meet your consciousness, peel off his masks, and be vulnerable. He can't do that until he goes through therapy and spiritual healing."

"That's so depressing!"

"I know. Just remember that if you continue to do the work and be the greatest version of you, then if you are star-crossed lovers, the Universe has ways of orchestrating the synchronicities to bring you two back together. You be the full-throttle you and forget about him. Detach from the outcome."

"Yes, I'm doing that. Are you dating other people now?"

"I am. It's been five years since Brigette and I last spoke or saw each other. When I yearn for physical touch, I date women who are safe, just plain safe. They don't stir up my deepest inadequacies or sexual performance issues. I can have sex with them and not be attached—the open-relationship thing. No commitments for now! Maybe one day, I'll be ready to face the rest of my unhealed parts and contact Brigette again, if she's even available. I will always love her until the day I die."

"Thank you for sharing the deeper layers of your story and thank you for validating my experiences. I have a deeper understanding now of men's insecurities and inferiority complexes. My girlfriends tell me to stop thinking about John since he's a married scumbag. They don't understand the spiritual connection part. They judge and criticize and keep saying, 'There are so many available men out there, stop obsessing over John.' I don't think they can imagine the level of connection John and I feel. We did have an amazing spiritual meditation experience and were physically affectionate. It brought us closer."

"I'm so happy for you! There were times I couldn't climax with Brigette. Parts of me took over to let me know I didn't deserve to experience so much pleasure with the love of my life. It's so fucked up how insecurities show up."

"This conversation increases my compassion for John and all the inner dragons he will have to slay. His rejection doesn't have anything to do with me. It's because he doesn't feel manly or alpha enough to be with me."

Pierre replies, "Yes, that's the truth. Here's another insight to help you see it from a man's perspective. I hope you won't be offended with more sexual metaphors."

"I'm okay with that."

"I'm glad you're allowing me to use sexual metaphors since men think about sex all the time. In a nutshell, my emotional penis is flaccid. If I want Brigette back, I need to grow the balls to make the emotional penis hard so I can show all the parts of who I am— especially the shameful secrets I've kept from her. When I can do this, this will align my parts with my soul, and I will feel oneness with myself and another. This feeling is transcendence and enlightenment. Achieving this can be scary because the emotional hard-on can go flaccid instantly if she rejects my vulnerabilities."

"Wow, you know how to pack a punch with your metaphor." Jill lets out a laugh. "Emily would sum it up as lack of Self-leadership dooming your career and love life."

"I'm a guy. I can say it this way. I own my shame, fears, and insecurities with you because I feel safe with you."

Jill replies, "Did you know that owning the shame and saying them out loud to the love of your life makes you a brave warrior? I realize with this conversation that John is not ready for this higher-level self-awareness journey, even though I feel like he's the other half of my soul."

"He'll be ready in his timeframe. It could be next week, could be six months, or five years from now. He may need to get bruised a little more and crash harder before he faces himself in the mirror and addresses his failure as a leader and lover."

"I agree. So sad. I remind myself that John's running away because he's so scared about what oneness with himself and oneness with me could mean—that he won't be able to hide anymore. His rejection has nothing to do with me—he loves me deeply. John has to slay his dragons on his own. Your vulnerability has been a godsend, Pierre," Jill says with heart-felt gratitude.

"I feel safe with you. You've inspired me to take maybe a baby step to contact Brigette. Let's keep each other posted!"

"Wow, that would be amazing if you dipped your toe in the water with her."

"Yeah, this conversation shifted my energy. Love you to the moon, Jilly! Au revoir."

"Love you too!"

They end the video call with air kisses.

◆　◆　◆

After the delightful and insightful video call with Pierre, Jill zooms out and writes out a psycho-spiritual explanation.

Even if John were divorced, based on the behaviors I've witnessed, there is no way he would entertain romance with me. John doesn't want to go into a relationship feeling like a beta and a fraud, which is what he feels like right now since he's not 100 percent on his game with his career and finances. His unresolved childhood issues make him fail.

It's too frightening for John to admit he feels like a failure to the woman he's in love with. If he got naked with the truth of his shortcomings and how he feels like a fuck-up, he would be afraid she would say good-bye. He doesn't feel good enough or rich enough. Rejection by the woman of his dreams would be unbearable, so it's safe to keep her at arm's length. I'm also stupid for obsessing over John since I shouldn't be in love with a married man. But, I'm future-oriented and am always thinking of new possibilities.

John is not 100 percent sure I would want a relationship with him (after divorce) after spilling his truth because I may not put up with his lack of multi-million-dollar success. Being a millionaire is how he identifies himself and his self-worth. His current reality is not congruent with the multi-millionaire self-concept. John may have exaggerated his successes all along to try to prove his alpha-ness to me. Instead of doing inner work that would have been constructive, he wasted his efforts on the outer "show," honing his skill at fooling others and even himself. He feels like a fraud and doesn't feel worthy of me. Therefore, he can't be radically honest because he can't face himself in the mirror.

As Jill reads back her assessment, tears of compassion fall freely. *I can love him and not be entangled. I'm ready to move on and find a man who cherishes me and my greatness.* Later that day, Jill gets an email from Pierre:

Jill,

I forgot to tell you a few other things. *The Seat of the Soul* by Gary Zukav became a bestseller because of Oprah. The book talks about the yearning to merge our personality with our soul, to come to oneness and enlightenment. The book is dense at first and may not make sense, but once you're ready for it, you realize it's one of the most influential books on spirituality. When I read it the first time, before Brigette came into my life, I didn't understand the concepts. I've been rereading it now AB—after Brigette. Now I get it. The yearning we all have is a longing to merge our personality with our soul, to become "whole," and to find the meaning of why things happened in the way they did.

I researched the Internal Family Systems model. What Zukav's book covers is about the Soul or Self merging with the *parts* of the personality to become one cohesive team—the Inner Team—that's on the same sheet of music with what the Soul/Self wants to achieve. Letting the Soul/Self lead is coming home to our essence and authentic self.

It's funny, as I did this research on IFS and how it relates to what Zukav wrote, I'm becoming more enlightened and encouraged. Maybe I will grow the balls sooner rather than later to contact Brigette. Perhaps I can do it safely by mentioning spiritual books like *The Seat of the Soul* to get the discussion started. If she gets my lingo, I'll know she's been working on herself, and it may be safe to re-engage.

The other excellent book I read was *The Mask of Masculinity* by Lewis Howes. I was the epitome of the masked investment banker asshole. My cocky ego— or shall I say my immature dick—ran the insecurity show. My ego made sure everyone knew how great I was and how big my manhood was. No wonder some men are called 'dickheads'! Ha-ha! ☺

Still love you,
Pierre

Jill replies:

Pierre,

Do you realize that if you have the exact conversation with Brigette that you just wrote in this email, she can gain respect for your courageous and confident vulnerability around the parts you're not so thrilled about? If you open the doorway with discussions about spiritual books, you'll see if she's emotionally and intellectually ready to move forward with spiritual love. -Jill

A few minutes later, Pierre responds:

Yeah. Good idea. Real quick—Zukav's follow-up book, *Spiritual Partnerships,* is very insightful. The book says the purpose of a spiritual partnership is not about romance per se; it's about the partner triggering all the frightened parts of your personality. The scared parts of us are still stuck in the past. Healing these inner child parts will unlock the couple's joint mission to make the world a better place. Spiritual love is not selfish; it's about creating synergy for the greater good of the planet.

Jill writes back:

Thanks so much. You give me hope!

In the following weeks, Jill's meditations and tears release her attachment to John. He is now stored away in a back compartment of her heart. She's ready to start a new chapter in love and career.

◆　◆　◆

In the meantime, John's life is imploding. His parts are in chaos. He has completely shut down, lost connection to Self, and is only going through the motions. He decides to offload the noisy inner critic into a Word document during his morning commute.

Oh, dear God, what are you doing to me? Are you messing with my head and heart by bringing Jill into my life? My ego made me self-sabotage. I'm so embarrassed she witnessed the worst parts of me.

I've pushed her away, and I didn't want to. My ego can't take her X-ray vision into my BS. I know she senses I'm keeping secrets. I'm not worthy of her. I find myself bragging to no end to remind her of what I've accomplished. Meeting her made me see what a loser I am. What a disaster getting caught and fired for breaking the rules at Zatuck. Then I blew the opportunity to be the hero in our business.

- Am I ever going to be good enough to be the man that the woman of my dreams deserves?
- What if another man comes along and sweeps her away? I'd be so crushed. I don't think I could survive the rejection.
- Will she still love me if I reveal all the bad things I've done?
- What if she rejects me after she learns how broken and insecure I am underneath my masks?

Her badass emails were too painful to read because she was right. Ugh! God, I can't believe I let an amazing woman witness my failure and see through my white lies of omission. I sure know how to screw up royally.

Chapter 30

Emotional Progress

October 2017

A month after the business and friendship failures with Jill, John is blindsided when Liz tells him she found a lawyer and has started the divorce paperwork. He didn't think it was going to happen for at least six years, after their youngest enters college. John also thought he would be the one initiating the break-up, not her.

"I've had it! I can't take being married to you," Liz shouts. "Get out and find an apartment!"

"Okay." John is stunned but instinctively knows there is no negotiating here.

◆ ◆ ◆

Now that John's life is in the toilet—getting fired, failing in business with Jill and Shelly, incurring financial damages from the divorce—he finally absorbs that *he* caused these failures. *Antonio was right. I had to hit rock bottom.* John reaches out to his best friend.

When Antonio answers the phone, John says, "I've bottomed out. I need help! I got fired, Jill left me, and my wife kicked me out of the house! I'm broke, drinking way too much, and I feel like crap! I'm borrowing money from my parents to pay the bills. Jill told me all along I needed to address my demons. I can't run away from myself anymore."

"Okay, I hear you, buddy. You're right. It's time to man-up and do the work. You seemed pretty impressed with the gal who ran the workshop on the Cape—call her!"

"I guess I better call Emily."

"You'll get through this. Hope is around the corner."

◆　◆　◆

John calls Emily to see if she's willing to take him on. She tells him, "Yes, I can fit you in. I love working with alpha males. I'll get you out of the dark tunnel."

John breathes a sigh of relief.

"But wait, you worked with Jill, and she probably shared all my dirty secrets with you."

"Yes, I've heard some of the stories, but of course, my work with Jill focused on her. I'm not here to judge or take sides. I've worked with many couples and business partners. I get curious and see what parts of you contributed to the struggles and explain things from the higher psycho-spiritual perspective so we can heal your parts."

"Great! When can we start?"

"Next Tuesday."

◆　◆　◆

During John's initial visit, Emily establishes the frame and psychological safety to let him know he's free to raise any fears and concerns about the Internal Family System process. "I'm going to hold space for whatever comes up and stay curious and connected. I'll never judge any parts that want to express."

"That's reassuring."

"Good. Let's start with a few deep, grounding breaths." John follows. "Now, I'm curious to see if there are any parts that may be concerned about going deep to get to know your inner world."

"Yes, there's a part that's concerned with going back into the past. I don't want to relive the pain." John shudders slightly, just from imagining the journey back to childhood.

Emily guides him to unblend from the armored part that's afraid to go back into the past to revisit the pain. This part is concerned that if he went back into old memories, he would not recover from the raw emotions. Emily talks directly to this protector.

"I want to reassure you that the Internal Family Systems model of accessing Self to heal parts is gentle and safe. John will not go into any vulnerable memories until all the protectors permit him to do so. If we encounter a scene that is a bit scary, we can place that little John in another room, and Higher Self can talk to little John through a window. My role is to facilitate you to access Self so that Self forms loving connections with your protectors and exiles. If an exile gets emotional, we can ask him to dial down the emotion so as not to overwhelm you. Everything we do is permission based; nothing is forced."

John and his protector feel relief with this reassurance. He's heard stories from friends who came out of therapy sessions feeling worse than when they went in.

"The IFS protocol is safe and transformative. You'll feel better at the end of every session. Progress will be made, unlike some methodologies where it seems like you're going around in circles talking to yourself." With that certitude, he is ready to dive in.

John shares how ashamed he feels with living a life of lies. He's tired of being called a narcissist. Emily reassures him that he's not a narcissist, he just has narcissistic parts in extreme roles protecting his low self-worth exiles who are still stuck in the past. She guides John through a meditation to unblend from the self-centered part so he can get to know it. Self-centeredness shares it is afraid that if it didn't do its job, John would be invisible.

Emily: "Does self-centered part know that if it keeps it up, you'll fail in your career and love life?"

John: "No, it doesn't have the updates that I've screwed up big time!"

John befriends and talks to Self-centeredness. Then, the self-centered protector shows the exiles it protects.

J: "I see the seven-year-old who was forced into tennis at age four. By the time he was seven, he was sick and tired of Dad's constant criticism during practices, haranguing him about not progressing faster and criticizing his emotional outbursts. The directive to perform for Dad's approval was a huge burden. It was all about Dad's image and not about how *I* felt about tennis."

E: "Do you see you've become like your dad in how you relate to others? Where it's all about you and your image?"

J: "I just realized that; so embarrassing." [Places his elbows on his knees and slumps down to cover his face. His eyes water.]

E: "Is this the seven-year-old crying now?"

J: "Yes, it's him that's emotional."

E: "If he's okay with it, acknowledge and hug him. Is this level of emotion okay for you?"

J: "Yes, it's not too bad. Both the seven-year-old and the four-year-old have been waiting for me to rescue them from the tennis court."

E: "Yes, they have. Do they know who you are?"

J: "I'll let them know. 'Hey, I'm the adult version of you.'" [Goes inward and silently converses with the exiles.]

E: "How do you feel toward them now?"

J: "I love them."

Emily continues to guide John to dialogue with the exiles. They let John know how badly Dad and the tennis coaches berated them. John's Self heals the vulnerable parts by witnessing their negative experiences.

E: "Please ask these parts what beliefs they took on as a result of the tennis court experiences."

J: "They said they took on beliefs of *I'm never going to be good enough* and *I'm only going to be loved when I achieve.*"

E: "No wonder Self-centeredness grew out of these wounds. This protector shouts from the rooftop to let everyone know how great you are so you can receive praise."

J: "That sounds about right."

E: "Self-centered part was developed at a very young age to cope with feeling powerless. The protector helped you get noticed and promoted. It no longer serves you, right? Bragging and not listening alienate people."

J: "Yes, Self-centeredness gets that now. It resorted to boasting to prevent rejection. But, boasting created rejection instead. A self-fulfilling prophecy for sure!"

Emily continues the session to help John unburden the exiles. The self-centered part released its grip by 50 percent, not 100 percent. There are other exiles self-centered part protect that haven't been retrieved yet. The self-centered part is happy to transform into a new role of humility when all the exiles it protects unburden.

Chapter 31

Protectors in the Bedroom

John loves the psycho-spiritual explanations of why his world turned upside-down, especially after Jill came into his life. He finally realizes that continuing to wear his alpha masks will block the achievement of his goals. John feels ashamed that Jill saw right through his BS. He feels horrible that he's been the common denominator of all the struggles with work and personal relationships.

John relives how just kissing and cuddling with Jill in Cape Cod and the SoHo hotel room felt like out-of-body spiritual experiences. Emily tells him, "You experienced the epitome of Self-to-Self, heart-to-heart, pure conscious loving connection, which has the power to take you into altered states of consciousness."

"Yes, it felt like we transported into another dimension. It was dreamy. I can relive those warm and fuzzy feelings over and over again."

"Beautiful! That's Self-led intimacy, nirvana, and enlightenment. No amount of money, status, and things can give you this ecstatic feeling. The more you do the work to heal and balance the inner family system of Self and parts, the more access you will have to this yummy inner state. Right now, the exiles' emotional scars hold you back from accessing greater Self-leadership."

"Now that I feel very comfortable with you, there is something I've been confused and embarrassed about," John continues.

"I've heard it all. Whatever it is, it's just a *part* we need to get curious about. I'm all ears with no judgments," Emily puts him at ease with her heart. John is visibly relieved.

"Reflecting on my relationships, including the most recent meditation experience with Jill, there have been times when I desperately wanted to climax, but it felt like I had armored soldiers guarding my orgasms. What's that about?"

"There are many reasons for blockages. A common blocker is a part that is preoccupied with the to-do list; Self is absent. Another part that prevents orgasm is the part that *needs* to reach homerun; this is attaching to an outcome. It's paradoxical; the more you overthink the orgasm goal—because you want it so badly—the more likely you won't come. When you're in Self and in the present moment and not thinking about the goal, that's when orgasms are effortless."

"I get that, but I feel like there are deeper layers behind those obvious reasons. After she came, when she started stroking me, I got out of my heart and into my head."

"You may have had parts that weren't ready to give a woman the pleasure of witnessing your pleasure. It's a form of control."

"Ahhh . . . that's my controlling part that wants to feel the power of not letting her witness my pleasure? I do have to lose control to climax, and my controlling part didn't want to feel powerless."

"Bingo!"

"That makes a lot of sense because I feel emasculated by Jill because she called me out on my rogue ways many times."

"If you feel powerless or emasculated, your control part can prevent your orgasms as a way of not giving her the power to make you come. Underneath this control protector is the younger John's that felt powerless. If Jill triggers these vulnerable John's, the control part can show up to hold you back from giving her the gift of witnessing your climax."

"This explains why I had performance anxiety issues in past relationships too."

"Your parts, instead of Self, run the show because they are afraid of feeling powerless. Many personal growth experts and books on how beliefs form say that the subconscious is ninety percent responsible for your results. What lurks in the subconscious are the beliefs the exiles imprinted from emotionally wounding experiences. When you don't do the work to have legitimate love affairs with your parts, it contributes to the inability to climax in leadership and love, literally and metaphorically."

John shakes his head and lets out a self-deprecating chuckle. "Yeah, that is what's happening for sure. Let's do the work on the part that wouldn't let me climax."

John looks at the wall and points to the poster of the cartoon by Sako Asko Emily showed at the Self-leadership workshop in Cape Cod.

"The first step to change is awareness. You're doing great, John. You will transcend these protector-based hiccups."

"I feel so hopeful with your guidance."

Emily guides him through the initial IFS steps to separate/unblend from the part that wouldn't allow him to climax with Jill. The part, to him, looks like a bowling ball at the end of his penis. Emily takes a marble from her desk drawer to represent his "bowling ball/no climax" protector.

Emily: "What would Bowling Ball like you to know about its job?"

John: "His job is to stop me from coming . . . [Continues to stare at the marble.] . . . to prevent Jill from having my semen . . . to show I'm in control . . . a barrier to emotional closeness . . . not give her the pleasure of witnessing my pleasure . . . can't give her the power of my semen. Oh boy, this sounds warped." [Slumps down and buries his face in his hands.]

E: "It's not sick. This part has a job to protect you. What's this part afraid would happen if it didn't do its job of holding you back from climaxing?"

J: "It will be harder to run away from the deep emotional connection with Jill. I will have to come clean and get naked with how phony I've been. That will be embarrassing!"

E: "What is this part afraid would happen if you came clean with everything and shed your masks?"

J: "I would be as naked as naked can be and she may not like it. She will conclude that I'm a fraud, an impostor, who is not good enough for her. Then, she would reject me."

E: "The fear of not being loved by her because you don't have as much anymore is the number one fear I hear from men; it's the top reason why men push great women away. What would happen if she rejected you?"

J: "I would feel so ashamed of how inadequate I am. The rejection would confirm that I *am* a loser after all!"

E: "Let the part know that you get why it had to protect you from climaxing."

J: [Silently looks at the marble and lets it know.] "Okay, he appreciates that I heard his story."

E: "What else does this part want you to know?"

J: [Continues to look at the marble.] "This part pushed away many great girlfriends. Even though Jill isn't a girlfriend, we've had a relationship, and my protectors pushed her away. She rejected me because I wore many masks. [Waits for the part to answer.] The part is sorry that it caused her to reject me. The inability to climax represents my failure as a leader. The part was too ashamed to release in front of the woman of my dreams." [Eyes water and then tears flow.]

E: "That's a great insight. Is this part ready to show you the exile it protects?"

J: "Yes. It's protecting the same four-year-old from the last session. He was forced to play tennis. Because he didn't have a say in the matter, he felt powerless."

E: "Jill, the beautiful, radiant light that she is, has repeatedly triggered one of your biggest core wounds. She's been a gift. She has urged you to look in the mirror. The powerless four-year-old has driven your parts into extreme nonproductive roles in the boardroom and bedroom."

J: "I see that. I want to solve this problem."

E: "Let's re-visit the four-year-old again."

Emily steers John to visit the four-year-old exile again who felt powerless with Dad due to how he was forced into tennis. The four-year-old had more burdens to release; he only partially unburdened at the last session.

"I feel like Jill has been the laxative that activated the stuck emotional poop to release," John says as he lets out a chuckle. "God, I can't believe I just said that!"

Emily sprays some of the water she just gulped down. His analogy is a surprise but accurate.

"That's a good one! You shut down and ran when you felt exposed because you didn't want her anywhere near your stinky crap. You need to clean up the poop with IFS hand sanitizer so you can go back into the bedroom with clean underwear. Oh my, you have me rolling here."

They crack up with laughter.

"This session has been so freeing and humorous. I feel so much lighter from healing the four-year-old. He's safe with me now, and Dad can no longer hurt him."

During the subsequent sessions, John discusses how he has a lot of trouble with focus and being impeccable with his words. He wishes he could be more structured and organized to get things done. He wants to regain trust and respect from others. Emily leads him to reveal the exile that felt neglected by his alcoholic mom. John got clarity on how he sought external validation through money, power, material things, and extramarital affairs.

Emily invites John to read Lewis Howes' book, *The Mask of Masculinity*. John recalls Antonio mentioning the title. This book will help him understand the masks men wear: stoic mask, athlete mask, money mask, sexual mask, aggressive mask, joker mask, invincible mask, know-it-all mask, and alpha mask. Shedding these masks via the Internal Family Systems model is a powerful way to free men from the emotional prisons of their past and into the freedom and joy of a Self-led "all parts are welcome!" life. Emily also recommends John read two other important books: *The Way of the Superior Man: A Spiritual Guide to Mastering the Challenges of Women, Work, and Sexual* by David Deida and *The Masculine in Relationship: A Blueprint for Inspiring the Trust, Lust, and Devotion of a Strong Woman* by GS Youngblood.

Chapter 32

New Beginnings

After the business and friendship divorce from John, Jill lets her network of connections know she is ready for a new position. Three weeks into her job search, Jill lands a senior marketing position at a digital marketing company. Before onboarding, she decides to go to Bali. A stay at a spiritual healing center will help her get centered, allow her to meditate, and release tensions built up from the three-year emotional roller coaster with John. A well-known personal growth guru will lead the weeklong spiritual retreat.

During a hot yoga session on the first day of the program, Jill notices a handsome guy with his shirt off. It's difficult for her to tear her eyes away from his physique. *He must take care of his body like a temple, with healthy nutrition and exercise. He is a man I can fall for, at least physically. Maybe I'll get to talk to him later in the week. He must be on a spiritual journey.* Jill's thoughts turn to sex—*What would it be like to make love to this man? The erotic goddess part of me is dying to come out and play.*

Low and behold, the next day, this handsome man sits next to her during the group lunch. "Hi there, my name is Ron." He looks at the name tag on her sky-blue linen tank dress that tastefully teases her cleavage. "You're Jill, nice to meet you."

"Likewise. Great to meet you, Ron," Jill says as she feels a slight flush in her face.

Ron looks to be in his forties, about two inches over six feet, with a full head of curly brown hair. The white polo shirt he wears hugs the curves of his well-defined biceps. He's not too muscular like the heavy-duty weightlifters, but muscular enough to make you sigh. The two of them hit it off from the get-go. All thoughts of John fly out the window. It turns out that Ron lives just outside NYC, in Stamford, Connecticut. He's a patent attorney on a mission to get his life centered after a difficult divorce five years ago. Jill and Ron are smitten. Occasionally Jill thinks about John, which makes her sad. *John is so dear to my heart, but I know we are not meant to be together. He's hurting, and who knows if he'll ever do the inner work. If he did, his finances, business, and relationships would improve, and then . . . oh, I have to stop this! I can't count on anything. I've released him once and for all. John's in a special compartment in my heart. He was a catalyst for me to become the woman I was meant to become. In the meantime, I cannot deny that I'm attracted to Ron, in different ways than John.*

Back in the States after the retreat, Jill and Ron embark on a full-blown romance, with minimal drama and lots of good times. Now, Jill can't imagine life without Ron. He's a great catch, humble and centered. He's worked on himself and is on a spiritual journey, attending at least two self-development seminars a year. *I like this guy; he's stable and successful. I can imagine marrying him.*

After eight months of a whirlwind romance, Ron pops the question, and Jill accepts his proposal. Jill secures a wedding date and venue for November 2018, three months after the proposal.

To clear the final residues of John from her heart, Jill writes a letter to him that she's never going to mail. Then, Jill writes a letter back, addressed to herself, a response she imagines would be an ideal one from John. She then feels the clean break and start anew with Ron. So, on an Indian summer day in October, she sits cross-legged. She closes her eyes on the beach at Cove Island Wildlife Sanctuary in Connecticut, meditating as she transmits the letter's message to John over the waves of air and water—*I love you always, John. I'll see you in the next lifetime. My heart is ready for my new love.*

Opening her eyes, Jill lets out a big sigh, then lies on her blanket and cries for the next thirty minutes. Afterward, walking through the beach grass, the release of energy feels therapeutic and freeing. She's ready to walk down the aisle next month.

As Jill embarks on wedding-related errands, she thinks about the mental bullet points demonstrating why Ron is the perfect fit for life partnership—*He's kind and sensitive and treats me with respect. I'm attracted to him. Although he's not a 9.5 out of 10 attraction on every level like John, he's still a seven or eight across the board in physical, emotional, intellectual, and spiritual attraction. He's much more even-keeled than John and doesn't have a lot of baggage he projects onto me because he has worked on himself. His financial stability and success are a reflection of a man solid in his mission and purpose. Being with Ron is safe.*

Chapter 33

All Parts Are Welcome

After six months of weekly IFS sessions and another six months of biweekly meetings, John is a "new" person. His increased self-awareness and self-healing have positioned his Higher Self front and center. Not only does he feel great, but others also notice his increased presence, connection, compassion, curiosity, and clarity. John receives many compliments. He doesn't fly off the handle or stonewall to the extent he used to. Emily notices his transformation as well, and she is thrilled that he's emerged from his darkest days.

One of the most critical things Emily teaches John is how to speak *for* his parts from Self. Emily reminds him that, "Parts are welcome at the appropriate time and in proper doses. A surefire way to fail is to *blend* into extreme parts where Self-energy is missing in action. When you know you have parts that can rub others the wrong way, it's best to let them know what to expect from you proactively."

Through IFS sessions, John got to know many of his protectors, including Pain in the Ass, Debate, Fear of Commitment, and Hater of Details. These parts can ruin personal and professional relationships if they are not proactively managed. Emily gives John examples of how to speak *from* Self's calm energy *for* these parts.

John practices: "I want to give you a heads-up that I have this debate part that may rub you the wrong way. I want to speak for this part with calm energy and not from the part. This part comes out when it wants to challenge the status quo. It wants you to think differently and go outside the box. Please don't take it as a personal attack. If you notice that this part needs to dial down a bit—because it can get argumentative and overbearing—please nicely ask this part to take a break. For example, I will say something like: 'Jane, you make a good point. Will it be okay if my debate part explores another perspective? I would like to have a healthy discussion of all possibilities, so we leave no stone unturned before making the final decision.'"

"That was good, John."

"I understand it now. When I speak *for* the part from Self, with calm energy, instead of speaking *from* the debate part, which can have combative or patronizing energy, the Self-energy I exude calms the receiver, so they don't feel the need to get defensive."

"Yes!"

John also learns how to speak for his biggest shortcoming: "Because I'm a visionary who likes to build colorful castles in the sky, you may notice I have a fear of commitment part that avoids committing and jumping into building one of these castles on the ground. I know this frustrates some of you who love to dig into the weeds and execute the hows. I permit you to call me out when I'm too much in the clouds, and you can ask me as many detailed questions as necessary. Your questions will help me gain more clarity on my ideas so I can commit to a plan of action. I need the brilliance of each and every one of you to bring my ideas to life."

Emily gives John an example from the romance department: "I love you. I love our time together, but I'm not ready for a long-term relationship. I need to work through my fear of commitment and abandonment issues before I jump into a serious relationship. Past relationships ending badly have repeatedly reinjured the three-year-old part of me who felt abandoned by the way my caregivers treated me."

John feels a bit overwhelmed. "How am I going to remember how to do this? It seems so complicated."

"For the last year, I've been assisting you with having conversations with your parts. This Self-led way of speaking *for* your parts is no different than telling stories about your parts. It's like telling a story about your seven-year-old son. When you externalize, or unblend, the parts in front of you, it's relatively easy to speak for what's going on inside you without feeling embarrassed about their roles, fears, and concerns. When you share your parts' stories, it gives others permission to tell you when they are frustrated with your parts. They learn it's okay to speak up, that you won't take it personally or get upset with them."

"I get it now. Because I'm more emotionally intelligent, it's easier to think on my feet to speak for parts. I don't have to remember a complicated formula, just stay present in Self."

"Exactly!"

"And I love how the IFS way is useful in all situations, especially the romantic ones." John thinks of Jill as he says this.

"Yes, it is quite powerful for building intimacy in and out of the bedroom," Emily says with a wink.

"If only Jill could witness my transformation—wishful thinking," John says with an air of sadness. "I questioned how Jill could be in love with such a flawed and cocky person like me, and now I know why she saw through my crap and loved me anyway. She loved my soul."

"She sure did love your soul!"

"She fell in love with my soul, my Higher Self. She was waiting for my parts to heal. I have no idea if she'll ever come back into my life. I saw on Facebook that she is getting married."

"Yes, she sent me a picture of her new beau. You never know what the Universe has in store for you in the future. Surrender."

"I have no choice but to surrender."

"Let me remind you of this. Every adverse event was a gift. It is empowering to believe that the Universe purposely gave you the adverse events of your life for the evolution of your soul. It is up to you to make lemonade out of these lemons. When you are fueled by lemonade, you hop out of bed to greet the day with a new attitude and meaning. The privilege of a lifetime is to be authentically you in your career and relationships."

"Thank you, that was perfect for reminding me to reframe my life story."

◆ ◆ ◆

October 2018

It's been a year since the beautiful "oneness" email John received while he was on the commuter train, where Jill said she felt ravished and cherished during their tryst in the SoHo hotel room. He has become very reflective and decides to flesh things out. *If I had the guts, this is the letter I would send to Jill.*

My dearest Jill,

I fucked up big time. My fears and insecurities got the best of me. I apologize for what an asshole I've been. My ego had me exaggerate previous successes so that you would be impressed. It backfired. Now I know you were not impressed since you saw right through me and called me out. I am eternally grateful for that.

You wanted to talk things out, but I was afraid that your brilliant line of questioning would make me admit how badly I was doing. You would catch me in my white lies and half-truths, so I avoided in-depth truth-telling conversations. I couldn't risk having you see what a loser I was! You deserve someone way better than me.

Your confidence, intelligence, humility, vulnerability, and courage scared the living daylights out of me. And . . . you have the nerve to be drop-dead gorgeous on top of that? I'm not good enough for you, and I don't know if I can ever become good enough. I needed your brilliance for our business, but I couldn't even make that work. WTF is wrong with me?! Emily shared that I couldn't climax in leadership, and I couldn't climax in love because I wasn't in a love affair with my burdened parts. She's so right!

You knocked me off my alpha pedestal. I am grateful that you shined the light on my phoniness. Otherwise, I may never have faced myself in the mirror. Thank you, Jill, for being you. You are beyond amazing, and I love you so much. Words aren't enough to convey the depth of how I feel about you.

John rereads the confessional. He feels sad and ashamed for how his protectors made him become a miserable loser, a loser who self-sabotaged the best thing that came into his life—Jill. In the past, feeling this misery meant he would have stepped into the nearest bar to numb the emotional pain. But now, his safe place is being in Emily's office, working through his emotions.

Chapter 34

Didn't See This One Coming

November 2018

On the plane ride home from their Mediterranean honeymoon on the island of Mallorca, Jill gets an uneasy feeling in the pit of her stomach. She likes to journal on most days, but she forgot to throw her journal into the suitcase with the rush of wedding activities. When Jill arrives home, she looks in her lingerie drawer, where the journal is usually kept; it's not there. She frantically searches her desk and bookcases—nothing. *My deepest secrets are in that journal. God forbid if Ron got a hold of it!* Finally, she glances at Ron's messy dresser, spotting something resembling a corner of a small, dark gray book under a t-shirt and one of his tchotchkes, a mug commemorating a bicycle race with his college buddies. She moves the T-shirt and the beer stein aside and opens to the last page she wrote in her journal. She's horrified that one of her most intimate passages about her love for John has been crumpled up.

First angry, then feeling ashamed, she confronts Ron and apologizes, only to be stunned to hear him say, "No, I'm the one who should apologize. The journal was laying on the driveway. It must have fallen out of your bag the day before we left for our honeymoon." *Shit! That was the day after the wedding, where I absentmindedly put the journal in my bag and didn't notice it was missing.* "I opened it and read it while you were out shopping. I decided not to bring it up during the honeymoon."

"No wonder I felt a block in your heart in Spain," Jill shares cautiously to make sure Ron doesn't go off on her.

"I should be angry with you, but I get how you feel a forever bond with this guy. But I can't play second fiddle to John. Have you been lying to me all along that you're over him—because I—"

Jill cuts in, "No, he's out of my life for good now—John and I are done. I have no clue where he is now."

"I don't believe that. But, never mind. Listen, remember how we talked about our most soulful relationships? How I didn't feel worthy of my ex-girlfriend—the one I was in love with?"

"Yes—" Jill says with a curious tone.

"My ex contacted me the week before our wedding and wanted to try again. I was torn and didn't know what to do. Then I had your journal. After I read it, I had such a swirl of emotions—anger, hurt, feelings for my ex, regrets, feeling both inferior in your eyes while superior that you were the one not being honest. I couldn't sort it all out instantly and just continued with the course we were on. I thought after making us 'official,' things might feel different, resolved, and smooth sailing. But, on our honeymoon, did it feel genuine to you?"

"No."

"We don't need to settle. At least I feel that I don't. You know I love you, but this is not the once-in-a-lifetime love we both deserve. Now I know we both need to be with other people."

"But why not try again to—"

"Why don't you try with John? I know you still love him, and I'm still in love with Karen."

Jill is stunned but can sense the truth in what Ron is saying. She hangs her head and says in a small voice, "Yes, I know we're both settling. But—"

"How about we get an annulment or a quickie divorce?"

"Wow," Jill says, reaching for the wall and sliding down to the floor, breathing heavily. After a minute, she looks up. "I thought I would be devastated, but I feel relieved. Now I know why people get cold feet right before a wedding. We should have canceled the wedding; but, neither of us was brave enough to address the elephant in the room."

"That's for sure!"

"Okay, I guess the Universe had our backs all along. Thank you for being so kind and gentle with this conversation." They move toward each other and hug.

The next day, they find an attorney and file for an uncontested divorce. As they walk out the door smiling, their lawyer says, "This is the happiest divorce I've ever seen. You'd think you were applying for a marriage license."

Jill and Ron decide to wait a bit before telling their friends and family about their decision. Since Jill had moved into Ron's condo in Connecticut just before the wedding, they decided she should move out and return to Manhattan.

Chapter 35

From Shallow to Deep

December 2018

Rearranging her belongings in her new Chelsea apartment, Jill feels shaky and sad to be alone again. Yet, another side of her is happy, free, and thanking Spirit for the chance to find a man who can meet her all the way. *I have no idea where John's at. He may be in an emotional ditch somewhere.* Jill trusts that the Universe will deliver a unique spiritual warrior who is ready for an awakened goddess. She feels grateful and happy that Ron was so honest and okay with dissolving the marriage so that they can both find a love that stirs their souls.

By late afternoon, she pours a glass of wine, sits on her balcony, and nods off.

When Jill awakens from her nap, she downloads her thoughts about what she wants out of a partnership. *I am writing this down to embody the feelings as if I'm already with my King, so the Universe can use my up-leveled vibration to manifest this special man.* She writes in her journal:

An ideal life with my spiritual warrior King means . . .

- I feel protected.
- I feel safe.
- I feel led.
- I feel cherished.
- I feel ravished.
- I feel witnessed.

- I feel loved.
- I feel safe to surrender.
- I feel safe to crack open my heart.
- I love his energy.
- I love his hugs and kisses.
- I trust his leadership.
- He listens well and knows how to hold space.
- He holds me tight through our emotional firestorms.
- He's conscious and present.
- He's confident and intelligent.
- He's handsome, healthy, and fit.
- He's spiritually evolved and always working on himself, or willing to.
- He's emotionally available.
- He's a lifelong learner.
- He smells good.
- He knows how to create sexual tension with the simplest gestures.
- He communicates clearly with radical honesty and vulnerability.
- He feels the slightest shifts in my energy and wants to know what's going on.
- He knows how to lead the dance of spiritual love and sacred intimacy.
- He's not afraid of hard conversations and loves conscious communication.
- We swirl in Self-energy.
- We are turned on by each other's fearless self-expression of all parts, especially the vulnerable ones.
- We're always curious, never furious.
- We laugh, sing, and dance.
- We are impeccable with our words.
- We talk nonstop when we want to, and also honor silence and space.
- We find God and oneness through sex.
- Our eyes sparkle when we look at each other.
- We transcend and get in touch with Spirit through soulful eye-gazing.
- Our hearts become one and melt into each other when we dance and make love.
- We are two evolved rare diamonds custom-made for each other.
- Beauty finally has a witness.

Jill decides to add another entry into her journal about the things Emily taught her about what men genuinely want from their women in a hetero-normative relationship. *Men are not hairy women. They want to be appreciated, respected, trusted, and admired.* Jill types these four desires that men wish into the phone to remind herself to give her man what he needs.

After this journal entry, Jill knows her warrior wish list is a pretty far-fetched list of attributes to expect in *one* guy. Still, she imagines being in this kind of relationship anyways since quantum physics teachings say thoughts activate feelings; and feeling the wish fulfilled is the key to allowing the Universe to pull in the desired outcomes. Jill meditates and wells up with tears of joy at how "right" and ecstatic it feels to be with her King. With hope for the future, Jill decides to see the new movie that is all abuzz, the remake of *A Star is Born*, with Bradley Cooper and Lady Gaga.

The movie stirs Jill to tears. *The chemistry between Bradley and Gaga is insane! I want their spiritual love! No wonder people can't stop talking about the movie. John and I have that kind of intensity. But a deep love like this may not survive.* As she leaves the theater, she notices many men have tears in their eyes, too. *Wow, I can see how Jackson's journey can hit close to home, where he buried his shame and unhealed inner demons behind booze.* Jill can't stop humming the movie's signature song, "Shallow."

Jill feels like the movie depicted a similar journey she and John traversed. John came into her life to activate her to the next level of growth and greatness while he tumbled down due to his unresolved emotional baggage.

As the weeks go by, Jill can't stop thinking about the film and often belts out "Shallow" at the top of her lungs. John is on her mind every day, but she's detached from needing to be in touch with him. *Is he divorced? Did he hit rock-bottom? Is he working on himself?* She's open to meeting a new man who will become her life partner.

Waking up in the middle of a dream about John, Jill is inspired to write a Self-led email and send a video of herself singing "Shallow." *I have nothing to lose. I want him to know that I still care.*

Jill's hands shake as she hits "record" on her iPhone. She finds the "Shallow" karaoke track on YouTube. She takes a deep breath to calm herself and looks into the camera. Jill introduces the video. "Hi John, how are you? I was moved to tears when I saw *A Star is Born*. I saw the parallels of what we went through depicted in that movie. The 'Shallow' lyrics hit me hard."

Jill proceeds to sing from her soul like Lady Gaga. After she finishes, she continues to look into the camera. "That song asks about your happiness. It also asks what you're looking for. I searched for depth of consciousness, and you gave me glimpses of that consciousness when you were present and playful. The song asks what you need to fill in your life. We yearned for validation, and we gave each other validation. But in the end, the primary validation we needed was self-validation and self-love. Great leaders need to have a healthy love affair with their parts, first and foremost. Sadly, your fears got in the way. We dove into the deep end of triggering each other, with no turning back. Through IFS sessions, I became more self-aware and a better version of myself. You were my Jackson, the main character in the movie, my catalyst. I send lots of love to you, my friend. And now, I'd like to read you the gratitude note I wrote. I'll send this to you via email, too."

My dearest John,

How are you? It's been a while since we've communicated. I miss you. I miss our friendship. Please note that there aren't any hidden agendas in this note. I want to share how deeply grateful I am.

You were brought into my life to activate the dormant parts that I didn't even know existed. I had been hiding behind many masks so I could feel like I was someone important.

Because of you, I became the person I was always meant to grow into, including becoming courageously vulnerable to express all that I am—including my darkness. You played a big part in activating me to the next level of my potential, and you helped to shine the flashlight into the badass egoic parts of me that were devoid of Self-leadership. Thank you.

In reflecting on my communications with you, I feel embarrassed at most of the things I said. My controlling ego, judgments, and criticisms messed us up. I was in my fear-based analytical head, and I had no idea how disconnected I was from my heart. My fear-based attachments to your success, my success, and our success ultimately doomed our success. I'm very, very sorry, John.

I learned that I need to surrender into my feminine heart. Unfortunately, I never felt safe to surrender to anyone because no one was ever there to catch me—not in my childhood and not in my previous relationships. My exes couldn't hold the container for me to surrender my emotions. Somehow, you were able to create the masculine frame I needed to surrender in Cape Cod and SoHo. The email I sent after that experience let you know how witnessed and loved I felt. I hope you cracked a smile.

I treasure the memories of so many beautiful moments of gazing into your loving soul's depth. We experienced the beauty of intimacy, transcendence, and unconditional love. I will cherish these memories for the rest of my life. Thank you.

I am grateful from the bottom of my heart for how you changed my life. As painful as it was for us, it was divine orchestration, and things happened exactly how they needed to happen.

I hope things are going well for you. The Divine in me sees the Divine in you.

With love always,
Jill
P.S. I'm single.

Jill reaches for a tissue as her tears of gratitude flow freely. She makes this video "private" on Vimeo and sends John the link via text. Afterward, she rereads what she wrote. *Holy moly! This vulnerable share is Self-led and from the heart. I made a U-turn and owned my part in the failure of our friendship and business partnership. Wow, the work with Emily paid off!*

John's phone dings as he cooks dinner, and his heart thumps when he sees Jill Morgan's text. He notices that it's a video titled "Gratitude." *What's this? Could this put a smile on my face? I'm emotionally ready for something more, now that I'm divorced and have done the deep work with Emily.* He turns off the stove burner and sits down as he opens the video file.

John's eyes water as he watches Jill belt out "Shallow" from her soul. He listens and is deeply moved. He watches the video two more times. *I've never had this depth of connection with anyone before. We came into each other's lives so we could become better versions of ourselves.* He takes a couple of hours to sit with and digest his emotions, stirred by her vulnerability. And—*I can't believe she's single! What on earth happened?* Finally, he finishes cooking and eats his dinner while consumed with emotions and memories of times with Jill. Unlike his previous short and cold email responses, he sends Jill a heart-led response.

My dearest Jill,

My soul was stirred with your singing and message. The Universe has us connected in powerful ways that I could never have imagined. I have been thinking about you A LOT in the last week. I miss you, too. I miss you, A WHOLE LOT! The last time I was truly happy was with you, in the SoHo hotel room.

Despite how badly I behaved, all I ever wanted was to be loved and to shower love onto others. Sadly, my parts didn't allow me to do that. I'm sorry.

You'll be happy to hear that I've worked with Emily for a year now. We went deep to address all the younger parts that drove my cockiness and lack of Self-leadership. I'm very sorry for the pain I put you through.

You were indeed the gift from heaven that helped me see how poorly I've treated myself and others. And, you were also the mirror that reflected the shadow parts of me that desperately needed fixing. Thank you. You also let me know that I could be conscious and loving when my parts stepped aside and trusted my Self-leadership to lead you in our beautiful experiences in Cape Cod and SoHo. I surrendered into those spiritual experiences just like you did. You showed me what pure bliss was. I'm forever grateful.

I am still a student of love, intimacy, and leadership. I'm confident that all the IFS work I've done will help me, and you, and us, to pave a new path forward—*if* there's a new path forward. I heard through the grapevine that you got married. But wait, now you're single? I'm confused.

There's no need to apologize for the things you said or did. The sequence needed to happen in the exact way it did. I have forgiven you and myself. Our souls' collision was the biggest gift the Universe delivered for our respective evolution. We were each other's catalytic awakeners. Thank you from the bottom of my heart for helping me become the real me.

The butterfly of the best version of me has emerged from the cocoon. Watch out! I look forward to sharing the details of my healing journey with you.

You are an amazing and exquisite soul, my sweet Jill. I wouldn't have become the (new) man I am today without your loving "sledgehammers." LOL ☺

Love you,
John
P.S. I'm divorced.
P.P.S. Any possibility we can catch up in person?

Jill hears the ding on her phone. Her heart skips a beat. Her eyes devour John's words. She's overwhelmed with the love she feels. *Wow, his email is so Self-led, raw, and vulnerable. There is so much love between us. What??? He ends the email with 'Love you,' not 'Best,' or some other lame business sign-off. And, he's divorced! Holy Toledo! There's a God after all.*

John,

Your heart-led response touched me deeply. I imagined us in a tight embrace, looking into each other's eyes and breathing in sync as our souls connect once again. How about we catch up over dinner at my place?

Love you too,
Jill

Chapter 36

Flirting Part Is Hot

In forty-eight hours, John and Jill will reunite. John's heart is so full of love, he can't contain the excitement. He keeps the connection alive via text.

John: I'm so excited about coming to your place. I bet we can heat up the kitchen without turning the stove on. ;)

Jill: Ooo la la . . . you're making me laugh and blush at the same time. And we can dance as we cook. You know I was instantly smitten with your sexy moves in that San Francisco hotel room.

John: I was smitten too. I've seen you blush; you're so cute! We may never make it to dinner, depending on the style of dance we do in the kitchen. Uh-oh, I better be careful what I text . . . I'm drinking wine now . . .

Jill: No worries, I have wine too. Drunk texting can't hurt; it spices things up.

John: Despite our differences and difficulties, you and I think very much alike. We're both passionate, which must be why I find you incredibly sexy. People talk about chemistry, but ours can cause an explosion!

Jill: We'll have to embark on a new chemistry experiment. Flow, presence, and letting things unfold organically, without attachment to the outcome. Attachment is what doomed us in the last iteration. Just saying . . . ;)

John: Sounds like a fun experiment. I'm sure heat will be part of the formula, too, but I concur that "presence" is critical.

Jill: Everything has prepared me for the most profound connection we can have.

John: I like that after all the disappointments, you're still committed to a relationship that includes vulnerability and appreciation for masculine-feminine dynamics.

Jill: Wow! I'm impressed with your spiritual insights. Can't wait to bask in your Self-energy! You'll witness all parts of me, including the emotional parts that can kick up a raging storm.

John: I want you at full-throttle! I want to bathe in your too-much-ness. I'm ready to witness your 1000w light, and I've got the skills to contain your raging feminine ocean of vulnerabilities and emotions. ;)

Jill: You're turning me on with this spiritual poetry! Sacred intimacy is a two-way dance, my friend.

John: I finally understand what is required to be that masculine "spine" for the feminine, sexy goddess that you are. I'm not afraid of you . . . anymore. LOL ;)

Jill: I'm blushing again.

John: In case you didn't know, your sexiness is distracting. It was hard for me to concentrate at work. I think back to the times I held you tightly . . . it was so natural to entangle into your energy, especially when we danced in my suite. It was perfect.

Jill: It felt natural to surrender and trust completely. Something about you . . .

John: I loved the way you allowed me to lead. Your comfortable femininity and sensuality made me feel masculine and protective.

Jill: The dancing was so hot and sexy. I felt protected in that polarized dance. Thank you for that experience.

John: There's something magnetic and visceral when a man meets a woman who is so natural, aware, and open.

Jill: The sexy goddess part of me feels so accepted.

John: You inspire my poetic part.

Jill: I LOVE how your poetic part makes me feel cherished and loved.

John: It was so beautiful to hold you tightly when we danced. Our bodies fit so perfectly together.

Jill: I don't know if you're aware of this now, but you've done an excellent job setting the masculine "frame" that makes me feel safe to express without the worry of judgment. I appreciate the show of confidence and humility.

John: Thank you for the glowing feedback. I have Emily to thank for teaching me about the masculine-feminine relational physics. It's comfortable and easy to openly share with you, unlike before, where I often went into shut-down mode.

Jill: I love your Self-energy and self-expression!

John: You've triggered so many strong feelings and desires, but you no longer push my insecurity buttons. IFS is a gamechanger!

Jill: I think you've finally risen to the level of gravitas I desire.

John: The King is ready to claim his Queen!

Jill: I want to let you know how much I appreciate your honest and transparent new communication style. It makes me so happy and I feel safe to be me. Who knew a conscious text exchange could express so much. Big hugs.

John: Thank you. Your compliments mean the world to me.

Jill: Okay . . . I need my beauty sleep now. I'm drifting off, imagining you cuddling right next to me . . .

John: Good night, sweetie. xoxo

Jill: Good night, my King!

With that poetic text exchange, Jill is convinced that John has become a Self-led, courageously vulnerable spiritual warrior and leader.

Chapter 37

Divine Leader-*ship*, Friend-*ship*, and Relation-*ship*

J ohn arrives at Jill's apartment with two dozen red roses. Jill greets him with a radiant smile that could light up Carnegie Hall. They embrace in a prolonged deep-breathing hug, rubbing each other's backs with their hands as they savored two days of sweet and flirty texts.

John is beyond happy that he hit rock bottom. It made him face himself in the mirror and embark on the necessary inner work. He has become a man who is sovereign in his masculinity, truth, and vulnerability. He's not ashamed of the depth of what he had to go through with Jill to unleash the compassionate warrior that was hidden behind the masks. *My only job tonight is to be present with no expectations, and allow Self-energy and playful parts to entwine with Jill.* John hears Emily's words ring in his ears—*Surrender! Stay curious. Zero expectations equal to zero disappointments.*

Over a candlelit, healthy, gourmet dinner with romantic music in the background, with legs touching, they gaze across the small table into each other's eyes, feeling safe and loved. John places his hand on Jill's. "I feel so happy and grounded now. I got my body back, got rid of the drinking problem, and dissolved my stressful marriage. My parts feel settled, welcomed, loved by me, and loved by you."

"Aww . . ." Jill says with tenderness.

John proposes a toast. "To our *Titanic*, the icebergs of emotional burdens broke, and our friend-*ship* and relation-*ship* resurrected from the bottom of the ocean, to sail into new unchartered territory."

"I love it, so poetic," Jill says with a wink. "You're still sipping your first glass of wine. That's great!" He pumps his arms and chest like a bodybuilder; they laugh.

"I've apologized to the long list of people I've hurt, including Liz and the kids. And, of course, I need to apologize to you for all the mistakes I made. I'm so, so sorry." John looks longingly into Jill's eyes to let her feel how remorseful he is; Jill feels it.

"I accept your apologies. Things happened the way they needed to happen. I'm sorry, too."

"I accept your apologies, even though you did nothing wrong, you were just a lovable badass," John replies, moving his chair over to be right next to her.

Jill puts her hand on his thigh and says, "I'm so happy for all the work you've done. Your energy is lighter, and I can *feel* the presence of your intoxicating soul."

I love this woman and how she receives me with open arms.

"About my divorce," Jill begins. "Ron found my journal and read all about you; then he confessed he was still in love with his ex. I settled when I married, even though he checked off all the boxes. I didn't know he had cold feet just as much as I did."

"Wow, Emily was right that the Universe had a grander plan. The timing of our reunion is amazing!"

John wants to be radically honest and transparent, and Jill squeezes his hand to let him know she will hold space for whatever he wants to say. He lets her know he had to conceal what a fraud he was. His intense love for her topped the Richter scale, and nothing he did—including shutting down and ghosting—was able to remove the chemistry and attraction he felt. "When I heard you got married, I was crushed and cried." John notices tears welling up in Jill's eyes.

"You're such a brave warrior to share the depths of your pain," Jill squeezes his forearm to reinforce that she meant that.

John continues, "Emily had me read *The Seat of the Soul*, by Gary Zukav. The book let me know how my ego, not my soul, ran the show. My ego failed me. The IFS sessions helped me find the real essence of who I was underneath the masks. I tapped into Self. I feel closer to merging my personality with my soul's deepest desires: to be loved, to give love, and to leave the world a better place than I found it. I want to do this with a spiritual partner who is on the same journey."

Jill responds, "I saw your soul from day one. I cringed every time I heard others talk negatively about you at Zatuck. Zukav's follow-up book *Spiritual Partnership*, helped explain what we went through. Our spiritual connection had the purpose of triggering each other's frightened parts so we could ascend to higher consciousness."

"That's an understatement! We drove each other craaazy!" They laugh at how things unfolded.

Jill continues, "My logical brain decided to marry Ron since it was a 'safe,' relatively non-triggering relationship. I was ready to settle down, and he's a good person. I didn't know if you and I would ever see each other again."

"I didn't know if our paths would ever cross again either. Now that we're back together, how about we take our time to rebuild our friendship, trust, and respect?"

"I'm on board with that. Let's not have any expectations and let things unfold organically."

"Agree," John says. "I love the 'ship' metaphor. We need to rebuild our friend-*ship* because the iceberg of my exiles' burdens crashed and sunk the leader-*ship*, friend-*ship*, and relation-*ship*."

"I recognized that early on. Can we call each other out when we don't feel Self from the other, so our friend-ship doesn't ever sink again?" Jill's proactive part asks.

"Of course, and we need to agree on the language. We can figure out that agreement the next time we meet. How about we also agree that we commit to seeking Emily's guidance when we can't resolve our differences?"

"I couldn't agree with you more," Jill says and raises her hand for a high-five on that idea.

"Let's resurrect our friend-ship and leader-ship *Titanic* from the bottom of the ocean and sail into love the right way! Then we can finally climax to the top of our potential in work and love," John says with a wink. Jill giggles.

"And we commit to the lifelong curiosity of each other's inner worlds. Get curious, not furious!"

They pick up their wine glasses and toast to that.

"And maybe one day . . . we can do business again, this time with Self-leadership in the driver's seat and not our immature and broken parts," says Jill.

"One step at a time, no need to rush."

"Yeah . . . my new marketing job is a good soft-landing spot for now," Jill shares.

"My new job, too. Not as lucrative as Zatuck, but at least it pays the bills and child support. By the way, I heard Shelly nabbed a great senior director position, and she's engaged."

"I'm happy for her," Jill says.

"Changing topics—I'm dying to kiss you right now. Can I kiss you?"

John reaches over and kisses her softly on her cheek. He finishes the remaining Merlot and refills his wine glass with seltzer. "My beautiful sweetheart . . . I know the secret to heal from the past for good."

"Oh, what's that?"

"Great, mind-blowing, cosmic, make-up sex, since it's kosher for us to take it to the next level finally."

Jill laughs. "As much as I would love to be made love to, we can't jinx rebuilding this friendship. We need to focus on closeness and being in the present moment, not focusing on sexual performance. I'm not ready to bare my body yet . . . and consummate, because it's not just about the sex, it's so much deeper. Orgasmic bliss would be coming to oneness. I'm not sure if I'm ready for that intensity today because it's scary, and there's no turning back."

"You're right. Maybe I'm not ready for that yet, either. The last time in bed was powerful and spiritual. We can cuddle on the couch with our clothes on and savor the closeness and pleasure. How's that?"

"Okay . . . that works for me."

◆　◆　◆

After they washed the dinner dishes while dancing to music from the '90s, they settled down again. The music switches to smooth jazz. They sit on the couch, not talking for a few minutes, just in awe that they reunited.

"I need to come clean about everything and be completely transparent," John says. "You asked for this a long time ago, and now I'm finally ready to tell you the depths of guilt and pain I harbored."

"Thank you. Go right ahead. I welcome the expression of all your parts, without judgments." Jill places her hand on John's upper thigh to hold space and be present, with curiosity.

John shares how he felt like a fraud attending two Ivy League schools; his dad pulled strings to get him admitted. He shares how he was caught with cocaine and almost expelled from school until Dad intervened once again. He tells stories of how badly he treated Liz, nudging her friends to leave his house when they were happily socializing, and the most embarrassing admission—his financial debt and years of robbing Peter to pay Paul. Jill keeps her eyes locked on him and breathes deeply to let him know that she's right there, not judging or thinking any less of him.

After it is clear that John has finished sharing, at least for now, Jill lets him know she has a few shameful stories. She admits that when they first met, and John was in bragging mode, she felt inferior and ashamed to have grown up in a blue-collar family.

After the mutual reveal of secrets, they hug each other tightly, opening the depths of their hearts with full transparency.

John has an epiphany. "Now that we've shared our deepest secrets, it's obvious that no one person is better than another. It doesn't matter if you are the CEO or janitor, male or female, all of us carry shame and secrets that make us feel insecure. With everything I've learned from Emily, it's so much easier to have compassion for others, no matter who they are, especially when they don't live up to our expectations. A Self-led person sees the sameness in all and gets curious instead of furious."

"Emily would be so proud that we are having this conscious conversation."

"Indeed! I feel emotionally and spiritually cleansed. I felt so guilty and ashamed for how I tried to impress you. Emily taught me to make decisions from a place of imagining being on my deathbed. Who do I need to come clean with and apologize to before I go to heaven? You were the first person that popped into my head."

"I'm in heaven with your radical honesty!" Jill reassures John that he's doing great. "I have no judgments about what you shared, only compassion. I know without a doubt that you will, and we will, soar to new heights. Your energy is one thousand times better than before. A good sign of great things to come."

"I feel so supported right now," he murmurs. "The real John was buried underneath so many wounds. Having only coins in my pocket instead of big bills made my bragging part come out with white lies. I was a fraud. I felt I wasn't worthy of you, and that stopped the pleasure release when we were in the SoHo hotel room."

"I dissected your lack of climax, and I came to a similar conclusion. Everything happened for a reason. You are a powerful spiritual warrior now, the real you, without masks. I'm the luckiest woman alive."

"Thank you, but I'm the lucky one. I feel seen and heard. It feels so good to peel off my masks and confess. If I didn't do this, the white lies of omission and half-truths would have eaten me alive. I didn't know if I had the guts to reach out to you again. Thank goodness you were brave enough to sing the song and send the note. Your rawness was beyond beautiful. Your video was the opening I needed to feel safe to get in touch since I didn't know if you had permanently deleted me out of your life."

"After seeing *A Star Is Born*, I had to reach out. My soul was ready to bare its deepest truths. I had nothing to lose and everything to gain. The 'Shallow' song is so poignant since it reminded me of our journey. I'm grateful my video gave you the opening to move forward," Jill says, and hugs him.

"I did have a part that was afraid to share my truths but that fear got overruled with Self's reassurance that you will not reject radical honesty."

"I will never, ever reject one-hundred percent transparency. The truth is extremely sexy and an aphrodisiac! White lies and half-truths are poison, and that's why I ran. You know by now that it's hard to hide from me because I'm intuitive, and I can see the psychology behind everything you do," Jill laughs.

"That's why you scared me. You have X-ray vision! I love you *because* you are such a magnificent badass! You did nothing wrong by calling me out on my loser leader behaviors; thank you."

They giggle, in awe of how fluid and natural this conversation has been. *This energy feels so good. I want to make mad love to her right now!*

John breaks the silence. "Heart-led Self-leadership *is* a spiritual journey. I had to face my darkness. The Universe had my back all along. It feels so good to be the soulful alpha warrior who doesn't need to wear masks anymore. I'm so proud I can laugh and cry and show my emotions without fearing judgment or loss of masculinity. Now I know the mark of a real warrior is his courage to be confidently vulnerable!"

"Hell yeah!"

"I love you more than you know, Jilly."

"No, I love you more!" Jill plants a kiss on John's lips. "Remember, we're not rushing into anything. I'm enjoying every intimate, emotional minute."

"Okay. Let's take it slow," John says.

"I thought I sabotaged our connection by being so blunt," Jill admits.

"No, you didn't. As much as I hated your words and cursed you out, I fell more in love with you because of your no-holds-barred transparency. You were you, and that's why I couldn't stop thinking about you."

Jill says, "It amazes me how only after meeting you did I learn to be my raw self."

"Love it! Speaking of rawness . . . will you go all-out naked with me on every level—physically, emotionally, mentally, and spiritually?" John asks.

"Hey . . . isn't this the type of spiritual question I should be asking?" Jill says with a grin.

"Uh-oh, I've caught up to you in the School of Consciousness. We're both at the college level now, moving onto graduate studies."

Jill giggles as they melt into deep French kisses.

"Hmm . . . more please," John begs.

"Soon . . . we're not done with the conversation yet!" Jill says with a tipsy wink. She takes another sip of wine and resumes, as the Spotify playlist lands on Rod Stewart's rendition of "Have I Told You Lately."

Jill's surrenders into John's presence and consciousness. He leads their bodies' sway to the music. They are one.

When the song ends, John says, "The age-old question, 'How much pain are you willing to go through to get what you want?' I'm willing to go through the pain all over again, to get this beautiful reunion!"

"Yeah, me too! Now I'm ready snuggle into my spiritual home forever."

"Uh, that would be me, right?" John asks.

She giggles and kisses him wildly as they move from the living room to the bedroom, with Self-to-Self energy rippling upwards in spiritual fireworks, with no protectors to prevent John from exploding in ecstasy.

◆　◆　◆

The day after their romantic rendezvous, Jill texts Pierre: I'm in heaven! John and I reunited. It was meant to be. And the 'you know what' was cosmic. ;-)

Pierre texts back: So happy for you! And I want you to know that Brigette and I are talking again. Things are looking rosy. I'm starting to get emotionally naked with her . . . hugs. xoxo

Jill replies: Yay!!! Glad our conversation gave you the courage to reach out. I can't wait to hear more.

Then, Jill texts the happy ending for two star-crossed lovers update to other close friends.

Two days after the romantic night with Jill, John texts Antonio: Ciao! You were so right; the truth has set me free. I confessed everything, and I got Jill back! The lovemaking was intense!

Antonio feels happy for his once-drunken friend: I knew it was going to happen when you finally decided to get real. There's nowhere to go but UP! Pun intended. ☺

John laughs: Yeah, now I'm in a spiritual love affair with my Higher Self and with Jill. Who knew it was so 'simple' to climax in love and leadership by first having a love affair with yourself. ☺

Important Caveat:
Why Self-to-Self Connection Can Fail
and What to Do About It

If your authenticity is not met, this means the receiver has not done the work to understand their emotions. This is why they don't know how to handle your rawness. Another reason why some people are scared of Self-energy is because they experienced traumas related to Self-energy. For example:

- A child in a trusting mood confesses something vulnerable to his parents, and he gets yelled at. So, the child takes on the belief that showing his authentic Self is not safe.
- A man gets turned on by his young, vibrant, playful niece in Self-energy; he molests her. As a result, this traumatized part of her takes on the belief that it is not safe to be playful and dynamic.

Here is what you can do if your vulnerability or Self-energy is rejected: make a U-turn and take of the part of you that feels hurt. If appropriate, thank the other person for letting you know that they don't feel safe with radical honesty and vulnerability: "Thank you for setting the boundary and saying 'no' to me," or, "Thank you for rejecting me and protecting yourself by saying 'no.'"

Courageous Love and Vulnerability:
A Path to Healing, Wholeness, and Enlightenment

If you desire a romantic partnership with growth, intimacy, and great sex, it is imperative that you do the deep inner work as Jill and John did. The ability to be raw, vulnerable, and authentic is the ultimate aphrodisiac.

The spiritual purpose of a romantic relationship is to push each other's buttons and reveal the unhealed exiles underneath these triggers. The primary healer for the exiles is your Higher Self. Because you were hurt in "relationship" during childhood, the secondary healing occurs in the context of a loving relationship. When you and your partner's exiles are respectively healed, witnessed, and loved through each other, consciousness expands; you can become a spiritual "power couple." The spiritual synergy can ignite a mission that impacts humanity. To learn more about the aforementioned concepts, read: *You Are the One You've Been Waiting For: Bringing Courageous Love into Intimate Relationships,* by Dr. Richard Schwartz (only available at www.IFS-Institute.com), and *Spiritual Partnership: The Journey to Authentic Power,* by Gary Zukav.

When you are ready to embark on self-development and transformation, you can begin the journey through books, videos, online programs, and in-person seminars. The foundation of Self-leadership is vital to unleashing greatness. You can find Internal Family Systems information on YouTube and the Internal Family Systems website, www.IFS-Institute.com. The IFS website has books, videos, and a directory of IFS therapists/IFS practitioners.

If you want to learn confident vulnerability in and out of the bedroom, please go to www.ClimaxLeadershipBook.com, where you will be taken to the "Great Love and Sex through IFS" YouTube channel. On this channel, Percy Ballard, MD and I role-play vulnerable and sexy conscious communication.

If you want to self-actualize and climax in love and leadership, sign up for the online course "Climax in Love: Be the Ultimate Warrior for a Goddess" or "Climax in Love: Be the Ultimate Goddess for a Warrior." To access these course, please go to www.ClimaxInLove.com.

Appendix A

Summary of Key Takeaways

(Download these lists at www.ClimaxLeadershipBook.com)

ENERGY

- Law of Magnetism/Law of Attraction/Law of Vibration: You will not attract what you want; you will attract who you are.

- A healthy love affair with yourself (self-love) raises your vibration. Your vibe attracts your tribe.

- Your energy (vibration) determines your results.

- The compilation of beliefs, thoughts, and feelings from your parts determines your aura—i.e., the energy you radiate.

- Changing your energy is an inside-out job that requires getting to know your parts and unburdening them from disempowering beliefs. When the energy from limiting beliefs release, your aura improves.

- Positive Self-energy attracts positive people and experiences; negative energy (lack of Self-energy) attracts negative people and experiences. Negative experiences are feedback for course correction. "What were my inner beliefs and self-talk that attracted this negative situation?"

SELF-LEADERSHIP

- Great leadership is first and foremost an inside-out spiritual journey of getting to know Self and parts. Reintegrating and falling in love with wounded and disowned parts are the keys to becoming an extraordinary authentic leader.

- Masked, egotistical, non-Self-led leaders are judged, criticized, and powerless.

- Trust and respect increase when you apologize from Self for the parts that misbehaved.

- The parts that cause leadership struggles are the same parts that cause romantic relationship challenges.

- Get curious, not furious. Seek to understand first, and then to be understood. Zoom out to a higher perspective and say, "I'm curious about xyz," instead of reacting with negative judgments and emotions.

- It takes two to tango. Drop the swords of criticism and judgment and make a U-turn to own your contribution to disagreements. Speak for your feelings with "I" language: "I feel . . ." (If you struggle with articulating your feelings, google "Feelings Wheel.")

- Using the "you" word makes the other person defensive or want to shut down. Defensiveness and stonewalling lead to stalemates, disconnection, and more conflicts.

- Self-energy is visceral. People feel your calm, curiosity, confidence, courage, clarity, compassion, connectedness, playfulness, perspective, patience, and presence.

- The journey to self-love (of your parts) opens the capacity to shower unconditional love onto others.

- Self-led leaders make U-turns to learn how their parts contributed to challenges and conflicts.

- Self-led leaders make heart-led apologies.

- Self-led leaders initiate difficult and crucial conversations.

- Self-led leaders validate others.

- Self-led leaders command a room.

- Self-led leaders have gravitas.

- Self-led leaders are the obvious choice for promotions.

- Self-led leaders are transparent, authentic, and confidently vulnerable.

- Self-led leaders are a joy to work for.

- Self-led leaders inspire, influence, and impact.

- The IFS tagline is: "All parts are welcome!" Parts want Self to acknowledge the hard work they do, and they want Self to lead and tell them which parts should be on deck for the situation at hand.

VULNERABILITY

- In love, Self-led confident vulnerability is the most potent path to closeness, pleasure, and transcendent experiences.

- In leadership, Self-led confident vulnerability is power, influence, and impact.

- Parts are your beliefs, emotions, thoughts, behaviors, and inner child parts. Courageous and confident vulnerability is speaking *for* parts *from* Self.

- Vulnerability requires real warrior courage to get "naked," and risking possible judgment or rejection. If the receiver rejects your authenticity, they are afraid of their vulnerabilities because they have not done the work to understand their emotions, flaws, and weaknesses.

- For self-aware souls who have done the inner work, experiencing vulnerability from their partner is an incredible aphrodisiac.

- Vulnerability is risky; the rewards are worth the risk.

- Vulnerability increases connection and intimacy.

- Vulnerability positively transforms relationships.

- Vulnerability is scary.

- Vulnerability is power.

- Vulnerability is courage.

- Vulnerability is sexy.

- Vulnerability is transparency.

- Vulnerability is radical honesty.

- Vulnerability is integrity.

- Vulnerability is growth.

PERSONAL GROWTH CONCEPTS

- The number one universal core human need is validation.

- The past is always in the present.

- What is hysterical is historical.

- Hurt people hurt others.

- Get curious, not furious.

- We are all broken and imperfect with similar fears, insecurities, and shame.

- You will never rise above your limiting beliefs. You can only grow to the extent you invest in your personal growth. The deeper the work, the greater the success.

- Peter Principle: You rise to the level of your incompetence.

- You can only love thy neighbor to the extent that you heal and love yourself.

- When you tenderly look at your darkness, you drop judgments and gain compassion for another's darkness.

- The iceberg of childhood burdens can sink leader-ship, friend-ships, and romantic relation-ships.

- A dysfunctional inner world lacks Self-leadership. Lack of Self-leadership is the root cause of leadership, love, and health struggles.

- The path to becoming an extraordinary leader (and romantic partner) starts with doing the work to have a spiritual love affair with yourself. This self-development process involves befriending and loving all parts, especially the wounded and disowned parts.

- Your outer world reflects your inner world. To change the external reality, do the work to transform your inner world (of dysfunctional parts).

- The Universe purposely gave you painful experiences for the evolution of your soul. It is up to you to connect the dots of your life looking backward so you can make lemonade out of the lemons of your life. Your core wounds helped you develop the unique gifts that only you can deliver to the world.

- Increased awareness and compassion for your parts means judging, criticizing, and blaming others significantly decrease.

- If you don't invest the time, energy, and money in self-development, your unhealed parts can get desperate and seek validation through "illicit" love affairs. These illicit love affairs include people, food, power, status, material things, alcohol, drugs, gambling, shopping, sex, etc. These illicit love affairs undermine your relationships, health, and career.

- If you want someone else to change, you need to lead the change. Your change activates a different response from the other person.

- What you love about another person is what you love about yourself; what you dislike and judge in another person is what you dislike and judge about yourself.

- Half-truths, white lies of omission, and lack of radical honesty will backfire and lead to self-sabotage and failure. It's the physics of Law of Cause and Effect—every action has an equal and opposite reaction.

- If you can't hold space for another person's emotions and vulnerabilities, you haven't done the work to acknowledge, heal, and accept the feelings you have disowned and locked away. A hallmark of courage is welcoming vulnerability—your own and others.

- Whole truths, radical honesty, and courageous vulnerability lead to intimate and fulfilling relationships.

- Self has the power to give you the courage to take risks and go beyond your comfort zone. It doesn't matter if you fail; the effort is the reward. Failure is "feedback" for course correction.

- The spiritual journey to wholeness, happiness, and greatness is about doing the work to peel off your masks.

- The spiritual purpose of a romantic relationship is to push each other's buttons and reveal the unhealed exiles underneath these triggers. The primary healer for the exiles is your Higher Self. Because you were hurt in "relationship" during childhood, the secondary healing occurs in the context of a loving relationship. When you and your partner's exiles are respectively healed, witnessed, and loved by one another, consciousness expands; you can become a spiritual "power couple." The spiritual synergy can ignite a mission that impacts humanity.

IN A NUTSHELL

- The Internal Family Systems Self-leadership model is an evidence-based, cutting-edge, robust methodology to help you become an extraordinary Self-led leader in all areas of your life.

◆ ◆ ◆

To learn more about how to become an extraordinary Self-led leader and lover, sign up for either "Climax in Love: Be the Ultimate Warrior for a Goddess" or "Climax in Love: Be the Ultimate Goddess for a Warrior." You can access these courses at www.ClimaxInLove.com.

Appendix B

The 8Cs and 5Ps of Self-Leadership

*Adapted from Internal Family Systems and
The Center for Self-leadership*

(Download this list at www.ClimaxLeadershipBook.com)

1. Clarity
- Maintaining objectivity
- Expressing your thoughts clearly

2. Compassion
- Relating to others openheartedly without the need to change them
- Feeling empathy towards the needs and burdens of others

3. Creativity
- Producing original ideas
- Entering into flow and creating from pleasure in the moment

4. Calmness
- Remaining calm and centered regardless of circumstances
- Responding to triggers calmly by speaking objectively for the emotion, not from the emotion

5. Curiosity
- Desiring to learn about others, without judgment
- Having a sense of wonder about people and the world

6. Confidence
- Believing in yourself with high self-esteem
- Believing you can handle whatever happens
- Not allowing past failures to thwart your journey to greatness

7. Courage
- Taking action despite fear
- Willing to explore one's inner world
- Taking responsibility for one's actions and having the courage to apologize and restore harmony

8. Connectedness
- Feeling a part of a larger entity such as a partnership, team, or organization
- Relaxing defenses, building trust, eliminating judgment and control
- Believing in something bigger than yourself to transcend circumstances

◆　◆　◆

1. Patience
- Giving people and situations the time to evolve and transform

2. Perspective
- Zooming out to a higher perspective instead of judging, criticizing, and blaming

3. Persistence
- Staying the course even when things get challenging

4. Playfulness
- Bringing fun and play into interactions when appropriate

5. Presence
- Staying in the present moment without being distracted

Appendix C

Internal Family Systems Information

Website

www.IFS-Institute.com

Find IFS Therapists and IFS Practitioners

www.IFS-Institute.com

IFS Books and Videos

www.IFS-Institute.com

You can watch Emily Liu in real-time Internal Family Systems client sessions. The videos are available at www.ClimaxLeadershipBook.com. Client sessions include: "Where Does the 'Don't Trust Men' Belief Come From?" and "Real Reasons Why Men Pull Away from Commitment."

There are many videos on YouTube about the Internal Family Systems model, including lectures given by the founder and developer of IFS, Richard (Dick) Schwartz, PhD, LMFT. Google "Internal Family Systems" and "Richard (Dick) Schwartz."

Appendix D

Recommended Books and Talks

BOOKS

How to Permanently Erase Negative Self-Talk: So You Can Be Extraordinary (author's first book under her former name: "Emily Filloramo"), 2015.

You're the One You've Been Waiting For: Bringing Courageous Love to Intimate Relationships by Richard Schwartz, PhD, 2008. (This book is only available on the IFS website: www.IFS-Institute.com.)

Introduction to the Internal Family Systems Model by Richard Schwartz, PhD, 2001.

Why Did I Do That? How You Make Sense and Why There Is Hope by Dorie Cameron, LICSW, 2009. (An illustrated book on IFS for children and adults.)

Self-Therapy: A Step-By-Step Guide to Creating Wellness and Healing Your Inner Child Using IFS, A New, Cutting-Edge Psychotherapy by Jay Earley, PhD, 2009.

How to Win Friends and Influence People by Dale Carnegie, 2011.

Triumphs of Experience: The Men of the Harvard Grant Study by George E. Vaillant, 2015.

The Mask of Masculinity: How Men Can Embrace Vulnerability, Create Strong Relationships, and Live Their Fullest Lives by Lewis Howes, 2017.

Dare to Lead: Brave Work. Tough Conversations. Whole Hearts. by Brené Brown, 2018.

The Gifts of Imperfection: Let Go of Who You Think You're Supposed to Be and Embrace Who You Are by Brené Brown, 2010.

Daring Greatly: How the Courage to be Vulnerable Transforms the Way We Live, Love, Parent, and Lead by Brené Brown, 2015.

Braving the Wilderness: The Quest for True Belonging and the Courage to Stand Alone by Brené Brown, 2019.

Wild at Heart (Revised and Updated): Discovering the Secret of a Man's Soul by John Eldredge, 2011.

Captivating (Revised and Updated): Unveiling the Mystery of a Woman's Soul by John and Stasi Eldredge, 2011.

I Thought It Was Just Me (But It Isn't): Making the Journey from "What Will People Think?" to "I Am Enough" by Brené Brown, 2007.

The Pain Behind the Mask: Overcoming Masculine Depression by John Lynch and Christopher Kilmartin, 1999.

I Don't Want to Talk About It: Overcoming the Secret Legacy of Male Depression by Terrence Real, 1998.

How Can I Get Through to You? Closing the Intimacy Gap Between Men and Women by Terrence Real, 2002.

Nonviolent Communication: A Language of Life: Life-Changing Tools for Healthy Relationships by Marshall B. Rosenberg, PhD, 2015.

The New Rules of Marriage: What You Need to Know to Make Love Work by Terrence Real, 2008.

Men are From Mars, Women are From Venus by John Gray, 2012.

Beyond Mars and Venus: Relationship Skills for Today's Complex World by John Gray, 2017.

The Way of the Superior Man: A Spiritual Guide to Mastering the Challenges of Women, Work, and Sexual Desire by David Deida, 2017.

The Masculine in Relationship: A Blueprint for Inspiring the Trust, Lust, and Devotion of a Strong Woman by GS Youngblood

The Seat of the Soul: 25th Anniversary Edition with a Study Guide by Gary Zukav, 2014

Spiritual Partnership: The Journey to Authentic Power by Gary Zukav, 2011.

The Untethered Soul: The Journey Beyond Yourself by Michael A. Singer, 2007.

The Surrender Experiment: My Journey into Life's Perfection by Michael A. Singer, 2015.

An Uncommon Bond by Jeff Brown, 2015.

Soulshaping: A Journey of Self-Creation by Jeff Brown, 2009.

Breaking the Habit of Being Yourself: How to Love Your Mind and Create a New One by Dr. Joe Dispenza, 2013.

Becoming Supernatural: How Common People Are Doing the Uncommon by Dr. Joe Dispenza, 2019.

You Are the Placebo: Making Your Mind Matter by Dr. Joe Dispenza, 2015.

The Biology of Belief (10th Anniversary Edition): Unleashing the Power of Consciousness, Matter, and Miracles by Bruce Lipton, PhD, 2016.

The Power of Your Subconscious Mind by Joseph Murphy, PhD, 2009.

Real Magic: Ancient Wisdom, Modern Science, and a Guide to the Secret Power of the Universe by Dean Radin, PhD, 2018.

Entangled Minds: Extrasensory Experiences in a Quantum Reality by Dean Radin, PhD, 2006.

Quantum Love: Use Your Body's Atomic Energy to Create the Relationship You Desire by Laura Berman, PhD, 2017.

The State of Affairs: Rethinking Infidelity by Esther Perel, 2018.

Mating in Captivity: Unlocking Erotic Intelligence by Esther Perel, 2007.

Wired for Dating: How Understanding Neurobiology and Attachment Style Can Help You Find Your Ideal Mate by Stan Tatkin, PsyD, MFT, 2016.

Wired for Love: How Understanding Your Partner's Brain and Attachment Style Can Help You Defuse Conflict and Build a Secure Relationship by Stan Tatkin, PsyD, MFT, 2012.

Attached: The New Science of Adult Attachment and How It Can Help You Find and Keep Love by Amir Levine, MD and Rachel S.F. Heller M.A., 2012.

Judgment Detox: Release the Beliefs that Hold You Back from Living a Better Life by Gabrielle Bernstein, 2018.

The Top Five Regrets of the Dying: A Life Transformed by Dearly Departing by Bronnie Ware, 2019.

The Seven Levels of Intimacy: The Art of Loving and the Joy of Being Loved by Matthew Kelly, 2015.

His Needs, Her Needs: Building an Affair-Proof Marriage by Willard F. Harley, Jr., 2011.

The Five Love Languages: The Secret to Love that Lasts by Gary Chapman, 2015.

Sexual Intelligence: What We Really Want from Sex and How to Get It by Marty Klein, PhD, 2013.

The Obstacle is the Way: The Timeless Art of Turning Trials into Triumph by Ryan Holiday, 2014.

Ego is the Enemy by Ryan Holiday, 2016.

Why Quantum Physicists Do Not Fail: Learn the Secrets of Achieving Almost Anything Your Heart Desires by Greg Kuhn, 2013.

The Road to Character by David Brooks, 2016.

Rocket Fuel: The One Essential Combination That Will Get You More of What You Want from Your Business by Gino Wickman and Mark C. Winters, 2015.

Why CEOs Fail: The 11 Behaviors that Can Derail Your Climb to the Top and How to Manage Them by David D. Dotlich and Peter C. Cairo, 2003.

The Dark Side of the Light Chasers: Reclaiming Your Power, Creativity, Brilliance, and Dreams by Debbie Ford, 2010.

The Secret of the Shadow: The Power of Owning Your Story by Debbie Ford, 2002.

The Shadow Effect: Illuminating the Hidden Power of Your True Self by Deepak Chopra, Debbie Ford, and Marianne Williamson, 2011.

A Return to Love: Reflections on the Principles of "A Course in Miracles" by Marianne Williamson, 1996.

Male Brain: A Breakthrough Understanding of How Men and Boys Think by Louann Brizendine, 2011.

The Female Brain by Louann Brizendine, 2007.

The Seven Principles for Making Marriage Work by John Gottman, PhD, 2015.

What Makes Love Last: How to Build Trust and Avoid Betrayal by John Gottman, PhD, 2013.

Eight Dates: Conversations for a Lifetime of Love by John Gottman, PhD, 2019.

A Man's Guide to Women: Scientifically Proven Secrets from the Love Lab About What Women Really Want by John Gottman, PhD, 2016.

Science of Trust: Emotional Attunement for Couples by John Gottman, PhD, 2011.

Getting the Love You Want: A Guide for Couples: Third Edition by Harville Hendrix PhD, 2019.

The Queen's Code by Alison A. Armstrong, 2013.

Making Sense of Men: A Woman's Guide to a Lifetime of Love, Care and Attention from All Men by Alison Armstrong, 2008.

Keys to the Kingdom by Alison Armstrong, 2003.

TED TALKS

"Power of Vulnerability" by Brené Brown

"Listening to Shame" by Brené Brown

"Monogamish: The New Rules of Marriage" by Jessica O'Reilly

"What Makes a Good Life? Lessons from the Longest Study on Happiness" by Robert Waldinger

Appendix E

Self-Led Courageous Conversations Framework

Step 1

Suspend judgment of what the other person is doing or saying. Take the birds-eye view and witness your thoughts and emotions.

- Identify the part that holds you back from initiating a conversation.
- What reassurance does this part need to let Self be courageous to initiate the conversation?

Step 2

Zoom out and observe the other. Get curious, not furious.

- Notice the other person's parts that are not favorable towards you. Suspend judgment, get curious, and understand that they have fears. (Their fears may stem from how you spoke to them in the past; they may feel unsafe to open up. If this is the case, start with: "I would like to apologize for how I've spoken to you in the past. I'm sorry.")

Step 3

Ask permission to set aside time for a conversation.

- "I'm curious . . . is it possible to set aside time to talk about xyz?"
  (Do not say, "We need to talk." This sentence can activate defenses because the interpretation is: "I'm in trouble; I failed; I did something wrong.")

Step 4

Use "I" language only.
(Speak *from* Self, for the part.)

- "I have a part that is active. Would it be okay if I spoke for it?"
- "There's a part of me . . ."
- "I'm feeling _____ [frustrated, afraid, confused, challenged, etc.]."
  (Google "Feelings Wheels" for feelings adjectives.)

Step 5

Do not blame or point fingers; make a U-turn into you.

- "Would you be willing to give me feedback on how I'm contributing to our challenging dynamic?"
- "What is the number one thing you need from me to solve this so we can communicate better?"

◆ ◆ ◆

TWO POWERFUL PHRASES TO INCORPORATE INTO EVERYDAY LANGUAGE

1. "I'm curious . . ."
2. "There's a part of me . . ."

◆ ◆ ◆

APOLOGIZING FOR A PART

"The (name the part) part of me had a temper tantrum when it was triggered by your (name their part) part and made me (name the negative behavior). I apologize for this part. I hope you can forgive this part of me." Example:

- "The mean part of me had a temper tantrum when it got triggered by your silence and made me unfriend you on Facebook. I apologize; I hope you can forgive this part of me."

◆ ◆ ◆

PSYCHOLOGY OF JUDGMENTS AND TRIGGERS

Identify the people you judge and criticize. Identify the people who trigger you.

- Family members
- Significant others (past and present)
- Kids
- Friends
- Bosses
- Coworkers
- Acquaintances

When you judge or are triggered, make a U-turn. The parts of someone you judge reflects the part of you that you don't like or don't have the courage to express. In other words, what you love in another person is what you love about yourself; what you dislike and judge in another person is what you dislike and judge about yourself. Ask yourself: "What is the trait or part of them that rubs me the wrong way? Examples:

- "She puts herself out there; she dares to fearlessly self-express. [Make a U-turn.] I wish I dared to put myself out there like she does. I'm playing small."

Or

"She spends so much money on expensive designer everything. [Make a U-turn.] Ohhh . . . I also have a shopping part that shops too much. I'm judging the shopping part of me that needs to show others 'I've made it.' I don't like this part that buys things I don't need, with money I don't have, to impress people I don't like. I'm not any happier after accumulating material things."

Judgments and triggers are not about the other person; they are about holding the mirror up to see the parts of you that need work. Judging others is a defense mechanism to help you feel "better than" and to feel significant.

◆ ◆ ◆

To learn more about how to become an extraordinary Self-led leader and lover, sign up for either "Climax in Love: Be the Ultimate Warrior for a Goddess" or "Climax in Love: Be the Ultimate Goddess for a Warrior." You can access these courses at www.ClimaxInLove.com.

Appendix F

Live Your Best Life: Identify and Remove the Inner Blocks

(Download the worksheet at www.ClimaxLeadershipBook.com.)

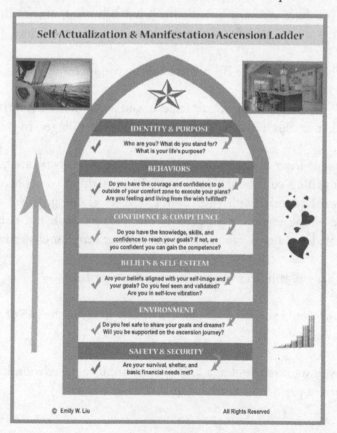

Claim Your Identity, Vision, and Destiny

1. From your HEART—not from your logical head with excuses and limiting beliefs— what do you passionately and *realistically* want if you weren't afraid and you knew you couldn't fail? What is the "music" inside of you that wants to express? [You have to know where you want to drive the bus of your life. If you don't have a clear, realistic/believable vision, you'll stay where you are because you haven't plugged the destination into your life's GPS.]

   In 3 months:
   In 6 months:
   In 1 year:
   In 3 years:
   In 5 years:

   If you have difficulty articulating what you want, answer this question: What are you afraid of if you clearly stated what you want?

2. Who do you have to BE to attract what you want?

3. Why is it essential for you to achieve your goals? What is your IDENTITY? What is this identity "lightning rod" that will get you out of bed?

4. Is your heart aligned with this goal? Do you really want this, or is this something you should do? [If this is something you should do and it doesn't resonate with your heart's deepest yearning, you're doing it for the wrong reasons; e.g., this is your parents' goal, not yours. Lack of heart-led passion can lead to self-sabotage and soul-sucking feelings.]

5. What will you *feel* when you achieve your goals?

6. How would you *behave* if you are already living in the end of your desired realities?

7. If you want to manifest a soulmate or improve the relationship with your current partner, what are the qualities you desire?

8. When your ideal soulmate looks at you from his/her perspective, would they be attracted to who you are now? If the answer is "no," who would you need to become to be attractive to this person? What's holding you back from doing the work to becoming your best self?

Find the Inner Blocks, Limiting Beliefs, and Negative Self-Talk

Your "Exiles/Inner Children" parts with their negative beliefs are the root causes of feeling stuck and the inability to believe you are truly worthy your ambitious goals. The ability to imagine future scenes and feeling that success as if you already have what you want gives the Universe the sign to orchestrate the twists-and-turns that can eventually lead you to the goals. To manifest the future, you need to identify the exile-caused inner blocks. Unfortunately, just saying affirmations will not work until the exiles wholeheartedly *believe* your assertions. Change your inner world, and your new outer world reality follows.

9. What challenges hurt the most that you want to solve right now?

10. What are the struggles costing you?
Psychological/Emotional Cost:
Physical Cost:
Financial Cost:
Spiritual Cost:

11. What are your current positive and negative beliefs about your life? [Examples: I am fat; I am cute; I am smart; I am not worthy; I am not enough; I am compassionate; I am controlling; I am a perfectionist; I am judgmental/critical; I am fearless; I am geeky; I am an overachiever; I am a loser; I am shy; I am attractive; I am average.]

I AM _____.
I AM _____.
I AM _____.
Life is_____.
Write out as many beliefs that pop into your head.

12. What are the beliefs of the best version of you that can manifest love (and keep) love, money, and success?

    I AM _____.
    I AM _____.
    I AM _____.
    Life is_____.
    Write out as many new beliefs you need to adopt.

13. What are your beliefs about LOVE?

14. What are your beliefs about VULNERABILITY?

15. What are your beliefs about MONEY, WEALTH, and HEALTH?

16. Are you willing to take risks, fail many times, and face the fear of the unknown to get what you want?

17. What would help your fears decrease or disappear?

18. On a scale of 1 to 10, how badly do you want to achieve your goals? [If the answer isn't a strong "9" or "10," you may not be ready to get uncomfortable to do the hard work to get what you want. It's essential to get to know the Fear of Change protector.]

19. Have you decided to do whatever it takes to end your struggles, including going outside of your comfort zone to take risks you've never considered before? [If the answer is "no," you are not ready to move forward yet until your hesitant parts overcome their fears.]

20. Is the pain of staying in your current state more significant than the pain of fear of change, fear of the unknown, fear of failure, and fear of success? [If the pain isn't bad enough, the mediocrity "nail" you've been sitting on hasn't gone deep enough to make you want to act. It's easier to live with the moderately painful "devil you know" than to live the unknown of your best life.]

21. Are you afraid of failure?

22. Are you afraid of success? What parts of your life will change if you do succeed? [Examples: My husband might feel threatened and divorce me if I'm thinner, more attractive, and more prosperous; the men at work will flirt with me and set me up for temptations; my girlfriends will be jealous, and I'll get kicked out of the tribe.]

23. Do you have a vested interest in staying the same? [Examples: If I remain heavy, I won't have to have sex with my husband; if I stay depressed, I won't have to be accountable to do something with my life; if I get too rich, I will be judged by my family and friends.]

24. Are you concerned with what others will think of you when you achieve big and are in the spotlight?

25. What other difficulties may arise if you overcame your challenges and lived your dream life? What relationships might be affected? Who might become jealous of you? [Examples: I'll be a bad mom if I'm successful because I won't spend as much time with the kids; my family believes rich people are not nice and I'll be judged if I'm too successful; my husband won't like it, and he will feel insecure if I make more money than he does; if I lost thirty pounds, I won't be able to afford a new wardrobe; if I get promoted, I will need to move, and my husband will have to leave his job; if I attract my dream partner, I'm afraid of exposing the real me because he/she may not like my flaws.]

26. What are the loudest negative voices ringing in your head from caregivers, teachers, coaches, peers, and siblings? How do these voices hold you back from fully expressing your personality and potential? [These negative voices are the root causes of why you haven't been able to achieve your goals.]

27. What, if any, cultural and religious messages from childhood hold you back?

28. When you look in the mirror can you say, "I love you so much; you're awesome; you're beautiful/handsome; you're the best thing ever created; we're gonna leave a unique legacy with the gifts born out of the deepest wounds"? [If you find it difficult to say how much you love and believe in

yourself, with healthy self-love, then this is the root cause of why it's been a challenge to manifest dreams in love, money, or success.]

29. How would you describe your childhood? [Examples: loving; tense; full of conflict; shame-filled due to abuse; I couldn't wait to go to college to escape the chaos.]

30. On a scale of 1 to 10, how big is the negative emotional charge from childhood adverse emotional events? ["1" is a minor emotional charge, "10" is a significant emotional charge. The greater the burden, the harder it will be to manifest your dreams unless you do the deep inner work to unburden the childhood traumas.]

31. What are your coping mechanisms for soothing and avoiding emotional triggers? (Examples: eating; shopping; drinking; sex/porn; gambling; working; getting angry; being controlling.)

Eliminate the Inner Blocks (via IFS) and Rise to Self-Love Vibration

These are the steps of the Internal Family Systems Self-leadership healing and transformation model.

1. FOCUS on part

2. UNBLEND from part

3. How do you FEEL towards part?

4. BEFRIEND the part

5. UPDATE the part

6. Find the part's FEARS

7. Find the SOURCE of the fear

8. WITNESS the fear

9. RECONSOLIDATE the emotional memory

10. RETRIEVE the "past part" (exile/inner child)

11. UNBURDEN the "past part"

12. INVITE new beliefs and qualities

13. REINTEGRATE original part/protector

14. Invite original part/protector to TRANSFORM

15. THANK parts for cooperation

You can watch real-time Internal Family Systems transformational sessions by the author, Emily W. Liu. The IFS sessions include: "Where Does 'Don't Trust Men' Belief Come From?" and "Real Reasons Why Men Pull Away from Commitment." These videos are available at www.ClimaxLeadershipBook.com.

When you sign up for "Climax in Love: Be the Ultimate Warrior for a Goddess" or "Climax in Love: Be the Ultimate Goddess for a Warrior," you will be guided step-by-step to remove the inner blocks that hold you back from your best life. Go to www.ClimaxInLove.com to access the courses.

About the Author

Emily W. Liu is the founder of Soar to Greatness Now LLC. She is the author of *How to Permanently Erase Negative Self-Talk: So You Can Be Extraordinary* (2015). She is a frequent keynote speaker and workshop leader, as well as working in private practice with individuals and couples.

Emily guides you to become an extraordinary Self-led leader through the doorway of your love life. She teaches you how to increase closeness, pleasure, and spiritual depth with courageous and confident vulnerability using the evidence-based Internal Family Systems (IFS) Self-leadership framework. Once you know how to do love right via the IFS model, you can use the same framework to take off your masks and be an authentic leader. When you are genuine and not afraid to show your imperfections, you can become an inspiring and impactful "real" leader that everyone loves to work for.

Emily is a graduate of Cornell University. Her background education includes Neuro-Linguistic Programming (NLP) and the cutting-edge, evidence-based Internal Family Systems Self-leadership framework. Emily "accidentally" found her life's calling as a Self-leadership mentor and healer after a 27-year pharmaceutical sales career. She lives in Boston, Massachusetts.

WEBSITES

www.GreatLoveAndLeadership.com
www.ClimaxLeadershipBook.com
www.ClimaxInLove.com

COMMENTS AND FEEDBACK REGARDING THIS BOOK

book@GreatLoveAndLeadership.com
book@ClimaxLeadershipBook.com

INTERVIEW AND SPEAKING INQUIRIES

speaking@GreatLoveAndLeadership.com

ALL OTHER INQUIRIES

Emily@GreatLoveAndLeadership.com

INSTAGRAM

www.Instagram.com/EmilyLiu444

LINKEDIN

www.LinkedIn.com/in/EmilyLiu444

FACEBOOK

www.Facebook.com/EmilyLiu444

TWITTER

www.Twitter.com/EmilyLiu444

YOUTUBE

1. "Emily W. Liu"
   www.bit.ly/emily-w-liu
2. "Great Love and Sex through IFS" (in collaboration with Harvard-trained psychiatrist Percy Ballard, MD)
   www.bit.ly/great-love-sex